Fear of Fire

Michael Harold Brown

Spirit Daily Publishing
www.spiritdaily.com
11 Walter Place
Palm Coast, Florida 32164

The publisher recognizes and accepts that the final authority regarding the apparitions in the Catholic Church rests with the Holy See of Rome, to whose judgment we willingly submit.

—*The Publisher*

Fear of Fire by Michael Harold Brown

Copyright © 2013 Michael H. Brown

Published by Spirit Daily Publishing

For additional copies, write:
Spirit Daily Publishing
11 Walter Place
Palm Coast, Florida 32164

or contact: www.spiritdaily.com

ISBN 978-0-615-83432-0

Printed in the United States of America   First Edition

To the Blessed Virgin Mary

"But the day of the Lord will come like a thief, in which the heavens will pass away with a roar and the element will be destroyed with intense heat, and the earth and its works will be burned up." (*2 Peter* 3:10)

1

Some years back, I wrote a book called *Tower of Light* based on what is called the "1990 prophecy"—an incredible missive received by an anonymous person during that year, a message that was dramatic, radical, and prophetic—startlingly so, in some aspects.

We await the fulfillment of the rest of it.

The prophecy stated that mankind was facing a "great new evil" that was being sent as a test by our merciful God, a new trial because, basically, we had failed the test of abortion.

It would be a test comparable to abortion, but different. It would arrive—at first imperceptibly—in four years and how we responded to it would determine the extent of coming chastisements.

Four years later, a sudden flurry of scientific discoveries and federal funding paved the way for a new great evil that indeed was—is—comparable in that it also has to do with reproduction and meddling with and in some cases destroying life but also is different: genetic manipulation— reordering God's Creation—and cloning. Since the prophecy, animals of all kinds—dogs, cats, cattle, monkeys (a sheep was the first)—have been cloned. Placed under a black light, and born with bio-luminescent enzymes (from such animals as fireflies and sea anemones), we have animals and plants that glow in the dark. We can now manufacture biological replicas, without two parents (or create offspring that have three parents). At the same time, the genetic structures of plants and animals have been altered, in some cases genes from various animals intermixed with one another (spider DNA, for example, with that of a goat, to create proteins) and genes from *plants* have even been inserted into those of *animals* (and vice versa)! Meanwhile, stem cells taken from aborted unborn babies have been used or proposed for use in medical procedures (including vaccines). *". . . an evil comparable to abortion—that is to say, that even if evils as great and widespread as abortion were to be eliminated, this is enough of an evil that it would present mankind with an enormous challenge,"* the prophecy had said.

It is not science fiction. It is not tabloid stuff. You can search for it on the internet (or in science journals).

The start of it can be traced, in many ways, to 1994.

And it was in the same period that something else from the prophecy was taking place.

Storms. Quakes. Disruptions in nature.

The 1990 prophecy had said that in this time of testing, during the "new great evil," there would be regional "chastisements" or warnings that would not be recognized by most people for what they were and since 1990 we have seen storms, floods, mudslides, tornadoes, climate swerves, and other events unprecedented in recent times. The prophecy was almost immediately followed by historic East Coast tempests, including the "perfect storm" and northeasters that put streets and highways in New York City under water, flooding parts of Long Island and lashing at Boston, as did winter blizzards. Los Angeles was hit by an earthquake whose epicenter was the very center too of the adult film industry. Central America encountered hurricanes with such floods that bodies floated from one country to another. Mudslides in Venezuela and elsewhere killed thousands. Hundreds of thousands sought highlands in Africa. Millions fled monsoons in China. *Tens* of millions fled monsoons in India. Massive tornadoes threatened American cities. Ice storms paralyzed southern Canada. Hurricane-force winds tore across England. Tremors rumbled along the "Ring of Fire." There was Hurricane Andrew. A massive quake devastated the New Zealand city of Christchurch. There was terrorism. There was the Fukushima disaster. There were the hurricanes in Louisiana, in Texas, in Florida—one summer, four major ones. The next year, "Katrina." Most recently, "Sandy."

Hardly anyone has pegged them as "chastisements." But they are. ("Sandy," by some derivatives, coming from "Cassandra," can mean "unheeded prophetess"). To say that 1990 began a run of events—just check out a list of storms in the 1990s alone—is an understatement.

Meanwhile, there has been a strangeness. There have been constant reports of unusual lights in the sky. There have been blazing auroras—usually confined to the Arctic, now seen down in Mexico. There have been unusual revelations (did you hear the audio of "Sandy's" winds through the Freedom Tower?). There have been earthquakes where there are not usually earthquakes. There have been close brushes with asteroids.

Strange times. We ignore these matters at our peril. We ignore them in our arrogance. We ignore them in our ignorance.

But they're there.

Even the mainstream media has taken up coverage of them.

There is unusual sunspot activity.

There are new objects discovered in space.

There have been strange, loud rumblings—noises in communities across the world that seemed to come from either the atmosphere or underground and resemble something alien or even like an ancient trumpet (known as the shofar).

One day soon, said the reputed prophecy, there will be fear of fire from the sky.

This will all lead, it added, to a breakdown of our "false" society.

A new world will emerge.

But before it does, there will be a personage of evil.

There will be an "antichrist."

There will be a new world order.

There will be a peasant lifestyle.

The evil will be broken by a manifestation of Jesus (as an apparition in towering light).

Or so it says.

We hold it all up for discernment.

But enough has come true to draw serious consideration.

Enough has come true to warrant a closer look at this and other prophecies.

Even the irreligious have noted a strangeness (some would say an eeriness) to our time.

There has been a fantastic rise of evil.

Bad has been made to seem good and good has been made to seem evil while we have encountered other watershed events like September 11 (which was also foreseen in the 1990 prophecy).

Could it be that our societies are completely off base—not just immoral, but founded in a way that contravenes God's Plan (and His Creation)?

Could it be that science is now His chief nemesis?

Could it be—as the prediction claimed—that there's a location north of San Francisco that is the center of Satan?

The 1990 prophecy was followed by what I have called an "addendum" in 2004.

The date was December 22.

It was days before the Great Asian Tsunami.

"There is going to be a major disruption in a region of the world that will affect everyone," it said. "The world is now seriously out of conformance with the Will of God and what He created and intended. There are those who would reconfigure the very creatures He has formed, and who meddle with the texture of life. For this reason, the Lord will allow a huge reorientation."

While the Asian tsunami was not precisely that "major disruption" (it didn't affect "everyone"), it tended to affirm a coming disruption in similar fashion.

The addendum warned again that in addition to all the sins of men, we are now totally out of conformance with the support structures of what is called nature.

We are trying to recreate Creation.

We are dabbling at the tiniest—and largest—levels.

We affect the immediate space around earth (see: space junk).

We affect microorganisms.

We are on Mars.

We have nano-technology.

Everywhere is the mark—and mayhem—of man and as a result, said the addendum, humankind will soon encounter something that will surprise all who have offered predictions.

"The angels have their instruction from east to west, and now a timetable has been set in motion," it intoned, as if from the Lord. *"When the huge light is seen, I will act in a way I have not acted before."*

That was the 1990 prophecy and addendum.

Note the economy of language. Note the substantial time between them (1990 and 2004).

Another was to come on September 25, 2010.

It was more poignant and dramatic yet.

It seems imminent.

It is the topic of this book.

"The trials of your time now head to the crescendo of meaning, whereby to each will be shown the imperfection of the past and the need for purification of the future," it asserted.

"In these transgressions is found the enemy of Creation, and the one who seeks to install his spirit as the spirit that conquers for all time.

"It is a final battle in which the trials of the future will serve as engagements complete unto themselves. Those who choose to ignore the dynamic of spiritual interaction will find themselves in a very confused state that will lead to more conflict. While love prevails, so does courage, and so does the uncovering of those spirits which now install themselves as guardians for those who have invited falsity into their hearts. The angels stand ready to assist those who unleash power with humility and belief.

"Only those in union with God will be able to see in the darkness which so many expected and that already is upon the earth. New Mexico I have ordained as a beacon of light and also the place near the water where the cross stands.

"In this time, expect the error of premature expectation, but not [error in] the truth of the expectation itself.

"For these times, you have the Rosary, and even more so, the praise. In union with God comes all protection, as the dark spirits are now allowed to materialize in full due to the pretense and aspirations of man. Not until the initial event will the curtain be drawn that reveals the entirety of the plan, and even then, it will be parted only slowly, in the woes of purification."

2

These words floored me when I first read them.

There was just something about the prediction.

It was more urgent, it seemed imminent ("stand ready"), it implied soon.

This wasn't to diminish the original, which was very powerful—the most potent locution I had read outside of a Church-approved apparition of the Blessed Mother.

Personal opinion.

And that addendum in 2004: it had been extraordinarily intriguing, with ideas and phraseology—twists of language—I knew were not characteristic of the person who had received it. Simply put: the recipient was not capable of it. We'll be revisiting these.

But the new message pumped powerful adrenalin into them.

It also pumped energy into older prophecies such as those from Akita, Japan; Kibeho, Rwanda; Fatima, Portugal; and LaSalette, France, that may not yet have reached total realization.

There were links—hidden ones, I was to discover—between them.

For many years, Christians around the world had been sensing that serious changes—watershed events—were in store for humanity; that something new and out of everybody's experience was about to occur in a world that was increasingly, gravely out of order. It was a world that ridiculed religion, disdained most Christian doctrines, misled its youth, promoted superficiality, celebrated pornography, had put up with free sex for now half a century, allowed millions of abortions, had lurid celebrities with names like "Madonna" (and rock bands like "Black Sabbath"), advertised sterilization, tolerated drugs (but not the Nativity), was immersed in evermore materialism (as exhibited by the rush to Wall Street in the decade leading up to 1990), seriously polluted what God had created, saw crime—serial killings—continue to ratchet upward, and made the symbol of the Cross yield to that of the dollar sign.

The list was relentless—and nearly without end.

Corruption remarkably similar to that during the Roman Empire and back even to ancient Nineveh and Babylon and the time of Noah was rampant across the "societies" of men (as the original 1990 message put it), and so—as with Noah, as in Babylon, as during the Roman Empire—chastisement from God, a "correction," very major events, seemed at hand.

The signs—the sins—were all around us.

There was Hollywood.

There was Las Vegas.

Some of those we elected to office had lower moral standards than old-time riverboat gamblers.

In Nevada, a brothel owner was elected.

Abroad, in other lands, people were savagely killed over money and politics or beliefs—beheaded by Muslims, firebombed in India, jailed in China for converting to Christianity.

There was always brutality and for much of history the cruelty had been more blatant. Back in early Christian times, believers had been eviscerated (gutted). Peter was crucified upside-down. We all know what happened to Jesus. In the Middle Ages, Joan of Arc was burned at the stake. Heads were displayed on posts across old London. Later, there was the guillotine. There was the rack. In the relatively sedate U.S., they'd hung people for stealing a horse; they'd tarred and feathered; soon, the electric chair.

But the modern and mass slaying of unborn—abortion, though declining a bit after 1990 (after mankind already failed the test)—trumped past transgressions (in number) and joined a list that seemed to know no bounds, running directly counter to what Christ had taught and what the Church of Rome—the oldest institution on earth, the oldest Christian faith—accepted as standards of what would cause one to be accepted or rejected by Heaven, standards of chastisement.

There was an epidemic of evil.

And so there was this inherent sense that *something* was soon to occur—a cleansing, a warning, an illumination—and it was only reinforced by prophetic inclinations in various denominations. Many, many Catholics and others felt it coming—during prayer meetings, at conferences, during Adoration.

Yet nothing monumental, nothing apocalyptic, nothing that saw societies fall, had yet happened.

It was like in Scripture when Christians in the first century felt events that Christ had foreseen were about to transpire. "The revelation of Jesus Christ, which God gave to him, to show his servants what must happen soon," said the Book of Revelation—in its very first passage.

It all seemed—the prophetic pulse—presumptuous.

At best, premature.

The question of the hour: How did God—how did the eternal entities in Heaven—view "soon," "shortly," "imminent"?

The dictionary defined "soon" as "within a short period after this or that time, event; before long; in the near future; at an early date, promptly or quickly."

"Time is short," was a constant prophetic refrain.

But was it really premature?

Granted, nowhere in the known Fatima messages was the word "imminent" or "soon" used but for those watching the sun dance, and then plunge, that day on October 13 in 1917—the sun falling: fire falling?—could be excused for speculating about the urgent nature of the message.

And, in fact, one part—to do with Russia turning atheistic—was to come true the following year (when Lenin arrived with his revolution), as was the part foreseeing an end to World War One.

But other parts of the prophecy had taken longer. The prediction at Fatima in 1917 of a sign that would precede a huge war had not been fulfilled until 1938 (when an incredible display of the aurora borealis across Europe, the Atlantic, and North America presaged World War Two), and if the "bishop in white" mentioned in the third secret, the man felled by bullets, had represented John Paul II (who was shot on the Fatima anniversary day of May 13, 1981), that prediction had taken six decades—sixty-four years—to materialize.

"Soon" was a relative word.

The Fatima secret—officials said—was played out. Its prophecies had been realized. Fire had been threatened but quenched, that flaming torch in the third secret, the fire held by an angel who had been ready to strike, due to the intervention of the Blessed Mother. This had come to pass. ("After the two parts which I have already explained, at the left of Our Lady and a little above, we saw an Angel with a flaming sword in his left hand; flashing, it gave out flames that looked as though they would set the world on fire; but they died out in contact with the splendor that Our Lady radiated towards him from her right hand: pointing to the earth with his right hand, the Angel cried out in a loud voice: 'Penance, Penance, Penance!'" recalled Sister Lucia dos Santos.) Fatima was largely focused on the rise of Russia, and arguably, a nuclear war with that nation—with the Soviet Union—had been averted (following the consecration of the world to the Immaculate Heart of Mary by John Paul II—who, before he could do this, was nearly killed on a Fatima anniversary day, adding to the intrigue). After that, Communism fell.

But many events in other reputed prognostications, which reached a crescendo in the late 1980s and early 1990s, had yet to happen.

There was also the mention of *fire*—and not just in the 1990 prophecy.

Many warned of it.

All saw truly major happenings.

Some sort of happening—*"the event to come,"* said the 2004 addition, and *"the initial event,"* said the follow-up in 2010—was on the horizon.

This is what we had to come to terms with. This was now the start of our contemplation. *"Soon the world will not be the world you know,"* said the original 1990 prophecy. *"A timetable has been set in motion,"* said the one in 2004. *"The trials of your time now head to the crescendo of meaning,"* said the latest.

What? When?

Whatever "soon" meant, we now faced another set of prophecies that implied urgency or directly stated it. Regional events did occur in the years immediately following the 1990 prophecy, as did the "great new evil"— and September 11 arrived eleven years after the same prophecy had said that the pride in New York would be broken. But now there was more to consider. Soon, it said, "the world will not be the world you know." It wasn't just the obscure "1990" missives. There were folks around the world who claimed strikingly similar "prompts" in the Spirit.

Was it always the Holy Spirit they were in touch with?

No doubt, many messages came from the subconscious: from folks simply peering around and taking stock of an errant, wayward, staggering world. It was a common perception that led to common expectations. The enemy also sent little "messages" to depress or dilute legitimate ones (or simply to delude the faithful). But there was a feel to its essence—to the undercurrent of prophecies—that resonated. If one accepted that, the next question got back to timetables.

When were all things going to occur?

It was as if there had been a lull.

Folks even had grown complacent.

When were the messages received from so many places through so many Catholics, since the early 1980s and in some cases before, going to play out?

We knew from Fatima that a timetable was impossible to set in stone. There were predictions that were short-term, prophecies that were mid-range, and others that were long-term. Vladimir Illrich Lenin's revolution came instantly after the last major Fatima apparition, and almost as quickly came the end of World War One, as the Blessed

Mother had foreseen to the children. This took twelve months. Others played out over decades. The Madonna had said if mankind didn't stop offending God there would be another great war and persecutions of the Church; the good would be martyred; there would be famine. And starting in the 1920s, Communists began an incredible campaign against believers of all stripes, and particularly Catholics, who were imprisoned, tortured, and slain by the hundreds of thousands. In 1934, the golden dome of St. Michael's Cathedral in Kiev was destroyed and other churches bulldozed, turned into grain depositories, or converted into museums of atheism—in direct confirmation of what the Blessed Mother forewarned, when she'd specifically cited atheists. Icons were smashed. Belltowers were yanked to the ground. By 1950, 4,119 Catholic churches in Ukraine (just one of the Soviet republics) were demolished or handed over to the Orthodox, who were controlled by Moscow. Thousands of priests were imprisoned or executed (some nailed to walls in mockery of the Crucifixion). In 1933 alone an estimated 4.6 to ten million Ukrainians died in a government-induced *famine* (their crops stolen by the Russians). By the most conservative estimates, twenty million were killed under Joseph Stalin, Lenin's successor. The important point here is the chronology. We see the time frame. A massive chastisement—in many ways, apocalyptic—unwound in fits, starts, lulls, and surges for three decades and then—after a long lull—proceeded to the shooting of the Pope in 1981 and the collapse of Communism. While not specifically naming Russia, John Paul II consecrated the entire world to the Immaculate Heart of Mary in 1982 and it was right after that Mikhail Gorbachev—who later became a great admirer of the Pope—rose to power and allowed Poland, East Germany, Czechoslovakia, Bulgaria, Romania, and Hungary to shake free from Communism.

All did so by 1990—the year of the new prophecy.

In 1991, the Soviet Union itself dissolved—and to universal astonishment Russia began a path toward Christianity (perhaps in fulfillment of Mary's prophecy that this nation would be "converted"). No longer was there the constant threat of a nuclear holocaust—not between the two superpowers, not for now. A "period of peace," as predicted, was granted to the world.

Thus the Fatima prophecies had stretched out over nearly a century.

Was this now true for the others that had come since Fatima?

When one looked into history, one saw the variance. In Wisconsin, in what would become America's first approved apparition, the Blessed Mother, in 1859, near Green Bay, had forecast a "punishment" that took place in 1871—twelve years later—with fire. In Kibeho, Rwanda, in 1982, another apparition of Mary prophesied a genocide that likewise materialized a dozen years after. *Did twelve mean anything?* Further back, before Fatima, there was the LaSalette apparition in the French Alps and its prophecy—in a Church-accepted secret from there—that exactly foresaw a famine and outbreak that began within a year while prophecies in a longer, far more apocalyptic, but unofficial secret from LaSalette, still waited to play out.

"God will strike in an unprecedented way," it said. "Woe to the inhabitants of the earth! God will exhaust His wrath upon them, and no one will be able to escape so many afflictions together. The chiefs, the leaders of the people of God have neglected prayer and penance, and the devil has bedimmed their intelligence. They have become wandering stars which the old devil will drag along with his tail to make them perish. God will allow the old serpent to cause divisions among those who reign, in every society and in every family. Physical and moral agonies will be suffered.

God will abandon mankind to itself and will send punishments which will follow one after the other for more than thirty-five years."

Some of this occurred soon after, as France suffered various uprisings and afflictions. But what about the rest— including a prediction in the secret that *"water and fire will purge the earth and consume all the works of men's pride"?*

3

There were thus the immediate, short-term, and long-term prophecies.

Was the same now true of the 1990 "locution"?

The prophecy had started out by saying that "a new evil the likes of which mankind has never before encountered" would come in four years time and would be "comparable" in its evil to abortion. It also mentioned chastisements that would "differ according to regions" and "not always or usually be immediately noticeable" for what they were.

Incredible it was to mull that over, for 1990 was arguably the starting point for an incredible run of regional disasters—particularly weather events—worldwide, events that were certainly not recognized as regional "chastisements." Were they forerunners to future augmented events?

In the two decades after 1990 the National Climatic Data Center logged one hundred weather and climate disasters that cost at least one billion each, for a grand total of $706.2 billion or well over half a trillion dollars. That said nothing, of course, about the tornadoes and winds that roared through 2012—about the $41 billion cost of "Sandy"—nor did it take into account other disasters such as the Los

Angeles quake in 1994. And it didn't count events in other nations—where the surge, where the explosion in weather, not to mention tsunamis, was more monumental yet. Those who didn't believe in coincidence could be excused for doing a double-take at the fact that "Katrina" was derived from a word that meant "purification."

There was more—much more—but we get the point: as in other cases, as with Fatima, and LaSalette, as in Wisconsin, and Africa, a number of events that could be tied to the prophecy occurred immediately or "soon" after—soon in human chronology. One that was man-made—September 11—was interesting because toward the end of the original 1990 prophecy it said, *"New York City is under an evil cloud and will be for 12 years. Do not go there. The pride there will be broken."* The Twin Towers—the pride of Manhattan—were destroyed just under twelve years later (and I myself, on the way to give a eulogy for a friend who died in the attack, was witness there to an unusual, engulfing cloud that was not typical New York smog).

4

And so one paid heed when a subsequent message said, *"The trials of your time now head to the crescendo of meaning, whereby to each will be shown the imperfection of the past and the need for purification of the future."*

According to the dictionary, "crescendo" meant the peak "of a gradual increase."

Like so many things about these prophetic messages, new and deeper meaning often evolved over time and I did not equate the word "gradual" with crescendo so much as simply the word "climax" or "peak" and yet it fit perfectly: starting in 1990—freezes in California, flooding in Texas— events had subtly grown. Over time, they had built up. There was a massive firestorm in California. There was a hurricane. Storms were increasing in intensity, with "mini-crescendos" such as a nor'easter in 1992, Hurricane Andrew (which was like a mile-wide tornado) that same year, and a blizzard in 1993 which slammed the entire eastern seaboard and closed every major airport east of the Mississippi for the first time on record.

This was the time of the "perfect storms."

By 2012, after an unusually warm winter, a blistering summer the previous year, and an unusually *cold* winter before that, the public agreed by a margin of two to one—sixty-nine percent—in a poll that the weather was getting more severe. They linked it to the climate, and for good reason: the jet stream, and oscillations over the Atlantic, were jumping all over the place. I called it a swerve or "gyration." The climate was going to various extremes and clouds, temperature, humidity, wind flow, ocean currents, rivers, and other players in our surroundings were going along with it.

Swerving. Gyrating. At the same time that the U.S. had a startlingly clement winter, Europe was bundled up against record lows and snow.

Clouds?

They seemed like harbingers. Was it an artifact—was it simply because so many people now had access to blogs and YouTube, as well as digital cameras—or were there clouds the likes of which most had not previously witnessed?

I received many photos. I saw the massive, towering ones. I saw the mammatus—which looked like a sky full of dumplings. I saw the towering black tornadic cells. I saw eerie dark stratus. Some seemed to arrive at peculiar times, with peculiar formations, even images. Scientists called this pareidolia: when a person believes he sees something in a cloud or other nebulous constituent and the mind subconsciously associates part of it with an object or person. I wasn't sure that was always the case. In fact, I knew it wasn't. I had seen photographs of silhouettes that looked startlingly like Mary or Jesus. Angels seemed prominent (and ready). The fluffs of cumulus, the wisps from high cirrus, formed their gowns, their wings. Let's say much could be tagged to interpretation. But *something* was going on. Something was being said. Nature—God through nature—seemed to be speaking;

hinting that all those weather events were no happenstance; as too folks often saw evil visages: demons. Meanwhile even secular news sites ran photographs of a sun flare that looked like an angel with trumpet to mouth and I recalled a formation of the aurora borealis that seemed like a gigantic, towering, prismatic angel streaming down in resplendent light—shimmering green, a blazing, incendiary red.

It had been the presentation of the northern lights that formed the great sign of Fatima, and so we paid attention to the auroras, which were fulgent, which were blazing toward the earth, into the magnetosphere, over whole continents, big time. Just because an astrophysicist could detail the physical mechanics behind solar radiation causing colorful mesospheric colors didn't mean that God wasn't behind those mechanics. Sister Lucia herself had seen the 1938 aurora and had stated in a letter to her bishop that "God manifested that sign, which astronomers chose to call an aurora borealis. I don't know for certain, but if they investigated the matter, they would discover that, in the form in which it appeared, it could not possibly have been an aurora borealis. Be that as it may, God made use of this to make me understand His Justice was about to strike the guilty nations."

A similar aurora had preceded an apparition in the French village of Pontmain (also in connection with a war) and following September 11, the sky illuminated in similar fashion.

I had spoken the night before September 11 to a crowd at a small church near Salt Lake City and during my talk found myself declaring that due to America's transgressions, fire was about to fall. I had said the same the day before in Sacramento. It was one of those intuitions out of nowhere, but soon, within hours, in a manner of speech, fire did rain down in Manhattan.

Red. It was the color of the hour. There was red in the auroras, there was red in the solar flares, there was red in the sun miracles, there was the red tide that turned ocean water afire—that made it look like blood, in places like Australia—and there was the actual blood that turned waters red as dolphins were slaughtered in Japan and red in unprecedented wildfires and in streaming lava from volcanic eruptions.

Fire. Such a thing about fire. And images. When I ran stories about formations that were claimed on various objects (walls, countertops, garages, windows, seashells, simply to discern), it was not surprising to receive e-mails questioning such or even complaining about such "nonsense." And in cases, nonsense, perhaps, it was. Certainly, many images that were interpreted as the Blessed Mother did not really look much like her. Holy figures were imputed each time anything vaguely resembled the profile of a human. Skepticism was understandable—even healthy.

A closed mind was not.

Those studying the annals of paranormal research knew that history was replete with phenomena whereby spirits seemed to inflect physical objects. There were signs from the other side—at wakes, at scenes of accidents, in hospitals. (*Don't forget me. Pray for me.*) As the theorist Haldane said, the world is not only stranger than we imagine, but stranger than we *can* imagine.

And God was throughout the mix.

He operated everywhere and on every level and so there was more than a slim chance that a substantial number of images, some ridiculed, some mesmerizing, bore a reminder of the supernatural, and when Jesus seemed to take form, or Mary, one immediately associated it with the eruption of so many other alleged phenomena such as weeping statues, healings, stigmata, apparitions, oil from icons, crosses on trees, or perhaps an unusual circular rainbow (over a church, say, on Divine Mercy Sunday).

I had once witnessed a rainbow that appeared on a totally clear day as my family was headed to the cemetery to bury a great-uncle. The rainbow was not really a bow but rather a multi-colored line that was parallel with the ground all the way to the cemetery (thereafter vanishing).

And so it was difficult to scoff at the many—the count-less—images.

Was Jesus speaking? Was Heaven preparing us for what the original 1990 prophecy said: a manifestation? The mystic Maria Esperanza had once told me that Christ was preparing to visit "everyone," and so one could ponder whether little, arguable inflections of holiness into the phys-ical realm might—*might*—presage that event.

It certainly seemed like everyone was having some kind of an experience—in forests, on shorelines, near water as it cascaded over a falls. And, yes, images were seen in fire. There were an *awful* lot of fire or storm-cloud photos that had what looked like angry, demonic faces. In the same shot, there might be what some saw as holy ones. A popular example was the shape of flames in a Polish campfire that looked just like the outline of a photograph of John Paul II (as he waved to a crowd).

Were these "snapshots" of a spiritual reality that surrounded us? The holy ones often came with a sense of sanctity—you could at times feel an anointing—or at highly meaningful times: on Hosts, in chapels. At night, people saw a Cross behind the crescent moon or a form in the light of the moon itself.

Speaking of fire, it was drawing right up to places of worship. There was a spectacular photograph of a fire in southern California near San Diego that shot high in the sky just beyond a Franciscan monastery but never touched it. In the Wisconsin apparition, the wildfire had destroyed miles of surrounding terraine and scorched the fence rails around a shrine built to mark the vision but—impossibly—never entered the shrine itself.

In my own city, at the church where I attended weekday Mass, a brushfire went right to the parking lot, and there was just this strange sense to it, to pulling up for seven a.m. Mass and seeing tall flames; a sense not just for that fire but for all that seemed to be coming in fits and starts—everywhere, gradually.

This was such a key word in the new *alleged* locution: gradual. Hurricane Iniki had given way to Hurricane Andrew which was to give way to Hurricane Katrina.

A quake in San Francisco had given way to one in Los Angeles which gave way to a big one in New Zealand which gave way to a gigantic one in the sea off Japan.

Graduation.

One worse than the one before.

But in fits and starts—a gradual trend not seen except when one took the long view of retrospection.

This threw off many who were feeling the "prophetic pulse"—and had, since the 1990s—but expected only the "big one."

There was *overexpectation*.

It was just what the newest message said.

We nearly wanted chastisement, purification, things to change more quickly than was turning out to be the case. We'd forgotten Fatima. We'd forgotten how long the major events could take. We had designed a time frame in our own way and so with each huge storm or a flooding of the Mississippi—which happened in such an incredible historic, biblical way in 1993—we were sure everything was going to "hit the fan."

It was only a matter of days, or weeks, or at the most months, was the constant speculation. Locutions came in a torrent. Most carried similar messages. Some were clear repeats. Others were so lengthy that only the most dedicated follower could be expected to spend time going through them. There was a lack of economical language. The same was true of apparitions. But they showed a great unrest—not just among active Catholics, but also evangelical Christian brethren—in the spirit. Something—some *things*—were going to come down. The 2004 "addendum" addressed this directly when in its unique (and economic) tone it said, *"The event to come will surprise everyone who has offered a prognostication."*

Clearly, no major private revelation foresaw it. Clearly, there was going to be a surprise. These were excellent people out there, involved in prophecy; you couldn't find better. But everyone, it seemed, was going to be taken aback; no one had it set in stone. But they knew *something* was coming. Scripture said that God does nothing before first warning through His prophets, and in fact He *had* warned— had been warning, arguably—for more than two decades; depending on which private revelation, one could say (not counting Fatima or LaSalette) for half a century. There were just all kinds of appearances by the Virgin—in Italy, in Spain, in South America, in Africa, in North America, in Ireland—all indicating the same trend, all with messages echoing the same theme. It was uncanny. I could visit a seer on a mountaintop in Ecuador and get the same basic tenor as in a remote Ukrainian hamlet where there were no phones or cars or radios and where they too were seeing strange occurrences with the sun.

As at Fatima, and like the weather, the sun was gyrating at various places. It was oscillating and varying. Sometimes—as at Fatima—it seemed to move, or turn colors, or throw off colors; sometimes there were *two* suns. Millions testified to seeing things they took to be a sort of pulse from the sun and a roundish dark spot or orb that moved in front of the solar radiation to shield the eyes, taken by more than a few to represent a Host.

I first saw the "sun miracle" at Medjugorje in Yugoslavia and not only did it toss off various colors for a distance several times its diameter but the surrounding mountains seemed swathed in a prism-like aura of multiple light. I happened to run into the football coach Don Shula and his wife on a vineyard and she was seeing what I was (he remained closed-mouthed).

Returning to the U.S., I consulted an expert at Columbia University who told me staring at the sun for the prolonged time pilgrims were staring at it should have resulted in immediate eye damage (it did not). Later, I would see it from many places around the world, including from my own yard, at dinner time.

Was it just something to do with the way the sun's rays bent as the sun neared the horizon?

Perhaps some was "natural." But once more, there was a different aspect to it. Often it seemed like a sign that major transformation loomed. Here we went again. "Soon." Other times, it seemed like a personal confirmation. How gradual was God? He was, of course, infinitely deliberate. We could look at the way He formed Creation. Moreover, the delay in anything happening could always be attributed to the intervention of Blessed Mary as well as His patience, His mercy. Recall that the Fatima secret showed Mary quenching—erasing—the angel's fire. A possibility—a major calamity—had been averted, and the 1990 prophecy had stated at its very beginning how the Lord allegedly was allowing the test of a new great evil in response to the Virgin's pleas—that while we had miserably failed the test of abortion (and no doubt endless other moral tests), this new one, which was "comparable" to abortion (to do with genetic manipulation, in my estimation), gave us, presumably, a final chance.

Did this mean that otherwise—without Mary—*preordained chastisements would have occurred by the 1990s? Like Fatima, had justice been quenched—if temporarily?*

Perhaps. But there was a difference. The Fatima secret—relayed to Lucia and the other seers on July 13, 1917—*foresaw* that the chastisement would be erased, at least for the time being. With the third Fatima secret it had not been the case whereby a prediction was made and then God reversed Himself. This was often asserted when a prophecy failed to materialize: that the foreseen events were conditional and had been eliminated due to prayer or some moral change. At major, approved apparitions, at least in recent centuries, if such was the possibility, this was explicitly stated. Appearing up there in Wisconsin, the Blessed Mother had told a devout Belgian immigrant girl, *"You received Holy Communion this morning and that is well. But you must do more. Make a general confession and offer Communion for the conversion of sinners. If they do not convert and do penance, my Son will be obliged to punish them."* The word "if" had made it clear: it was conditional—and announced as such. The same held true with the first LaSalette prophecy (about a coming potato famine), which had started with the word *"if"* before spelling out what could only be described as doom. *"If my people do not wish to submit themselves,"* it had said, *"I am forced to let go of the Hand of my Son."* Note the similarities to Wisconsin—which occurred, in an entirely different part of the world thirteen years later. At Fatima the Blessed Mother had warned in the second secret that *"if what I say to you is done, many souls will be saved and there will be peace."* If not, there would be great conflict, as indeed there was, when a second world war arrived. On the Fatima anniversary day of October 13, 1973, at Akita, Japan, Mary reportedly had told the locutionist there, Sister Agnes Sasagawa, *"if men do not repent and better themselves, the Father will inflict a terrible punishment on all humanity. It will be punishment greater than the deluge, such as one will never have seen before."* Again, there was a condition, an escape hatch. The 1990 prophecy put it this way: *"How mankind responds to this new evil will determine the extent, length, and severity of the first chastisements."*

But here was the rub.

The 1990 prophecy, while conditional (*"how mankind responds"*), did not say "if." It only referred to potential easement in duration and severity.

Certain events—chastisements—were going to occur. The same was indicated at the alleged (always note the word "alleged") site of Medjugorje. There, a disaster in one seer's set of secrets had been eliminated, it was said, but others that were set to follow had to occur due to sin in the world. They were set in stone. Likewise, the events foreseen as the initial ones in the 1990 missive were stated definitively as occurrences that—after some kind of scare to do with the sky, and strange rumblings—would be followed by *"another chastisement"* proportionate to mankind's response. It was obvious that the regional chastisements— spoken about in plural—were considered as a collective phase, for it was followed by the forecast that *"this, according to mankind's response, will then be followed by another chastisement."*

The regional events were one aspect; there was also a subsequent chastisement.

Would that chastisement be a singular happening or an aggregate of several?

I couldn't tell.

One could say this:

Other events in the message did not contain a similar proviso. The prophecy had flatly and boldly—startlingly—predicted that our technology would be dismantled, that society would be reduced to a simpler state, that the world was not going to end but change (dramatically), that a new world order would come, affected by an antichrist but followed by a powerful series of events in which Christ was also going to manifest to break Satan's power. In the 2010 addition to the original prophecy, the "crescendo" seemed to indicate that indeed the massive weather and seismic events since 1990 were the aforementioned regional events or precursors to them, and it was these events—which built so piecemeal—that would now reach a "crescendo."

What it didn't say was whether that crescendo would mean a single high-point event (a natural disaster, but on a greater scale than any which living men had witnessed); a sudden flurry of events (linked by timing or similarity); or a new kind of chastisement altogether. Actually, it wasn't even clear if natural disasters were what would hit a peak. The locution of 2010 used the word "trials." *The trials of our time.* For certain, devastation by hurricanes or blizzards or droughts was a trial. A trial could be a cross, a crucible, a gauntlet, which disasters and other physical hardships brought. But it could have meant many other things as well. A trial could be a formal examination before a tribunal, which might come with persecution. It could be a test of faith, patience, or stamina (through subjection to suffering). As such, it would refer more to the spiritual dimensions. It would refer more to the battle with evil. It would refer more to sin. We certainly were surrounded by it! Was this what was set to reach a crescendo—evil? Was evil itself a chastisement, about to peak? If so, how?

No one yet knew. But that it was connected to moral evil—turpitude—seemed clear too from the subsequent phrase that said we would be shown *"the imperfection of the past and the need for purification of the future."* Clearly, the "trials" involved our vast and irreconcilable imperfections. We had gone too far for complete remission. Now here it became even more interesting. It did not say simply that the *"trials"* would reach a *"crescendo."* It said that the trials would reach the *"crescendo of meaning."* Meaning could indicate "intention, sense, or significance." It was meant to convey something. The logical assumption was that chastisements were designed as an expression of God's displeasure *with* that imperfection. The dictionary—intriguingly enough—said a meaning also could be "an implication of a hidden or special significance." The weather and seismic events could fit that. The allowance of sin, of darkness, could also be seen as a chastisement. But it was not clear if the 2010 message was even referring back to those regional chastisements of the first prophecy. One might argue that the new message—presumed to be authentic, presumed to be from an angel, or the Lord—indeed referred chiefly to a test of evil, which was certainly prevalent in our era. A similar notion was in play at Medjugorje, where the Blessed Mother was quoted as calling the current time "the hour of the power of darkness" and as saying that "darkness reigns over the whole world." Somehow, this crescendo was going to illuminate for us the mistakes of our past. It was also going to show the need for future *"purification."* Did that mean societal mistakes—and purification—or personal cleansing; or both?

As usual, the words operated on several levels—the clear mark of potential authenticity. Each word, each syllable almost, had to be digested. It was weaving—uncannily—a very complex scenario with precious few words. *"The trials of your time now head to the crescendo of meaning, whereby to each will be shown the imperfection of the past and the need for purification of the future."*

One could even speculate that something physical—something in the real, tangible, visible world—would occur to open up or illuminate our consciences.

Or, it could be in the realm of morality. Might there be something so evil on the horizon that it would collectively take mankind aback?

Evil had been relentlessly building up. Blatant? How about a massive pagan ritual that was camouflaged as the half-time show at the 2012 Super Bowl or the occult underpinnings in the Olympic ceremonies that same year in a stadium called the Cauldron where a gigantic satanic figure was hoisted far above the ground: As one person from England wrote me, "There was the reading from the writer of the Harry Potter series, then the bad night dreams of the children. Horrible black satanic demonic creatures roamed, then near the end there was black smoke and more black demonic creatures seemed to crawl out of the floors/sewers. England has more witches and warlocks than priests now."

The same demonic images were celebrated from New Orleans at Mardi Gras to the annual lascivious carnival in Rio to actual events in San Francisco and Greenwich Village that openly relished—advertised—debauchery (see the annual Halloween parade there, disrupted in 2012 by "Sandy").

Something evil or bad was approaching that would show everyone how errant mankind was turning and the wrong course of "progress": the technological mistakes. Every reading of the prophecy brought more intrigue. Importantly, the "crescendo"—whatever it was, in whatever regard—was not presented as the conclusion of coming disturbances but only a demonstration of the need for *"purification of the future."* The trials were "heading" to that summit, that peak—heading, not necessarily there quite yet. But use of the word "now" indicated a new phase. If nothing else, we were going to understand the reason why what happened occurred. The burning question: what might arrive to show the need for major transformation? What would cause "each" person to suddenly realize past mistakes? Might it be something supernatural, as so many expected, something skyward? They even called this the "illumination." From as far back as the sixteenth century, when Saint Edmund Campion of England spoke of "a great day that would reveal all men's consciences," a coming day of enlightenment had been foretold, pointed out one author. Known as the "warning" and the "mini-judgment," it was purported to be the day in which God would supernaturally illuminate the conscience of every man, woman, and child on earth. "Each person, then, would momentarily see the state of their soul through God's Eyes and realize the truth of His existence, after which, it is said the world will never be the same," noted the back cover of a book on the topic. "This predicted event is now said to be imminent, as talk concerning the certainty of this miracle has intensified." In the dark, brightness—of some sort. Physical? Spiritual? A combination? As for darkness reaching a peak, many believed there would come a time when demons would visibly show themselves and there would be three days of actual darkness (warded off only by blessed candles). Such concepts were believed by a not insignificant number of serious Catholics. How drastic a "crescendo" was in store? Could it also and simply be a final stage whereby evil found its essence and expended its most power: began to rule the world?

5

We were already close. It was not the dark age of Stalin. It wasn't Nazi Germany. It was not Ukraine in the 1930s, granted. That was when evil became about as material as evil could get.

But in the sphere of morality, it was hard to imagine a worse era.

For in the current time it was to blaspheme in any way one saw fit (this right protected by law), okay to put graphic acts of sex on television (there to be viewed by youngsters), to take organs from "donors" who technically were still living, to charge exorbitantly for medication, to terminate an unborn just before birth, to create vaccinations from stem-cell lines (derived from aborted fetuses), to sell baby parts, to assist the ill and aged with suicide, to worship as a witch (in the military), to sell the most profane pornography on the internet, to peddle actual curses (and create an entire theme park devoted to wizardry), to publicly prevaricate in order to sell a product (such that virtually every advertisement possessed some level of deception), to distribute food that was contaminated (or dangerously synthetic), to lewdly portray the Pope, to "tweet" religious hatred, to make fun of nuns in a movie, to mock the Blessed Mother, to put a Crucifix in a bottle of urine (as a work of "art"), to smear a portrait of the Virgin with feces, to ban religion from the workplace, to prohibit mention of God—or the wearing of a Cross—at school, at games, in the workplace; to mandate that Catholics allow birth control; to forbid criticism of homosexuality (and same-sex marriage), to deface the body (so many tattoos, often with demonic images), to self-mutilate (one man had horns sewn into his head). What a trial it was, to observe the craze of vampires, to watch teen idols turn into public harlots, to hear the hatred spewed forth on radio and TV (or blogged on the computer screen), to read the almost certain profanity in the public comments at the end of internet news articles, to watch the rich grab for yet more money; to witness the startling corporate disregard for human health, and to stand by as they changed the genetic structures of frogs and cats and dogs and crops (to list a few evils).

What more could happen? Was the 2010 prophecy simply saying that all these things were now about as bad as things could get or that they were simply nearing a summit (*"head to the crescendo"*)? Was the peak we approached the crescendo of noticing evil among those who were spiritually attuned and watched such things and had for years, for decades? Some said it coincided with the prophecy by Pope Leo XIII, who back in the nineteenth century on October 13, 1884 had heard Satan ask for a century during which he would test humankind. October 13 was again also what would be a crucial Fatima anniversary. Some wondered if perhaps the special century or period allotted by God to Satan—who according to legend had been heard by the Pope to boast that if given enough time he could destroy the Church, and drag all of mankind to hell—had started in 1917. If so, it would end in 2017. *If.* It seemed unlikely that anyone could pin a specific year on the start nor that it would be precisely a hundred years. It seemed a manner of speech. It may have started with LaSalette—where it said the devil was being unloosed. Who was the Pope during the apparitions of Fatima? Pope Benedict XV, named after a saint associated with fighting evil. Now, as the period moved toward a conclusion, as of this writing, the pontiff was Pope Benedict XVI.

It was important to note that a crescendo or peak in "meaning" meant that we were nearing a time when the "trials" of our times became most *meaningful*. This might lead one to recall how at Fatima Sister Lucia reportedly had advised that it might be best to release the third secret after 1960 because then it would be more understandable (*mas claro*): in a word, more meaningful.

It was difficult to tell what she had said and what she had not, but she certainly had made it clear that we were in the midst of a gargantuan spiritual struggle.

Three years before the onset of that uproarious, rebellious decade, in 1957, the Fatima seer had told a priest named Father Augustine Fuentes that the devil was "in the mood for engaging in a decisive battle" and was particularly after those planning on entering the priesthood, making them delay or cancel entrance into religious life, while among the laypeople he was removing enthusiasm for sacrifices and dedication to God.

Astonishing it was, looking at those words in retrospect, for it was in the late Fifties and Sixties that so many priests who would later become sexual abusers—satanically harming our young, and nearly destroying Catholicism—were being ordained or in the seminary. Were the words of the second LaSalette secret also relevant?

Here it had been said that *"the priests, ministers of my Son, by their wicked lives, by their irreverence and their impiety in the celebration of the holy mysteries, by their love of money, their love of honors and pleasures, have become a cesspool of impurity."*

Harsh stuff. It made you look twice. On second glance, it made you wince.

That "secret"—never accepted by the formal Church (though believed by two popes who read it)—had also warned that an occult spirit, *"Asmodeas and his like"* (Asmodeas has traditionally been the name of a major demon), would turn convents into "grazing grounds" and—even more to the point—and that *"the devil will resort to all his evil tricks to introduce sinners into religious orders."*

There would be a "time of darkness" and the Church would witness "a frightful crisis." Indeed! What could possibly horrify the many excellent, devout, holy parishioners more than a pastor caught abusing the altar boys? The number of times this occurred—starting in the Fifties, and carrying through with a vengeance into the lust-bust 1970s—was nothing less than historic, arguably worse than even the corruption scandals (selling pastorships, selling waivers to priests so they could marry) of the High Middle Ages. It was frightful. It was dark. We were seeing the gates of hell. I couldn't possibly summarize the scandal, for every day articles came across the screen of my computer, some too disenchanting—and graphic—to read. One could come to no conclusion other than that Satan had distorted the sexuality of men who'd entered seminaries or lured those who had such a proclivity to start with and were enrolling in the priesthood to find a purpose or safe haven.

In the LaSalette message—the *unapproved* part—it claimed that Satan and a "large number" of his demons would be unloosed from hell in 1864. Was this what Pope Leo XIII was referring to? In this realm, could one really peg specific years—for something operating in an area that was timeless? A "century" meant an extended period. Definitely,

1964 was as much a time of entry as 1864—if not more so, with the explosion of music, drugs, sex, and occultism that overtook our youth like a tsunami. It was part of a "crescendo." The build up had been gradual—with certain points of special intensity. Lucia said this was "a decisive battle against the Virgin. And a decisive battle is the final battle where one side will be victorious and the other side will suffer defeat. Hence from now on we must choose sides. Either we are for God or we are for the devil. There is no other possibility."

So this was strong affirmation of both the original prophecy of December 1990 and the latest one in 2010: great darkness, *unusual* darkness, was reaching new heights. A peak could mean that after the crescendo there would be a gradual climb down on the other side but that was only a possibility. It could also mean a far less than gradual conclusion—indeed, a cliff. Certainly, sin was now more flagrant, more "out there," more pronounced, than in modern recorded history. Was it as bad as ancient Rome or in Babylon or Egypt? There was no way to tell. It was a different but likewise blanketing darkness. Paganism. Idolatry. It came in many forms! The 2010 prophecy also coincided strikingly with Fatima in the mention of trials with evil and that *"in these transgressions is found the enemy of Creation, and the one who seeks to install his spirit as the spirit that conquers for all time."* Worded differently, it nonetheless said the same thing: it was a final battle, the end game. The devil sought *"to install his spirit"* as the spirit that would prevail—forever. Very strong, unusual language. The word *"transgressions"* basically confirmed the word *"trials"* as in this context meaning sin. Trials. Temptations. Could there ever have been more? Were there really any worse temptations in those ancient temples with prostitutes in Babylon or with those seductresses on boats that sailed the Nile past Cairo or in the snares and travesties of emperors in Rome?

Transgression. A time of evil. Transgression meant evil-doing, turpitude, depravity; it meant crime, to breach the law; it meant terrorism and "abomination." The latter was a synonym that brought to mind *Matthew* 24 and the "abomination of desolation," for it was in that passage—when Christ prophesied—that we see the clear notion of massive future events, as too in *Luke* 21. "Nation will rise against nation, and kingdom against kingdom. There will be powerful earthquakes, famine, and plagues from place to place; and awesome sights and mighty signs will come from the sky," said that chapter—which at one point, perhaps referring to destruction of the Temple, called the events "imminent." Some of these events arguably transpired with the Roman war on Israel—and destruction of the Temple around 70 A.D. That was nearly twenty centuries ago. But clearly other aspects had not yet occurred, not in a literal way, at least not globally. Might the Black Death later have qualified? Or the world wars (as a "terrible calamity")? Or simply what Jews went through during the destruction of Jerusalem (when in fact Halley's Comet hung in the sky, like the sword of Damocles)? "There will be signs in the sun, the moon, and the stars, and on earth nations will be in dismay, perplexed by the roaring of the sea and the waves," said Jesus. "People will die of fright in anticipation of what is coming upon the world for the powers of the heavens will be shaken [*fear of fire?*]. And then they will see the Son of Man coming in a cloud with power and great glory" [*"a series of supernatural events similar to the apparitions"?*]. The reference to famines, quakes, and roaring seas could be taken as something that already had occurred—regionally: For example, the eruption, in the first century, of Vesuvius (which caused not just fire and three days of darkness and sudden death at Pompeii but also huge sea waves). But if taken literally, *Luke* and *Matthew* both seemed to preview something much larger, something that preceded Christ's coming "on a cloud" (as Mary was so often depicted, during apparitions, at places like Fatima, where she arrived with her feet on a luminous cloud) and this had not yet occurred. As for the mention in 2010 of "transgressions," it was interesting if coincidental that a secondary definition for that word was "the spreading of the sea over land as evidenced by the deposition of marine strata over terrestrial strata."

The main meaning of "transgressions," however, was evildoing and as Bishop Luigi Negri of San Marino-Montefeltro, Italy, speaking to the Vatican's newspaper, *L'Osservatore Romano*, noted, "There is diabolical presence in the mentality that dominates this society of ours . . . a fundamentally atheist mentality, diabolical in the sense that says 'If you take God away, man will realize his full potential.'"

A diabolical presence was dominating our cultures. In the 1960s, it was as if the devil had been conducting a camouflaged ritual—the drugs like a witch's *pharmakeia*, the spirit of rebellion reminding us of *1 Samuel* 23 (which likened rebellion to the spirit of witchery, which might also be said of radical feminism), the rock music beating like a drum in deep voodoo Africa *(Sympathy for the Devil)*, and the sexual revolution like a mass, modern rite of saturnalia, which led to the need not just for birth control (*pharmakeia* again) but also, by 1973, legalized abortion (like a mass human sacrifice). It was precisely what the 1990 prophecy had implied, and the volcanic eruption of darkness was also mentioned by a famous Rome exorcist who pegged an upswing in reported possessions as well as the uncountable cases of demonic infestation and *oppression* as running in parallel not just with the occult or actual Satanism but hedonism and the influences of "Western consumerism" (this was Father Gabriele Amorth). Added a well-known French exorcist, Father Joseph de Tonquédec, a Jesuit, "There are a vast number of souls who, while not showing signs of demonic possession, turn to the exorcist to be relieved of their suffering, such as stubborn illnesses, adversities, all sorts of misfortunes. Those possessed by the devil are few, but these unhappy souls are legion."

6

She was right, Lucia: a final battle was about to start. She said she was given to understand that. What was in her secrets would become clearer in the 1960s (when as it turned out the world was nearly torched during the Cuban missile crisis). But let's focus on what she called a great "diabolical disorientation." So extensive was the infiltration and then permeation of darkness that it defied summary. This raw evil, descending like a torrential rain, overcame the floodgates and ran in parallel with the urgency of the third secret and a punishment that in 1957 she said was "imminent." (The missile crisis occurred in 1962).

That was the word she used. Imminent.

And it meant impending, threatening, at hand, over-hanging, near, ready to occur at any moment: the events in that still unknown, mysterious secret that turned out to have been a vision as through a mirror of that "Angel with a flaming sword in his left hand" that "flashing" gave out "flames that looked as though they would set the world on fire."

We see immediate similarities with the 1990 prophecy.

"The angels have their instruction from east to west, and now a timetable has been set in motion," the 2004 addition had said.

The 2010 update said that the trials of our time *"now head"* toward a denouement, toward some kind of event or events—toward an *"initial event."*

As in the Book of Revelation, angels did God's bidding when it came to chastisement.

Seals were broken.

"Secrets" materialized. In *Revelation* was talk of angels who spent wrath upon the earth, and one whose coming caused the earth to become "illumined" (*Revelation* 18).

The Fatima secret had an escape clause in the way of the Blessed Mother's intercession, but looking back at 1957, we can see with crystal clear vision what was imminent—and perhaps what the angel's torch symbolized.

Just five years later came a crisis in which Russia and the U.S. found themselves on the brink of all-out nuclear war. President John Kennedy himself wasn't sure he'd survive it. Missiles were just ninety miles from Florida. And the U.S. demanded their removal in a standoff that had the two nations and the rest of the world gnawing fingernails to the quick. The weapons had been discovered by a spy plane on October 14. It could not have *been* clearer. Fire was about to fall. But the torch had been quenched. There was enough prayer. Something tipped the scales. But there we had it. The Lord had been ready, said Sister Lucia, to chastise the world "in a terrible manner" and she had even repeated the warning that Russia would one day be the instrument of chastisement if it was not converted and that many nations would disappear from the face of the earth. If, in saying that, the Virgin had been referring to the actual physical annihilation of nations, it was something that nuclear warfare was capable of accomplishing, or close to it. Or was the Blessed

Mother referring to the disappearance of sovereign countries, as occurred when Communists absorbed Ukraine and Belarus and Latvia and Lithuania and Estonia and formed the daunting evil empire called the Soviet Union along with the Eastern Bloc of Poland and Czechoslovakia and East Germany and Yugoslavia?

No matter. The secret (the revealed visual part, at any rate) had played out. It had been a conditional prophecy and the condition was prayer and consecration. It showed Our Lady dousing that flame! There were similarities with the Miraculous Medal messages to Saint Catherine Labouré in 1830. Like Fatima, the prophecies were fulfilled during the same century as the apparitions (one within a week). Mary had told Catherine that the times were *"very evil,"* that the whole world would be plunged into *"every kind of misery,"* that the devout would largely be protected but that there would be "victims" among the Paris clergy, including the hierarchy (here she wept tears). *"The streets will flow with blood,"* Mary said. *"Monseigneur the Archbishop will be stripped of his garments. My child, the whole world will be in sadness."* The seer said, "I wondered when this would be, and I understood clearly, *forty years."*

That same year of 1830 a revolution erupted—in fact a week after the apparition—and another in 1848; Archbishop Darboy was murdered in 1870—precisely forty years after the prediction—as was another archbishop named Affré. A third, Archbishop de Quélen, had to flee for his life.

Thus, again, were the events staggered over a period.

Thus were they also accurate—astonishingly.

There were those who felt that only part of the third secret had been released, that besides the image of the angel and Mary and the Pope there also had been text with a prophecy that was in line with *Matthew* 24 and *Luke* 21—

verbal, as opposed to just images, spelling out disaster—and it had been said that when questioned in Fulda, Germany, by a small group about the contents of the third secret, Pope John Paul II, according to a bimonthly Christian journal called *Stimme Des Glaubens* (the "Voice of Mission Faith"), had commented (again in 1980, two decades before the secret was released) that people should not long to know the secret "if it is a question of a message where it is said that the oceans will entirely flood certain parts of the earth, that from moment to moment millions will die."

Flooding? Oceans? There was no image like that in the revealed part of the secret.

If true (I saw no indication that the interview had been recorded), the next question was whether the Pope was alluding to the actual contents of an undisclosed secret text—or something from elsewhere. It *is* known that the great Pontiff (himself a mystic) had studied the secret a few months after Fulda at Gemelli Hospital while recovering from the attempted assassination on that Fatima anniversary. What made the purported Fulda remarks all the more startling was the similarity to an apocryphal "version" of that secret said to have been surreptitiously obtained and published by another German publication, *Nueues Europa,* on October 15, 1963 (and later denounced by Sister Lucia as a hoax). In that "text" was the claim that in the second half of the twentieth century a "big, big war" would occur and "fire and smoke will fall from the sky and the waters of the oceans will be turned to steam—hurling their foam towards the sky, and all that is standing will be overthrown. Millions and more millions will lose their lives from one hour to the next." Half of mankind, it said, would die. The living would "envy those who are dead."

Later, when the actual secret was released, it had that vision of persecuted priests, of the bishop in white falling, of an angel ready to torch the world, which implied fire and most probably nuclear war (since Fatima was so centered on warnings to do with Russia), but no actual words. No text. Nothing about "millions" dying, nor about the twentieth century; nor the oceans. Some claimed there were two Fatima "third secrets": one the vision (which was released) and the other text that accompanied it (as the other two parts of the Fatima prophecies were composed of text). If John Paul II had not read the actual third secret (which was basically a description of a vision), nor a secret, never-revealed text, one must speculate that he had seen the purported *Nueues Europa* report or was referring to the prophecy granted in what would become an approved miracle to the nun Sister Agnes Sasagawa in Akita, who asserted that on October 13, 1973 (again, a Fatima anniversary), she heard Mary warn in locution, *"As I told you, if men do not repent and better themselves, the Father will inflict a terrible punishment on all humanity. It will be a punishment greater than the deluge, such as one will never have seen before. Fire will fall from the sky and will wipe out a great part of humanity, the good as well as the bad, sparing neither priests nor faithful. The survivors will find themselves so desolate that they will envy the dead."*

Both Sister Agnes and the *Nueues Europa* "secret" mentioned Church problems: persecution and dissension. *Nueues Europa* said *"cardinals will be against cardinals and bishops against bishops"* while the Akita message a decade later foresaw that the devil would infiltrate the Church in such a way that one would see *"cardinals opposing cardinals, bishops against bishops. The priests who venerate me will be scorned and opposed by their confreres . . . churches and altars sacked; the Church will be full of those who accept compromises and the demon will press many priests and consecrated souls to leave the service of the Lord."*

Had Sister Agnes—tucked away in a remote cloister (more than five thousand miles away)—seen the *Nueues Europa* story (this was of course in the days before the internet), or had she indeed been granted the same prophecy as was in a written part of the third secret—the "text" that supposedly never has surfaced? It was difficult to believe the Vatican was deceiving about this, though there were entire books charging it had: that there was the secret describing the image Lucia saw in 1917 and another with the text of a message from Mary as the vision unfolded like a movie or hologram (in her words, in a luminosity, "something similar to how people appear in a mirror when they pass in front of it").

Curious it was that when an ambassador to the Vatican from the Philippines, Howard Dee, questioned then-Cardinal Joseph Ratzinger about the third secret (again, years before its release), the future Pope told Dee it was similar to the message of Akita. (Dee confirmed this to me personally.)

Was it "similar" simply because the Fatima image—the torch—and the Akita message both involved the threat of an engulfing fire? Or was he comparing two texts?

Skeptics implied the latter. I believed the Vatican. But I was aware that the rejected part of the LaSalette message, like Akita and the supposed Nueues Europa secret, saw internal Church crises (LaSalette foresaw "filth" as well as the occult entering seminaries and convents) along with global disasters (including great changes in the climate). The Vatican understandably does not seem to like prophecies that reflect negatively on the Church or that are overly apocalyptic. Such events were the kind that many expected and seemed like the sort of major matters implied in the 1990 prophecy as well as the locutions of 2004 and 2010.

Major, major events—of some sort.

The word "now" also played into the 2004 missive. *"The world is now seriously out of conformance with the Will of God and what He created and intended,"* it intoned. *"There are those who would reconfigure the very creatures He has formed, and who meddle with the texture of life. For this reason, the Lord will allow a huge reorientation. If not for the action of Heaven, what God has created on earth will soon be damaged beyond recovery."*

That there allegedly was alarm in Heaven and that it related to a world that was "now" seriously astray implied—once more—that action would "soon" be taken. Indeed, we see the word "soon" crop up in the last line quoted above.

In keeping with historic apparitions, it seemed evident that there were parts of the 1990 prophecy and additions that might occur right away, others that would take years, others that were longer term, accruing to a major transformation. That was one scenario—and certainly, already, regional events were taking place; already, there had been 9/11; already, there were remarkable developments as far as genetic manipulation. You could tell from those nineteenth and twentieth century apparitions that soon meant "before long" and you could also tell this from what was swelling up around us.

Tick, tock. Sin after sin. Outrage after outrage. Even without reading prophecy, one had to ask: how could God take it? There were atheists who equated belief in the Creator with belief in Santa, placed screaming headlines against Him on billboards or buses, who did everything to keep His existence away from the mindset of our young—our yearning, confused youth, who to their credit were starting to assimilate the notion that many of their parents had been brainwashed by nihilism. Nothingness. It had come out of the drug culture. It had come out of philosophy—the philosophy that had such roots in France, where all those apparitions had been. It had come out of a greatly weakened Church that ploughed forth with an academic and cerebral approach that failed to reach them.

"Cool" was now equated with disbelief. Comedians ridiculed Christianity. On one show was a naked woman with a manger between her legs. Excuse the explicit nature. It was the only way of realizing the depths. Others had skits that painted priests in the lowest possible way. There were plays about nuns. There were more comedies. A reality show focused on Mafia wives—glorifying evil. Another had featured Ozzie Osbourne—whose claim to fame included an ode to Satanist Aleister Crowley and whose albums included a song called *Sabbath Bloody Sabbath*. This fellow was now mainstream. Once, during a meeting with recording executives, Osbourne bit off the head of a bird (a love dove). No wonder he appeared in a documentary called "The Decline of Western Civilization." Other rockers were just as outrageous. The two-finger sign of the devil was everywhere—at concerts, at wrestling matches, at any sort of game. Religion was no longer just questioned; no longer was it simply ridiculed. It was being replaced by occultism. To analyze the approach of popular culture to Catholicism one had only to watch a video called "Like a Prayer" in which the singer-actress cavorted in a blatantly sexual manner in a church with a weeping male statue that came alive to seduce her for sex at the altar as she danced with the blood of the stigmata oozing from her hands in front of crosses that were set afire.

This was Madonna, and when you Googled her name, she by far tallied the most search results, way above those for the real Madonna.

No doubt about it: she was a Cleopatra. She was the one who performed at the Super Bowl as a neo-pagan priestess surrounded by slaves in ancient Egyptian-Babylonian occult motif, replete with a headdress and two horns. Her promotion of sadomasochism and transgenderism—blurring the sexes—was lauded. Such were our days—as they dwindled.

This was perhaps topped only by the debacle at the "Grammys" that same year as another hugely popular singer named Nicki Minaj showed up onstage with an escort dressed like the Pope for a mock Confession and exorcism.

Most vulgar was the part that showed a scantily clad female dancer stretching backwards while an altar boy knelt between her legs in prayer. A man posing as a bishop walked onstage; Minaj was shown levitating. A Christmas carol was sung in a lewd way. "None of this was by accident, and all of it was approved by The Recording Academy, which puts on the Grammys," complained the Catholic League. "Whether Minaj is possessed is surely an open question, but what is not in doubt is the irresponsibility of The Recording Academy."

There was Lady Gaga—an extraordinarily lewd performer who *Time* listed as one of the hundred most influential people in the world, singing of her love for Judas (and at one point suffering a concussion when she was struck by a pole on a set replete with a glowing Cross). When she went to Africa, a large organization of churches protested, worried that she would inspire Satanism. Of course, little came from complaints about blasphemy, no surprise to those who for years had watched society—or better, the societies of men (for these were international stars)—extol a performer who grabbed his groin area while performing for youngsters and represented companies such as Pepsi. The entities portrayed in his hallmark video, *Thriller* (he as werewolf, with glowing eyes), said what needed to be said. There had been an invasion. It tempted fate. It would cause—did cause—fire (didn't his hair burn in one Pepsi commercial?) No wonder then that one other pop star, Britney Spears, sang a song called "Till the World Ends."

Note the original 1990 missive in which it explained that *"the very artifice of your societies is false and against the accordance of God's Will. This artifice shall not last."*

Going back to the 1960s, a cartoonist had become famous for a character that looked like a classic devil.

Going back to the 1960s, we recall *1 Samuel* where it says that the spirit of rebellion "is as witchcraft" (15:23).

And *now* to the present, a president of the United States was endorsing homosexual marriage, *Time* magazine was carrying a lascivious cover photo showing part of a woman's anatomy, Argentina was making trans-sexualism a legal right (covered by health care), nuns were supporting Melinda Gates' crusade to contracept much of the globe, opposing homosexual adoption had become a hate crime, the state of Washington was taking "bride" and "groom" out of wedding certificates, a famous professional wrestler was telling those who supported traditional family values to "drink bleach," the U.S. was forcing through a health-care-birth-control mandate, and revelations emerged of late-term abortion on healthy twins (because twins were "anomalous" and threatened "mental health"). At the same time, a Catholic broadcaster in the Philippines was murdered, California was considering a ban on therapies to turn homosexuals heterosexual, a historic mission church in Santa Cruz was vandalized, a relic of the True Cross was stolen, Chinese were selling the powdered remains of aborted babies in pill form (as an aphrodisiac), witchcraft was being recognized as a valid religion for military personnel (there was a same-sex marriage at the West Point chapel), the biggest novel for women revolved around sado-masochistic sex (extolled in publications such as *The New York Times*) and a new film called "The Perfect Family" was said by the Catholic News Service to contain "pervasive anti-Catholic prejudice, sacrilegious humor, a benign view of premarital sex and homosexual acts as well as of same-sex marriage, an abortion theme, and some rough language."

It was a synopsis of our culture. Normal fare. Daily news. No big deal. The evil that surged into the Sixties was now fully legal, pervasive, and refined; it was now entrained in our "societies"; it was institutionalized.

And had to be purged.

There were men who (thanks to technology) became pregnant. There were babies with three genetic parents.

It was difficult to recount all this. It was serious. Depressing? No. With prayer, there was a buffer. With prayer, there was clarity. With prayer, there was the knowing that all had to come to a *crescendo*. But challenging? Yes. Moreover, it just scratched the surface. Evil had risen and was rising in all directions. Prayers were needed— urgently—for society, for the performers, for our youth (and for their parents). No one wanted to condemn. God and only God could judge. Who knew what demons a person was born with, what burdens of psyche, what spiritual malnourishment? It was not for us to judge; it was for us to pray; it was for us to love the sinner—but not the sin itself. There was so much of it—so much ego, so much rancor, so much wanderlust, so much humanism (as opposed to humanitarianism)—that it was difficult to see anything but a major reorientation. This was the term used by the 2004 addendum. We needed to be "reoriented"—and in more than cultural ways. There was the word "soon" in prophecy as well as "now"—"in or after a short time, in a little while, before long."

"Soon the world will not be the world you know," said the original locution.

"The world is now seriously out of conformance with the Will of God and what He created and intended," said the second message fourteen years later.

"The angels have their instruction from east to west, and now a timetable has been set in motion," it said, adding: *"If not for the action of Heaven, what God has created on earth will soon be damaged beyond recovery."*

Pointedly, the most recent one in 2010 said that *"the dark spirits are now allowed to materialize in full due to the pretense and aspirations of man"* and that *"while love prevails, so does courage, and so does the uncovering of those spirits which* now *install themselves as guardians for those who have invited into their hearts falsity."*

Soon. Now. To this one could add "already." That word was also conspicuous with the prophecies. In the 2004 missive it said that *"a very dramatic effect already is in progress as regards the support structures of what man calls nature."* In the original 1990 prediction, a voice understood to be that of Jesus said He would manifest in the future as some sort of extraordinary apparition—series of apparitions—like those of *"My mother, who already nurses Me."*

That had been seen in 1981 at the onset of apparitions at Medjugorje (where the first day she was seen holding a Child) and perhaps it indicated a timetable.

If he was "born" in 1981, when would He be 33?

Placing a year on it was of course a fool's errand. But here, once more, was seen immediacy.

Already, some parts of the prophecy had occurred right away (those storms, landslides, and quakes), some had unfolded within a dozen years (9/11), and other parts were in the longer term—precisely like the apparitions at Fatima, LaSalette, Wisconsin, Kibeho, and Rue du Bac in Paris.

Lo! It was an evolution as with God everything evolved, unfolding according to a plan and a timetable only He could formulate and understand and only He could change.

Not even Jesus knew when the end of the world would come but He certainly knew about the "event" or events on the horizon; He and His angels knew about chastisements. That was seen in *Luke* 21 and *Matthew* 24. The initial 1990 prophecy started with the voice of an angel, before switching to His; a decade later, in 2004, the addendum said, to repeat, *"The angels have their instruction from east to west, and now a timetable has been set in motion."* I was intrigued that an unofficial seer from the apparition site in Rwanda (one who had not won formal Church approval) quoted the Lord as saying, *"My anger with them shall be fierce, and it will be carried forth by my seven archangels, who will take it to the four corners of the planet. My archangels will visit my anger upon all the people who have refused to repent their sins, and there will be much suffering and tribulations."*

The use of the word "timetable" was potentially crucial. For the definition of this word meant "a schedule listing the times at which certain events, such as arrivals and departures at a transportation station, are expected to take place," or "an ordered list of times at which things are planned to occur." That meant we were speaking about a series of events set to a definite plan. It was a list, a lineup. Things would be ticked down and set off. There might be cancellations, certainly delays, but the majority of items would most likely—in most schedules—take place. With evil rose trends like an oven thermometer did with heat. In Rwanda one alleged visionary (this one not formally approved by the Church, which thus far sanctioned only three of the original seven seers) claimed the "last judgment" was at hand and that there would be "many earthquakes in all the corners of the globe. In some places the sun will beat down so relentlessly that the earth will dry up and crops will fail year after year. Winds will carry away all the soil, and never-ending rains will bring great flooding. Hunger will grip many nations. Many will fight each other for food, and scores will starve to death." This was still in the future, but it tied in with the "breakdown" in society, foreseen in 1990, and like other apparitions, like Fatima and LaSalette, the stages were staggered over time. Some occurred very quickly, such as the 1994 genocide, and also, perhaps, the spread of AIDS, for in 1982 the Blessed Mother had allegedly told another unapproved Kibeho visionary named Agnes Kamagaju that the people needed to renounce fornication and "make their bodies an instrument destined to the glory of God and not an object of pleasure at the service of men" or there would be disaster. The message was that due to sexual sin and materialism we were "*rushing*" toward a critical point of some sort; the seers were told that "*you must prepare while you still have time!*" An approved one said she was told that Mary came to pave the way for her Son—at least in the telling of a priest who studied the apparitions, which were accepted by Rome in 2001. That event—a manifestation of Jesus—obviously had not yet occurred, but shortly after the prophecies were given was the ghastly Rwandan genocide (a "last judgment" for hundreds of thousands) and even before that came the eruption of HIV, which some traced to truck drivers who were infected by prostitutes on the Kinshasa Highway—combining both concerns of the Blessed Mother: sexual impurity and materialism. The seers had been shown village after abandoned village—which came to be both as a result of AIDS, which emptied so many huts, and then the mass genocidal mania. As for the sun: extremes were being visited upon nature and there were now solar storms and flares and geomagnetic reactions that were turning the skies ablaze from the Arctic to Mexico with the northern lights at the same time that uncanny heat—waves and waves of it— visited many areas. In May of 2012 it was reported that a huge sunspot that dwarfed the earth was unleashing a series of powerful solar flares as it moved across the surface of the sun. The sunspot, AR 1476, was 60,000 miles across, so large that when first seen from NASA's Solar Dynamics

Observatory spacecraft, scientists dubbed it a "monster." These monsters, as well as swerves in climate, became commonplace, calling back to the Middle Ages, a similar period of heightened solar activity (and warming) that was followed by a plunge in temperature during what they called the "Maunder minimum" (when sunspots suddenly vanished) and a tremendous eruption of bubonic plague (or "Black Death").

The pundits, the radio hosts, the rabble-rousers whose only cause was political, missed the point. It *was* warming. Could some of it be from man? Of course it could. The level of carbon dioxide in the atmosphere was increasing twice as fast as in 1960 (two versus one parts per million each year). But much of it seemed to be from activity on the sun— perhaps even energetic forces we were not yet capable of detecting. Those who argued over climate needed to be ashamed of themselves: the tug of war, the stridency and error on both sides, were missing the point that natural upset—on earth and in space—was intensifying. Politics. Money. Matters were seen only in these terms as materialism and worldliness blinded. Evidence was building not only of erratic climate but of ancient gyrations on the sun— for example, thirteen hundred years ago—that had caused storms dozens of times greater than any seen in modern times, including even a solar event in 1868 that fried telegraph lines across the United States (in some cases shocking operators) and another in 1989 that blacked out Quebec. I was told by officials at the United States Space Weather Prediction Center it was plausible that a major ejection from the sun could take down the entire continent's grid. "A solar storm capable of bringing the world to a standstill is not far away, says a leading UK space weather scientist," noted a report from an English newspaper. "While Earth's electrical equipment has withstood a number of these flares from the sun in the past, the world is not prepared for a truly damaging storm, says Mike Hapgood, a space weather scientist at the Rutherford Appleton Laboratory near Oxford, England. Speaking about his research recently published in the international science journal *Nature*, Hapgood said there was a good chance a stream of highly charged particles from the sun was headed straight toward Earth. He warns this has the capability of plunging the planet into darkness."

Did he say "darkness"?

This was a mainstay of the prophetic pulse: that something involving darkness was coming. I heard it at speaking events. I saw it in my mailbag. Just as many expected an illumination, so did they believe that one day there would be three days of absolute darkness (as happened to Egypt in *Exodus*). The notion had been particularly popular among mystical nuns in cloisters during the 1700 and 1800s. "I had a dream my mom and I were exiting a local supermarket at night in the snow," a woman from Buffalo wrote me. "People were running and pointing to the sky around the corner. We walked over and saw two giant red suns in the sky. I thought, how could the sun be out at night and why are there two? Suddenly everything went pitch black. I noticed a tiny point of light high in the sky . . . like a twinkling blue star. The light began to grow and descend and as it descended it became a Cross. As it got closer I saw it was Jesus on the Cross. When it arrived in the parking lot, much to my astonishment, He walked off the cross and suddenly there were children everywhere running toward Him. I woke up and had no *idea* what this dream could mean but it felt like a premonition. I've only shared this with a few people but felt the need to finally share it with you."

Was all this just because of the subconscious, something that had been read earlier? In St. Faustina's messages from Jesus was the prediction that "before the day of justice arrives, there will be given to people a sign in the heavens of this sort: All light in the heavens will be extinguished, and there will be great darkness over the whole earth. Then the sign of the Cross will be seen in the sky, and from the openings where the hands and the feet of the Savior were nailed will come forth great lights which will light the earth for a period of time." I heard from one man in Huntsville, Alabama, who in 1994 (recall the "great new evil") claimed to have witnessed some sort of veil that darkened half the sky (and the year before that, angels in a mass of clouds).

Something causing darkness—and fire (or fear of it)—seemed to be on the way (along with the strange loud rumblings).

"It is a final battle in which the trials of the future will serve as engagements complete unto themselves," said the 2010 afterword, using the same term, "final battle," that Sister Lucia had deployed. A cosmically historic struggle was unfolding. It was no longer in the future. That was clear. When Sister Lucia had uttered her prediction, it still was imminent ("about to unfold"). Now it had come. The prophecy said as much, relating that evil spirits were *"now allowed to materialize in full"* and that *"only those in union with God will be able to see in the darkness which so many expected and that already is upon the earth."*

As foreseen, the darkness had come. In some cases, it was darker than many expected. Overnight (particularly since 1990), America had gone from a Christian nation to a secular one that tolerated less public Christianity than did *Russia.* A greater turnabout was hard to imagine. How many in 1981, the year John Paul II was shot—or before then, in the Fatima-foreseen holocausts by Communists during the 1930s and 1940s, would have guessed that one day Russia would not only shed Communism but also atheism to such an extent that the Russian *government* would pay to rebuild many churches destroyed under Stalin and release photographs of Vladimir Putin and Dmitry Medvedev lighting holy candles or wearing icons or kissing the ring of an Orthodox Christian priest?

It was implausible. Both had taken place. No one had seen it coming. Virtually no one thought they'd live to see the mighty and atheistic U.S.S.R.—the evil empire, as great a threat to humanity as ever existed in human form—dismantle, let alone make a sharp turn toward Christianity; no one but the Blessed Mother, who in 1981 at Medjugorje, when asked about Poland, had said, *"There will be great conflicts, but in the end the just will take over."* Regarding the U.S.S.R. she had added, *"The Russian people will be the people who will glorify God the most. The West has made civilization progress, but without God, as if they were their own creators."*

That was utterly remarkable because in 1981 the Iron Curtain and U.S.S.R. were at full force. So was the evil one, who—perhaps starting to get antsy, knowing he approached the end game—was stirring in a big way. It was the year President Ronald Reagan and the Pope were shot and it was also the year that both Kibeho and Medjugorje began and at both places, the devil showed himself: an incredibly intense hailstorm swept through Medjugorje the night before the first apparition—so severe it sent villagers onto the dirt roads tossing Holy Water (as a storm had also lashed Fatima the night before its concluding apparition)—while in Africa vandals targeted statues of Mary at Catholic churches across Rwanda immediately before the apparitions, which were then accompanied by strange sights in the sky, the sun pulsing and spinning. When I visited, I was told of occurrences extraordinary even by the standard of Marian apparitions. In addition to striking sun miracles that had been observed by tens of thousands were instances in which the sky turned half bright and half dark, like a split screen, during apparitions (recalling the report from Huntsville), and at another point when villagers had asked for a sign, the moon and stars darkened suddenly and so totally—so precipitously—that the thousands gathered at the apparition had to feel their way home.

That occurred—as sort of an apocalyptic preview—during an apparition with Agnes Kamagaju on November 30, 1982. "The archives said that Agnes begged Jesus in tears to return the moon, and Jesus was not happy," said Immaculée Ilibagiza, a Rwandan genocide survivor who closely followed the apparitions. "The stars all disappeared at eight p.m., and Jesus told the people to light up their earthly lamps, but those who were there said that they left around 11:30 p.m. still wondering if they could get back and find the way out; it was thick dark until next morning."

"The world is on the edge of catastrophe," the Blessed Mother told another approved seer, Marie-Claire Mukangango, who would die in the genocide while trying to protect her husband. *"Cleanse your hearts through prayer. The only way is God. If you don't take refuge in God, where will you go to hide when the fire has spread everywhere?"*

A brink. The "edge" of catastrophe. Edge implied something that fell quickly—though it might be the edge of a widespread circumstance. It went back to words like "soon," "now," and "imminent." There was the constant theme, at Kibeho, that we are running out of time. Agnes had been given "secrets" and the reason for secrets, she explained, was that Jesus wanted the intercession of seers but "didn't want other people to live in fear. He says in the end He will show many signs and He is showing many signs already. The time will come when the message will be listened to. Most of the secrets are from Jesus. He shares them as a friend would share secrets. He shows things to me when He wants prayer and fasting. They unite me with Him. Most of the secrets involve everyone in the world. Love is huge. It is above everything. He wants us to pray from our hearts. He says we should love Our Lady. He wants us to be standing in prayer and strong in faith. The world is good but there are bad people in it and the bad is continuing to grow. He is coming because things are bad and we are lost. There are many signs and He says our eyes are not open. There are secrets that will be revealed to certain people prior to them happening. We need to wake up to God's Love. He has spoken about the end of the world but more than that about the end of each person's world" (as during the genocide, as during the horror that was so precisely presaged and that she so narrowly escaped).

7

Clearly, this had been—in the language of the 1990 prophecy—a *"regional chastisement"* (as also was a brutal ethnic war that would erupt in Yugoslavia, around Medjugorje) that started after the prophecy.

In the case of Medjugorje, the chastisement had begun within weeks of the 1900 missive.

The African holocaust—much greater—came a few short years later.

Between 800,000 and one million were killed in less than a year.

That was a higher daily rate than the Nazi holocaust.

The apparitions at Kibeho had been preceded by that vandalism, which the bishop of Nyundo, Monsignor Aloys Bigirumwami, described as a "diabolical fury directed against the Mother of God between 1979 and 1981. The wild iconoclasts removed and broke all the statues which were in the churches and at the crossroads throughout the whole of Rwanda."

Now we were seeing such things—religious vandalism—in the U.S.

New York. California. Massachusetts.

Paint poured on statues; images blackened.

In Florida, a huge paranormal reflection that precisely fit the proportion of Guadalupe and appeared without explanation on a glass office building in Clearwater (covering nine contiguous panes of glass) was destroyed by a young man with a slingshot.

Other saboteurs attacked "miraculous" sites in Chicago and New Jersey.

At the same time, the West was drenched in the kind of materialism that was strongly warned against at Kibeho, where Mary told the seers she had chosen this village precisely because of its poverty, saying that Kibeho was one of the few uncontaminated places left on earth—this place of huts made with mud bricks and thatched roofs, parents sleeping on makeshift beds, kids on the dirt floor, some houses with corrugated tin for roofs but none with running water, which was carried by bucket from streams, the food consisting largely of fruits like bananas and avocadoes which were omnipresent and had not been infused with fungicides, insecticides, and fertilizer; the meat from the cows and goats that bore no antibiotics, no growth hormones (for those fortunate enough to have one). Similarly peasant conditions also had been in place at Medjugorje, more advanced than Kibeho but still without wide use of modern bathrooms or televisions, thatched roofs here too (though on walls of stone and mortar, over cement floors), most of the homes without electrical power at the time of the first apparition, which brought to mind the part of the 1990 prophecy that said, *"Soon the world will not be the world you know . . . not . . . a barren world, or one depopulated, but of the end of your technological era.*

"Many inventions of mankind will be broken down and there will be more of a peasant attitude and way of life everywhere," it had said, adding (in what seemed like the words of Jesus): *"Know this about the world: I would not*

appear on television, nor ride in a car, nor travel in an airplane. Would I come in such a manner? Would I live in such a world? You think of the changes in very simple ways, without realizing the fundamental mistakes of mankind. The very artifice of your societies is false and against the accordance of God's Will. This artifice shall not last. Your very conceptions of happiness and comforts are a great evil and falsity. They will not stand."

It was as if the "poverty"—the simplicity of both Kibeho and Medjugorje—stood as examples of what was to come upon the rest of the world.

On May 31, 1982, the Blessed Mother told approved seer Marie-Claire, *"What I am asking of you* [the world] *is to repent. If you recite the Seven Sorrows chaplet, duly meditating upon it, you will receive the strength to truly repent. Today, so many people do not know how to ask for forgiveness, but instead they persistently put the Son back on the Cross. This is why I have come to remind you of these things, especially here in Rwanda, because here I still find humble people who are not attached to money and the riches of the world.*"

At Medjugorje, conditions were simple (peasant) and life flourished, the birds plentiful, and singing, the figs and fields and vineyards remarkably verdant in spring, the sparrows halting their chatter—remarkably—at the moment of apparition.

Nature was still natural. But that was not in the devil's plan. It was at Medjugorje that the Blessed Mother told the seer Marija Pavlović that *"Satan desires to destroy not only human life, but also nature and the planet on which you live."* He was out to destroy Creation. He won out to compromise nature. He wanted to quash it. Why couldn't Christians get this? Why were so many swayed by secular commentators who were awash in materialism and argued that good conservatives must disregard concern for the ecology, for the environment, and that otherwise they would hurt the economy. Remarkably, pro-lifers were brought into this train of thought in a world where everyone was suddenly at odds and where there was now only black or white and no more compromise or balance or common ground and if one was in favor of "nature"—wildlife, protecting God's greenery—that somehow made them the enemy because they were lumped in with "tree huggers" and those who sought to limit population growth.

Scripture said to take what was good and to leave the rest.

Instead, the baby—the environment, God's nature, His Creation—was being tossed out with the bathwater.

It was now nearly *unchristian* (certainly unpatriotic) to express concern for the alarming and growing ecological peril—the plastic patches far out in the ocean, the albatrosses with bottle caps filling their stomachs, the vanishing tuna, the manatees with motorboat scars (it was now how they were identified), the millions of birds that slammed into cell towers every year, the bees and butterflies that were dangerously diminished because of pesticides and perhaps all the electromagnetism in the air, the fish that were in so short a supply that "sportsmen" now had to tear the hooks out of their mouths and toss them back, the Florida panthers that numbered under a *hundred*, the sea turtles that were caught in commercial fishing nets (nets that extended for miles ripping apart coral on the bottom), the vanishing forests in the Amazon, the Caribbean and its bleached coral, the near-extinction of many species of shark, the silt pouring from the Mississippi into the Gulf, the algae blooms, the red tides from synthetic fertilizers, the leaking underwater oil and gas wells, the poaching of gorillas to the point where *their* numbers were nearly down (in Africa—Rwanda) to the level of panthers . . . the slain elephants, the vanishing rhinos, the fading chimps.

Did anyone really think that God created inconceivably magnificent creatures and landscapes so that we in our self-ishness could cause them to go extinct?

That was not subduing the earth or having dominion over animals (*Genesis* 1:28); it was abusing them; it was eradicating them for short-term profit (or pleasure).

When I was in Rwanda I had been driven to a national park by a mission priest and had climbed a mountain to view a family of gorillas and up there in the high rainforest felt so close to God.

Aquinas had said it: Nature was His first temple.

I felt the same way kayaking among egrets and herons and turtles and manatees and alligators and enjoying the incredible beauty while picking up stray Styrofoam that floated near feeding water birds and the ever-present plastic bobbers or bottles or beer cans or fishing line that was non-biodegradable (that way because it was stronger, easier to manufacture, more convenient).

It had *beneficial* aspects.

Use a bottle once and throw it away even though it was said that every piece of plastic ever created was still around in some form (if it had not been incinerated) and would virtually last forever, disregarding the nature that God had so ingeniously fashioned.

So now—implied all three major 1990 prophecies—God would act to *save* His Creation. He would act to save our souls. Eternity was what was most important to Him. The earth—granted—was a passing place. We could not fashion Heaven here—no. The "new heaven and new earth" were in the future.

Or were we approaching it?

Did that figure into the purification?

I felt we were at the end of an age. But what did an "age" mean?

No one knew—not really. What I knew was there was that sense of imminence.

"Soon the world will not be the world you know."

There was "soon." Or I would hear, in many messages, that the "cup" was filling or already full or even "over-flowing." Again and again I heard the echo of the words, "time is short." That phrase was throughout messages since the Miraculous Medal and now was the sense that the contents of the cup were beginning to pour down the sides as seen in the smaller disasters that would become larger ones and that one day would pour in a torrent—if not a flood, with fire. Lava. Stones striking one another. Did we realize there were 32,000 volcanoes *on the ocean floors?* Of course, the vast majority were inactive, at least for now. Were their caldrons the "cup"? I didn't like the notion that we were in some sort of end game but when I was writing my book *The Final Hour* on Mary's messages since 1830 it was simple to notice the heightened urgency of her warn-ings and during the writing of that book I had heard a little voice tell me to call it "the final hour" which I immediately and strongly resisted as something that would lump me in with end-of-the-worlders though the words came to me three times and I finally gave into the title when less than an hour later I was at daily Mass and the reading that day was from *1 John* 2:18:

"Children, it is the final hour; and just as you heard that antichrist is coming, even now many antichrists have appeared; from this we know that it is the final hour."

Some translations said "last hour." Same difference. As with the messages of Medjugorje, the scriptural passage had begun with "*children*" and there was no question of the urgency; at Kibeho Marie-Claire's key message had been "repent, repent, repent," bringing to mind how John the Baptist had come immediately before Our Savior, saying, "repent, for the Kingdom of God is at hand." Medjugorje had begun on the feast of John the Baptist! The cup runneth over and even those who had near-death experiences—whether Catholic, Protestant, Jews, Hindus, Buddhists, Muslims, agnostic, or in some cases even atheists—were coming back with this same idea: transformation was in the wind. One of them—the atheist Howard Storm (now a minister who builds churches, including Catholic ones, in the Third World)—claimed he was told on the way to hell, (after his duodenum ruptured in Paris, and he was rescued by Christ and placed in the care of several angels) that God was disappointed with the response of mankind to the great event of His Son's first coming and was now discouraged specifically by the United States which had been so materially blessed (so that it could export its know-how to the rest of the world) but which had instead "hoarded" wealth and as a result would be reduced to a Third World country (in the course of the following one to two hundred years; this said in 1985).

"They made it very clear to me that God had given this country the greatest blessing of any people in the history of the world," said Dr. Storm, who had taught art at Northern Kentucky University before his experience (which caused him to leave academia for ministry). "We have more of God's blessing. Everything that we have comes from God. We didn't deserve it, we didn't earn it, but we happen to be the wealthiest, most powerful nation in the world. And God gave us all this so that we could be the instruments of God's light in this world, and we are not instruments of light. In other countries people see us as purveyors of exploitation, military might, and pornography. They see us as completely hedonistic and amoral—we have no morality. People can do whatever they want wherever they want with whatever they want. Our amorality is a cancer on the rest of the world, and God created us to be just the opposite. People get mad at me for saying it, but God is very unhappy with what we're doing. When I came back from the experience I was almost out of my mind trying to convert people. God wanted a worldwide conversion thousands of years ago. God pulled out all the stops two thousand years ago with Jesus. From God's view, that was the definitive moment in human history. And the impact of the prophets and teachers and the Messiah has been a big disappointment to God because people have by and large rejected it. I was told that God wants this conversion. And if we don't get with the program fairly soon, He is going to have to intervene in some ways that from a human point of view are going to seem cataclysmic. God is really tired of what we're doing to one another and the planet and to His Creation. We were put in this world to be stewards and live in harmony with His creation and one another and we don't realize the important spiritual consequences of what we do when we raise a child in a faithless society. I asked how [purification] would come about, and they said it would be simple, that our society is very dependent on a lot of very fragile things—energy grid, transportation. In each geographical area of the United States people used to be relatively self-sufficient as far as agricultural products. Now, how long would any state survive without the transport of food and energy? What would happen if these very complex and delicate grids of our economic system would begin to break down. We've created a society of such cruel and self-centered people that the very nature of civilization would begin to break down. The angels showed me that what would happen is that people would begin robbing the grocery stores, hoarding goods, and killing one another for gasoline and tires, and as a consequence everything would break down and would end up in chaos. God is changing the world now. God wants worldwide conversion. God is going to awaken every person to be the person he or she was created to be. Those who accept God's Will shall flourish and those who deny God's love shall perish."

When Storm had asked if America would lead the world in this change, he allegedly was told that "the United States has been given the opportunity to be the teacher for the world, but much is expected of those to whom much has been given. The United States has been given more of everything than any country in the history of the world and it has failed to be generous with the gifts. If the United States continues to exploit the rest of the world by greedily consuming the world's resources, the United States will have God's blessing withdrawn. Your country will collapse economically which will result in civil chaos. The world will watch in horror as your country is obliterated by strife. The rest of the world will not intervene because they have been victims of your exploitation. They will welcome the annihilation of such selfish people. The United States must change immediately and become the teachers of goodness and generosity to the rest of the world. Today the United States is the primary merchant of war and the culture of violence that you export to the world. This will come to an end because you have the seeds of your own destruction within you. Either you will destroy yourselves or God will bring it to an end if there isn't change. The United States has been given the opportunity to be the peacemaker of the world. With the medical, agricultural, manufacturing, and scientific knowledge, the United States could teach less fortunate countries how to give every person food, clothing, housing, medical care, education, and economic prosperity. The United States has the power to help every person in the world access clean water and hygienic waste disposal. There are millions of people in the world dying for lack of things people in the United States take for granted. This is not God's Will. God wants you to know that every person is your brother and sister. God wants every person to have the same chance for fulfillment that a person in the United States has. God sees the people of the United States becoming increasingly greedy, self-centered, and uncaring. There must be a turning to God or the reign of the United States will end."

That was in 1985—calling for this change "immediately."

If it was true that we only had one to two centuries (at most), a half a century already had passed and there was no sign of reversal: the U.S. was still in an era of economic exploitation—Wall Street skyrocketing and ever-younger and ever-greater numbers of people "making" huge amounts of money by switching paper back and forth in banks, hedge funds, leveraged buyouts, stocks, commodities, mortgages— the era of the movie *Wall Street* and investment banking: making money without helping others or even producing a tangible product ("growing" it as on a tree).

As commodity brokers grew rich on grain, and cocoa, and coffee, small farmers suffered.

It was the time of the corporate raiders and playing games that allowed a very few to reap profits as companies were dissolved as cash cows or loaded with debt while thousands of those who actually worked lost their jobs.

Money materialized out of thin air.

There were now "factory farms."

There was even a firm called The Money Store.

Not only was greed increasing, it was reaching fantastic heights—such that being wealthy became the dominant standard by which a person was judged.

Money, money, money. Mammon. Couldn't we remember what Jesus had told the rich man? Couldn't we recall how He Himself had lived?

In doing business, we had lost human contact.

There was the answering machine that morphed into voice mail that morphed into computerized switchboards that went with store websites with no listed phone number as we became robotized barcodes; with a tap on the keyboard, we all had access to material things.

God gave us what we need. Satan (who wore Prada) gave luxury. And was he ever handing it out! It was one of his oldest ruses; had we learned nothing from Babylon? Had we learned nothing of how he tempted Jesus?

Making things as cheaply as possible via mass production reached proportions no one could have expected, back when the first cars rolled off assembly lines, back in the day of the first televisions. Now, everything was mass-produced —and disposable. Anything that made money was seen as a "good" and anything that opposed it was Communist. The Popes opposed it. The humble opposed it. But this was a tsunami! God's Creation was now incurring an onslaught it had never previously witnessed, and one that would keep increasing with every passing year—to the very present moment.

And so: peril. Great peril. "Immediate" peril. God was merciful, which meant patient. He was slowly giving us indications. As the uproarious Eighties ended—having refined the evils of the Sixties and Seventies—there were regional events, and they kept increasing, as if the earth itself shook with grief. Billowed. Bellowed.

After the apocalypse, claimed Storm, earth would be returned to more of the natural state intended and a vastly simplified humankind—far fewer in number—would be far closer to nature, similar to how many Indians had been. Many who had near-death episodes spoke in terms of a "transformation." One came back to claim that "currently the earth suffers from evil and abuse heaped upon it. It suffers from the misuse of its energy by man, and this abuse has taken its toll. Mankind has now changed the nature of the energy within and surrounding the earth. Like a magnetic force, this energy is beginning to pull and distort the earth's harmony, throwing natural forces off balance. As dire and unavoidable as it sounds, we must not become fatalistic. We have the power to reverse this process. As I came back from death, I was shown many catastrophes that await the earth if mankind collectively continues to break universal laws. If we do not return to the truths of God, seasons will continue to be altered, earthquakes will split the earth, floods will rage, disaster will follow disaster, and all this will be a direct result of our collective disregard for universal laws. Our actions magnified by billions of souls will literally change our environment, first spiritually, then physically. These catastrophes are not for our punishment; they come as natural results of our choices. We determine our own destiny and will face the evil or good that we create. I was told that denying our Creator, Who is God Himself, would be the foremost cause of these consequences. So I was given to know that calamities need never occur if we bring ourselves into harmony with God and the universe. We can restore the spiritual balance of our creation if we choose to."

But had we?
Was there a turnaround?
We could—*should*, must—pray for it.

But it was currently a long, long way off, if it was coming, and though one always had to wonder if, with words like "planet" and "energy," there was New Age infiltration (or perhaps better said, "contamination") with some of these near-death prophecies, in other ways the words were jarringly similar to LaSalette, where Mélanie—again, in the unapproved part of her messages—had said in 1846 that *"the seasons will be altered,"* that the earth would produce nothing but *"bad fruit,"* that the stars would lose their regular motion, that there would be massive earth-quakes which would *"swallow up mountains,"* and that *"water and fire will give the earth's globe convulsions."*

Two near-death researchers, Dr. Craig R. Lundahl of Western New Mexico University and Dr. Harold A. Widdison of Northern Arizona University, quoted a woman named Reinee Pasarow who "died" and returned in 1967 as stating that "the vision of the future I received during my near-death experience was one of tremendous upheaval in the world as a result of our general ignorance of the 'true' reality. I was informed that mankind was breaking the laws of the universe and as a result of this would suffer. This suffering was not due to the vengeance of an indignant God but rather like the pain one might suffer as a result of arro-gantly defying the law of gravity. It was to be an inevitable educational cleansing of the earth that would creep up upon its inhabitants, who would try to hide blindly in the institu-tions of law, science, and religion. Mankind, I was told, was being consumed by the cancers of arrogance, materialism, racism, chauvinism, and separatist thinking. I saw sense turning to nonsense, and calamity, in the end, turning to providence. At the end of this general period of transition, mankind was to be 'born again,' with a new sense of his place in the universe. The birth process, however, as in all the kingdoms, was exquisitely painful. Mankind would emerge humbled yet educated, peaceful, and, at last, united."

Another quoted by the researchers (a man who died in 1993) said we could expect some of nature's "most disas-trous upheavals" (in the words of Lundahl and Widdison), along with "major disruptions in relationships between individuals, families, and nations." The cataclysms would be "unparalleled" in history "unless we stop being so materialistic and learn to love ourselves and others" (said the authors).

Another named Christine Monsen saw the earth enveloped in "layers of dark haze" that was growing thicker as she watched, a darkness that was explained to her as being evil and which takes us back to the words at Medjugorje, where the Blessed Mother was quoted on July 30, 1987—that same year as Monsen's near-death vision—as saying that *"darkness reigns over the whole world"* and the year before had described *"this unfaithful world walking in darkness."*

8

Now came the key question: just how dark was it and how apocalyptic would Heaven's response be?

At a Eucharistic Congress in Philadelphia in 1976—as Cardinal Karol Wojtyla—Pope John Paul II had said:

"We are now standing in the face of the greatest historical confrontation humanity has ever experienced. I do not think the wide circle of American society, or the wide circle of the Christian community, realize this fully. We are now facing the final confrontation between the Church and the anti-Church, between the Gospel and the anti-Gospel, between Christ and the Antichrist. This confrontation lies within the plans of Divine Providence. It is therefore within God's Plans and must be a trial which the Church must take up and face courageously."

Four years later, he had made the alleged comment on the third secret in Germany.

Later, as Pope, he would develop the theme of darkness more fully when, on May 13, 1982—a year to the day after he had been shot, during an apostolic visit to the Sanctuary of Our Lady of the Rosary, in Fatima—he gave a homily that said, "Today John Paul II, successor of Peter, continuer of the work of Pius, John, and Paul, and particular heir of the Second Vatican Council, presents himself before the Mother of the Son of God in her Shrine at Fatima. In what way does he come? He presents himself, reading again with trepidation the motherly call to penance, to conversion, the ardent appeal of the Heart of Mary that resounded at Fatima sixty-five years ago. Yes, he reads it again with trepidation in his heart, because he sees how many people and societies—how many Christians—have gone in the opposite direction to the one indicated in the message of Fatima.

"Sin has thus made itself firmly at home in the world, and denial of God has become widespread in the ideologies, ideas, and plans of human beings. But for this very reason the evangelical call to repentance and conversion, uttered in the Mother's message, remains ever relevant. It is still more relevant than it was sixty-five years ago.

"The successor of Peter presents himself here also as a witness to the immensity of human suffering, a witness to the almost apocalyptic menaces looking over the nations and mankind as a whole.

"In the name of these sufferings and *with awareness of the evil that is spreading throughout the world* [my italics] and menacing the individual human being, the nations, and mankind as a whole, Peter's successor presents himself here with greater faith in the redemption of the world, in the saving Love that is always stronger, always more powerful than any evil. My heart is oppressed when I see the sin of the world and the whole range of menaces gathering like a dark cloud over mankind, but it also rejoices with hope as I once more do what has been done by my Predecessors, when they consecrated the world to the Heart of the Mother, when they consecrated especially to that Heart those peoples which particularly need to be consecrated. Doing this means consecrating the world to Him Who is infinite Holiness. This Holiness means redemption. It means a love more powerful than evil. No 'sin of the world' can ever over-come this Love. Once more this act is being done. Mary's appeal is not for just once. Her appeal must be taken up by generation after generation, in accordance with the ever new 'signs of the times.'"

As in the 1990 prophecy, he used the term "societies" and announced an intention (as requested at Fatima) to dedicate mankind to the Immaculate Heart of Mary. This he would do as a consecration of the whole world and "espe-cially to that Heart those peoples which particularly need to be consecrated," an obvious allusion to the Godless Soviet Union (which he sought not to antagonize—and provoke—by name). A formal consecration was effected on March 25, 1984, one that Sister Lucia said was accepted by Heaven and one that was followed two quick months later on the Fatima anniversary of May 13 by an incredible explosion at the Soviet's Severomorsk Naval Base that destroyed an esti-mated two-thirds of the missiles stored for use by the U.S.S.R.'s Northern Fleet: the worst naval disaster since World War Two. That wasn't all. In quick succession the U.S.S.R.'s leader, Communist hardliner Konstantin Cher-nenko passed away, a Soviet Defense minister who master-minded invasion plans for Western Europe had suddenly (and mysteriously) died, and reformer Mikhail Gorbachev (who John Paul II speculated was a closet believer) rose to power—leading to nuclear treaties and overseeing the demise of the Evil Empire.

In 1989, the Berlin Wall—inconceivably—was torn down.

It was astounding and impossible and was only one piece in what seemed like an expanding puzzle.

Had Russia been consecrated exactly as prescribed?

There would always be debate. What we know is that extraordinary events—events pertinent to the message of Fatima—followed.

There would be no torch struck against the earth (for now).

That brought us to the other controversy: *Had the secret been completely released?* Did the image of an angel ready to rain down fire on humankind constitute the entirety of the secret (along with the symbols of Church persecution, and the shooting of a man in white)—or had there been an accompanying text, one that added details to the vision but one so frightening, so volatile (whether about Church issues or worldly ones), that it had been buried deep in some archive? The second secret of 1917 had ended with the words, *"In Portugal the dogma of the Faith will always be preserved etcetera"* and etcetera meant "and so forth": that there were other things. Yet, unlike the other secrets, the third secret, as released in June of 2000, bore no words. If there was accompanying text, might it have involved those words allegedly uttered by John Paul II at Fulda?

Sister Lucia wrote the secret in 1944—after undergoing two months of what was described as anxiety and a "block" against doing so. What would have been so upsetting that the seer couldn't bring herself to jot it down? Was it simply the image unveiled by the Vatican in 2000, or was it upsetting because it had to do with an internal Church crisis? One prelate, Cardinal Mario Luigi Ciappi (theologian from the pontifical household from 1955 to 1989), was quoted as noting that "in the third secret is predicted, among other things, that the great apostasy in the Church will begin at the top." (Others have even speculated that it had to do with the antichrist.)

One fallacy: that Sister Lucia instructed that the secret be opened in 1960. What she'd said was that it should not be revealed before then—and that the Pope could reveal it after 1960, if he so chose (it was not a demand). She had said it would be "clearer" by the Sixties, and three years before onset of that decade, in 1957, when a monsignor was delivering the envelope containing the secret to the apostolic nuncio in Lisbon, he was said to have examined the contents under a light and determined that inside was a smaller envelope and in that a sheet of paper. On it was what he discerned as Sister Lucia's handwriting, which he calculated to span twenty to twenty-five lines of text.

The priest charged with preparing the definitive recounting of Fatima, Father Joaquin Maria Alonso, speculated before its release that "if it concerned internal struggles in the heart of the Church itself and great pastoral negligence by the highest members of the hierarchy, one can comprehend that Lucia would have had a repugnance all but impossible to overcome by natural means." Indeed, it took a special appearance of the Blessed Mother sometime in 1943 or 1944 to free Lucia's hand so she could write it. Added this Fatima expert: "If in Portugal the dogma of the Faith will always be preserved, it can be clearly deduced from this that in other parts of the Church these dogmas are going to become obscure or even lost altogether. It is quite possible that the message not only speaks of a 'crisis of faith' in the Church during this period, but also like the secret of LaSalette, that it makes concrete references to internal strife among Catholics and to the deficiencies of priests and religious. It is also possible that it may imply deficiencies even among the upper ranks of the hierarchy."

But there was no "smoking gun," and one could see how the vision of a Pope falling under a hail of gunfire would disturb an intensely loyal nun—greatly. While the image had no text, neither had a vision reported by a second Fatima seer, the young girl Jacinta Marto, who during a supernatural experience after the formal apparitions had "seen" a Pontiff in a large house with stones and curses hurled at him. Why, some asked, was it stated that the secret had been kept at the Vatican's Holy Office, while others said it was in a wooden safe at the papal apartments (a box famously photographed by *Life* magazine upon a visit there)? Did that not imply two different communications on the secret? On a number of occasions Sister Lucia herself expressed irritation with those who alleged conspiracies. "It upset her that there was so much speculation about the secret," wrote one of the nuns who lived with her, Sister Maria Celina de Jesús Crucificado. "Before it was revealed, she used to say rather sadly: 'If they would only live the most important part, which has already been revealed! They are only interested in what has yet to be said, instead of fulfilling what has already been asked for, prayer and penance!' After the secret had been revealed, people began to express doubts as to the authenticity of the text. One day I said to her: 'Sister Lucia, people are saying that there is yet another secret.' She replied: 'Some people are never satisfied. Take no notice! If they know that there is yet another secret, let them reveal it! I know of no other!'"

The business of secrets and rumors attached to them was at best tricky business and in recent times even hovered over Saint Bernadette of Lourdes—who, it was claimed by others, including a highly questionable supermarket tabloid (drawing, supposedly, from an obscure German newsletter for clerics called the "Schwarzer Brief"), had written a five-page letter to Pope Leo XIII just before she died in 1879 with hitherto secret predictions from Mary correctly foreseeing the invention of electricity; the horrors of Nazi Germany; and men landing on the moon. It was supposedly found by a French priest, Father Antoine LaGrande, who came across a metal box at the Vatican during research on Lourdes in 1997. On the fifth sheet—went this assertion—Bernadette was rumored to have said, "Your Holiness, the Virgin had told me that when the twentieth century passes away, with it will pass away the Age of Science. A new Age of Faith will dawn around the world. Proof will come at last that it was Our Lord Who created the world and man, and this will be the beginning of the end for the scientists, in whom the people will cease to believe. Millions will return to Christ, and as the numbers of believers swell, the power of the Church will grow as never before. Also causing many to turn their backs on science will be the arrogance of physicians who use their knowledge to create an abomination. These doctors will find the means to combine the essence of man and the essence of a beast. The people will know in their hearts that this is wrong, but they will be powerless to stop the spawning of such monsters. In the end they will hunt scientists down as ravening wolves are hunted."

It sounded contrived and the supermarket tabloid was one known to actually fabricate articles (as opposed to simple exaggeration). The verbiage didn't sound like Bernadette. Unlike Fatima, Lourdes had no messages about world events. Moreover, the supposed prophecy as reported in the tabloid had foreseen a "final clash" between Muslims and Christians in which five million would be killed before the year 2000. In fact, the seer once had explicitly stated that while she did possess "wonderful" secrets given to her on February 23, 1858, she would go to her grave with them, that it "wasn't even for the Pope." And so this all seemed like a bizarre contrivance.

One did have to say, however, that whoever had penned the predictions seemed almost to have read the 1990 prophecy, which likewise foresaw the great rise in alteration of Creation and the fall of technology (and called science God's greatest "nemesis").

So had Pope Paul VI.

Unbeknownst to most of the world, the pontiff had called it the "smoke" of Satan, and it had entered the sanctuary. "There is no longer trust in the Church," the Pope said during remarks in June of 1972 and the following November. "They trust the first profane prophet who speaks in some journal or some social movement, and they run after him and ask him if he has a formula for true life. Doubt has entered our consciences, and it entered by a window that should have been open to light. Science exists to give us truths that do not separate us from God, but make us seek Him all the more and celebrate Him with greater intensity. Instead, science gives us criticism and doubt. Scientists are those who more thoughtfully and painfully exert their minds. But they end up teaching us: 'I don't know; we don't know; we cannot know.' The school becomes the gymnasium of confusion and sometimes absurd contradictions.

"There was the belief that after the Council there would be a day of sunshine for the history of the Church," added the Pope in the wake of Vatican Two. "Instead, it is the arrival of a day of clouds, of tempest, of darkness, of research, of uncertainty. We believe that something preternatural has come into the world precisely to disturb, to suffocate the fruits of the Ecumenical Council, and to impede the Church from breaking into the hymn of joy at having renewed in fullness its awareness of itself."

Famously, the Pope had remarked that "from some fissure the smoke entered the Temple of God."

It was a remark that was as famous as it was misunderstood, for while most interpreted it as focused on matters such as liturgical abuse—and heresy—in its actual, full context, which was made available by a translator named Father Stephanos Pedrano, it seemed chiefly directed at the sort of exaggerated rationalism and intellectuality which smothered belief among the shepherds as well as laity and led to the abuses of modernism (from which sprouted, yes, liturgical abuse but also libertine sexuality, feminism, and, in those seminaries, as well as now the rectories, horrifying scandal).

Bad fruit.

Instead of faith, there was now skepticism. Instead of exorcism, there was psychology. We were blasting away from the supernatural like a rocket (like Apollo, which had an uncomfortable aura around it). As if as a warning, there was the coincidence that a leading rocket scientist was a practicing Satanist. But really the point: skepticism. A rapidly shrinking view of the world (minus God). Nothing was accepted unless it could meet the narrow protocols of a laboratory, which by definition were limited to the mechanical, for they could not *see*—could not measure, could not replicate—the non-physical. When Vatican II opened the windows of the Church to such modernism, it was looking to shake away dust from its deep past Christian faith, to open itself to the new ways of mankind, but instead science and its philosophy of doubt had come with it.

In so many ways, something preternatural—"aberrant, existing outside of nature, psychic"—had infused itself and was transforming seminaries and it was remarkable how those locutions starting in 1990 paralleled this fuller context of Paul VI's remarks (available only recently).

It was Jesus Who said by the fruit we would know them (that "wisdom is vindicated by her works," *Matthew* 11) and among the fruits of science—and certainly there were some great contributions—were what seemed to have been indicated by that Fatima secret: fruits such as potential nuclear annihilation. Now also: genetic manipulation. And synthetic chemicals, pumped into the ground, into the water, into the atmosphere, without mercy. Science had given us radiation. In no way was it sustainable. The explosion of a hundred Hiroshima-sized bombs (there were thousands) would be enough to turn the entire global sky a roseate dusk, overcast for months.

9

Instead of a light to the world, science seemed ready to light a torch.

We had been given a light, but an explosion came with it.

That was the third secret. There had also been LaSalette and its secrets, particularly the unofficial ones that mentioned a crisis in the Church and even antichrist. At Akita (as also in that *Neues Europa* "version" of the Fatima "text"), one of the two main messages spoke about "cardinals opposing cardinals, bishops against other bishops." Any number of times, the idea of a split in Rome—cardinals against cardinals—seemed to be a mainstay of "revelations." And to a degree, there were factions and mounting tensions. In 2012 a controversy erupted when the papal butler stole papers from the Pope's desk about problems at the Vatican bank, issues that reflected negatively upon Cardinal Bertone and perhaps even Benedict XVI in what some saw as a concerted attempt—a conspiracy—to alter the Vatican power structures (and prevent Cardinal Tarcisio Bertone of Italy from controlling choice of the next Pope). Cardinal Bertone had described it as a "ferocious" and "organized" attack. There also had been disagreements in the hierarchy on apparitions such as Medjugorje. "The events of recent days about the Curia and my collaborators have brought sadness in my heart," Benedict said at the end of one general audience—in words that stunningly brought to mind that vision reported by Fatima seer Jacinta Marto, who saw a pontiff praying alone in a room while people outside "shouted ugly things and threw rocks through the window."

At the same time, the Vatican was the subject of news stories that had to do with the mysterious death of a girl whose father worked at the Vatican and who disappeared.

Some believed it was related to a sex ring and may even have involved a priest.

Investigators searched for her remains in the tomb of a Mafia gangster who had been buried at a Rome basilica (after making a substantial donation).

"The priests, ministers, of my Son, the priests by their wicked lives, by their irreverence and their impiety in the celebration of the holy mysteries, by their love of money, their love of honors and pleasures, the priests have become cesspools of impurity," the alleged LaSalette secret had said harshly. *"The sins of those dedicated to God cry out towards Heaven and call for vengeance, and now vengeance is at their door, for there is no one left to beg mercy and forgiveness for the people. There are no more generous souls, there is no one left worthy of offering a stainless sacrifice to the Eternal for the sake of the world."*

The prophecies seemed to weave together—as in the Fatima secret, *"penance, penance, penance,"* also three times at Lourdes (*"penance, penance, penance"*), as at Akita, *"penance,"* the same at Kibeho, and when he read the LaSalette message, Pope Pius IX was reported to have said, "if you do not do penance, you will all perish"!—but the LaSalette secret conveyed by *Mélanie* was in a class of its own and it was hard to discern it and even decide what the actual position of the Church was, except to say that at the very least there needed to be caution. It was that severe. It was that dramatic. It was reported by a scholar named Sandra L. Zimdars-Swartz that as she was writing hers down (for Church authorities), Mélanie had asked how to spell "antichrist," a word that was in a version of her secret that was contained in a little booklet with an imprimatur and a commentary but one that was soon condemned by the larger Church. Twice, in 1915 and 1923, the Vatican prohibited circulation of a brochure containing Mélanie's controversial and more apocalyptic prophecies (the one on a coming famine was approved), was later published in another brochure minus the troublesome commentary (which seemed anti-clerical), but leaving the faithful confused as to the Church's stand on circulating the alleged prophecy itself. There were claims that Mélanie had written various versions of the secret—with varying lengths—elaborating on it years after the approbation, perhaps under the influence of sisters with whom she stayed and who were immersed in prophecies (including one of the antichrist and three days of darkness) from cloistered French religious that dated back to the late eighteenth century.

What was clear was the harshness: words so strong about the Church, priests, and nuns that, like the commentary, they could be—and were—classified as "anti-clerical." In addition to saying many priests had fallen into "cesspools of impurity," it went on to quote the Blessed Mother as warning, *"Yes, the priests are asking vengeance, and vengeance is hanging over their heads. Woe to the priests and to those dedicated to God who by their unfaithfulness and their wicked lives are crucifying my Son again! The sins of those dedicated to God cry out towards Heaven and call for vengeance, and now vengeance is at their door, for there is no one left to beg mercy and forgiveness for the people.*

There are no more generous souls, there is no one left worthy of offering a stainless sacrifice to the Eternal for the sake of the world . . .

"The chiefs, the leaders of the people of God, have neglected prayer and penance, and the devil has bedimmed their intelligence. They have become wandering stars which the old devil will drag along with his tail to make them perish. God will allow the old serpent to cause divisions among those who reign in every society and in every family . . .

"Churches will be locked up or desecrated. Priests and religious orders will be hunted down, and made to die a cruel death. Several will abandon the faith, and a great number of priests and members of religious orders will break away from the true religion; among these people there will even be bishops . . . In the year 1864, Lucifer together with a large number of demons will be unloosed from hell; they will put an end to faith little by little, even in those dedicated to God. They will blind them in such a way that unless they are blessed with a special grace, these people will take on the spirit of these angels of hell; several religious institutions will lose all faith and will lose many souls . . .

"The vicar of my Son will suffer a great deal, because for a while the Church will yield to a large persecution, a time of darkness, and the Church will witness a frightful crisis. The true faith to the Lord having been forgotten, each individual will want to be on his own and be superior to people of the same identity; they will abolish civil rights as well as ecclesiastical; all order and all justice would be trampled underfoot and only homicides, hate, jealousy, lies, and dissension would be seen without love for country or family. The Holy Father will suffer a great deal. I will be with him until the end and receive his sacrifice. The mischievous will attempt several times to do harm and shorten his days but neither him nor his successor will see the triumph of the Church of God.

"All the civil governments will have one and the same plan, which will be to abolish and do away with every religious principle, to make way for materialism, atheism, spiritualism, and vice of all kinds. The year 1865, there will be desecration of holy places. In convents, the flowers of the Church will decompose and the devil will make himself like the king of all hearts. May those in religious communities be on their guard against the people they must receive, for the devil will resort to all his evil tricks to introduce sinners into religious orders, for disorder and the love of carnal pleasures will be spread all over the earth . . . For a time, God will cease to remember France and Italy because the Gospel of Jesus Christ has been forgotten . . . Suddenly the persecutors of the Church of Jesus Christ and all those given over to sin will perish and the earth will become desert-like . . . Tremble, earth, and you who proclaim yourselves as serving Jesus Christ and who, on the inside, only adore yourselves; tremble for God will hand you over to His enemy, because the holy places are in a state of corruption. Many convents are no longer houses of God, but the grazing ground of Asmodeas and his like. It will be during this time that the Antichrist will be born . . . Rome will lose faith and become the seat of Antichrist . . ."

10

It was obvious that part of Mélanie's unofficial secret pertained to events in 19th-century France, where there were to be persecutions, uprisings, and crises in the Church as France sought to secularize in an atmosphere that was anti-clerical and often Masonic while massive, large-scale persecution came the next century in places like the Soviet Union due to Communism. The secret even mentioned 1864 as a year when demons would be loosed. By the 1930s, many religious orders in the U.S.S.R. had been disbanded, and as for "cruel deaths," priests in republics such as Ukraine were being nailed to walls.

But there were also aspects of LaSalette, the more apoc-alyptic, the more fiery ones, that had not yet taken place and that therefore seemed to pertain to other stretches of history, including, perhaps, the current one. Tantalizing it was how the message made clear it was speaking of multiple societies when it said that there would be *"divisions among those who reign in every society and in every family,"* just as, again, the 1990 prophecy mentioned *"societies"* in the plural. But above all else was that focus on the Church itself, problems that stretched into our own day, that indeed cascaded upon us: problems that one is loathe and sad to mention, much less discuss, but problems that had to be addressed in order to understand the veracity of prophetic elements.

An *"infiltration"*? *"Transgressions"* of the enemy?

It was a horror when a grown man ravaged the innocence of a youngster and beyond a horror when the assault was carried forth by someone who represented or was said to represent the Good Lord. Never before had there been such an invasion. It was astonishing that the Church survived it. It had proven that Catholicism was built on a rock. It proved that Catholicism was stronger than the gates of hell. It was a white martyrdom for the many, many good priests, the many pure priests, the many dedicated and selfless priests who had to watch the unfolding of a scandal in which altar boys and other youth—usually teens, some as young as five or six—had been molested in rectories or sacristies and even in the confessional. Between 1950 and 2002 there had been at least 10,667 allegations against 4,392 priests in America alone. The vast majority of assaults were homosexual. The numbers, stark though they were, constituted less than four percent of the 110,000 or so priests in ministry in that time, and almost a fifth of the cases went unsubstantiated. Some were disproved. Most dated back decades. Too many relied on the highly questionable phenomenon of "repressed" memory. Worldwide, the percentage of abusive priests had been under one percent.

But these—those accused of an abomination—were priests. These were the men whose hands had been consecrated. These were the men who facilitated the transformation from unleavened bread to His Body. It was an abomination of desolation in the temple and if this was not the spirit of antichrist, it was challenging to imagine worse. In Boston one priest had assaulted a hundred and thirty children. John Paul II had declared such acts to be *"delictum gravius."* You could also say *"tempus muliebre."* No perversion was more damaging. Youngsters used in such a manner frequently experienced lifelong emotional upset. Some committed suicide. Others themselves lapsed into a "gay" lifestyle and, in some cases, became priests who perpetuated the villainy. Over a period of fifty years—starting in the 1950s, bolting upwards in the 1960s, and hitting high stride in the 1970s—the problem had haunted sixty percent of religious orders and ninety-five percent of the dioceses. This is what came in, when one opened the window to the world. Dioceses went bankrupt. In Texas, a priest was accused of trying to hire a hit man to silence one of his victims. In Ohio, another priest was found guilty of murdering a nun whose body was discovered with more than thirty stab wounds (some cross-shaped) and covered with an altar cloth in a chapel sacristy on Holy Saturday (in what seemed like an evil rite). Said LaSalette: *"The devil will resort to all his evil tricks to intro-duce sinners into religious orders, for disorder and the love of carnal pleasures will be spread all over the earth . . . ."* There was Ireland—where sexual abuse raged in at least eighteen Catholic institutions. There was Canada, where a bishop was found guilty of possessing child pornography (when his laptop was searched at an airport). In Arizona, a parent filed suit over the shooting of a son who had allegedly been abused by a priest, a cleric who had starred on a Catholic television network. Another priest who had been a television celebrity stood accused by at least two bishops as he moved from diocese to diocese. Lightning was hitting across the landscape. It cost U.S. dioceses alone $2.5 billion in settlements, lawyer fees, and new abuse regula-tions—enough to bail out struggling schools. Instead, schools, convents, and churches closed. Most damaging was the great harm to Church credibility. In a Good Friday address, Pope Benedict XVI called it "filth." Asked the Pope, "How are we to explain the fact that people who regularly received the Lord's body and confessed their sins in the sacrament of Penance have offended in this way? It remains a mystery."

It was a powerful word, "mystery," but one that seemed to have been explained at LaSalette, if one accepted the "secret." (*"May those in religious communities be on their guard . . ."*)

So yes, transgressions. Yes, infiltration. Did it reach up to the Vatican? No evidence yet of that. But when it came to persecution, the scandals had left Rome vulnerable to attack (already, the leader of Ireland had withdrawn his nation's Vatican ambassador). "When the prophetic secrets of the Blessed Mother are revealed in Medjugorje, the Catholic Church will find itself in a great ordeal, as much for the world as for the faithful, and a little of this suffering has already started," said seer Ivan Dragičević when he was interviewed on August 14, 2012 by Father Livio Fangaza on Radio Maria. "Satan is stronger than ever today, and he particularly wants to destroy the family and the youth, because they are the foundation of a new world. Presidents and leaders have their power from God; too many of them are using it for their own interests. The result is a disordered society. Without God, the world has no future, this is why [Our Lady] invites us to return to God and turn to the future with God, in order to maintain peace and harmony. A government without God is anarchy. It is a deceiving government. It is therefore necessary that God be present in the government, and in the first place. Since the lack of God is prevalent in a lot of places, peace is constantly threatened. The most terrible war is the one waging in the human heart. The emptiness of God gives Satan a space bigger than ever."

The Church faced an ordeal. A "great" one. Ordeal was defined as "a primitive means used to determine guilt or innocence by submitting the accused to dangerous or painful tests believed to be under supernatural control" (according to the Merriam-Webster dictionary) or "a painful or horrific experience, esp. a protracted one. An ancient test of guilt or innocence by subjection of the accused to severe pain, survival of which was taken as divine proof of innocence."

In customary law, as earlier said, an ordeal meant "a test of guilt or innocence in which the accused undergoes dangerous or painful tests believed to be under supernatural control. Ordeals by fire or water are the most common. Burns suffered while passing through fire (as in Hindu custom) or rejection (i.e., being buoyed up) by a body of water (as in witch trials) would be regarded as proof of guilt. In ordeal by combat, as in the medieval duel, the victor is said to win not by his own strength but because supernatural powers have intervened on the side of the right."

Did this mean more scandal or greater defamation, greater dissension from within, more falling away of the faithful? While Akita, Fatima, and Medjugorje indicated problems for Catholicism (it was said to be in some of the "middle secrets" at Medjugorje), the 1990 prophecy and Kibeho did not—although the original 1990 prophecy certainly warned of persecution. *"After this breakdown of false society will come persecution of Christians and also a new world order,"* it said, stating that an "antichrist" would be trying to affect that order. Already there were glimmerings that opposition to things such as adoption of babies by gay couples or marriage between homosexuals might be a "hate crime"—in effect that professing views espoused in Scripture could one day be against the law. Meanwhile, the seething hatred for the Church was seen in commentary or blog boxes below news articles that had anything to do with bishops or the Pope.

So did the concern that a malefic force might at the same time be within the Church structure, which had become heavy with bureaucracy, which at times made it seem impenetrable. Still, one had to recall the words of Pope

John XXIII, who had said that "distrustful souls see only darkness burdening the face of the earth. We prefer instead to reaffirm all our confidence in our Savior Who has not abandoned the world which he redeemed."

Jesus would never abandon His Church. Were there problems? Even priests admitted there were. Many now forgot their Breviary. Too few said the Rosary. Meetings in board rooms had replaced novenas. Thus was discernment compromised. There had been no rush to humility. There certainly was no sackcloth. In Ireland, the Church acted just as it should when the papal legate apologized for the abuse scandal at one of the world's most renowned spots for penance, Saint Patrick's Purgatory (where legend had it Saint Patrick had been tempted by the devil).

But too much of LaSalette, it seemed, had already come to pass. As foreseen by Jacinta and LaSalette, popes had suffered a great deal. There even had been that attempt on John Paul's life (*"The mischievous will attempt several times to do harm and shorten his days . . ."*). There was the incredible spectacle in America of the federal government— the world's most powerful political entity—trying to force the Church into allowing its institutions to issue referrals for birth control and make sure their health insurance policies covered it (*"All the civil governments will have one and the same plan, which will be to abolish and do away with every religious principle, to make way for materialism, atheism, spiritualism, and vice of all kinds."*)!

This was all on the heels, as everyone knew, of a tremendously widespread effort to eradicate any trace of Christianity from public view—whether in classrooms where crosses and Rosaries were banned or court buildings or parks or in the songs sung at games, even at military gravesites. Statues of Mary were contested even when they were on private property (in certain gated developments). Each year, it grew intense during Christmas. It was okay to display huge images of Buddha or New Age symbols at public universities or teach yoga at the grammar level, but Christianity was taboo. In Times Square in December of 2012 was a towering billboard paid for by atheists that said "Keep the Merry" above a picture of Santa Claus and "Get rid of the myth" over a picture of Jesus Crucified. There were even efforts to take "God" out of the Pledge of Allegiance, or do anyway with the Pledge to begin with. America the beautiful: was God still shedding His grace on it? Was He crowning us with brotherhood? Or had we squandered that (as Storm said). What about all the coarse language? What about all the bickering on radio and TV? As for New Age, there were dozens of Catholic retreat houses and convents that taught hypnosis, color therapy, reiki, enneagram, rolfing, and other esoteric beliefs. One prayer center near Chicago offered therapeutic massage, holistic facials, and Zen Shiatsu (which tapped into the "energy" points around the body). There also were "labyrinths" consisting of concentric circular paths that were supposed to be a "mirror" for where we were in our lives. Dominican sisters in Texas offered tai chi along with the labyrinth (their literature used the ying-yang symbol). Meanwhile, Benedictine Sisters in the Midwest named their retreat property the Sophia Center (after the feminine form of God) and in Ohio a former motherhouse at a Catholic high school was converted into a retreat center that offered yoga, quigong, reiki, and other "wellness" programs. (*"Many convents are no longer houses of God, but the grazing ground of Asmodeas and his like,"* said LaSalette, referring to the name of a demon.) Most troubling: at one Catholic conference in the Midwest, a practicing witch was listed as a speaker. In Colorado were reports of nuns who prayed to the east and west each morning—a New Age invocation geared to the gods of nature—and in New York rumors that a crystal had been placed by a nun in a Blessed Sacrament chapel.

In Seaford, New York, was a visiting female evangelist who reportedly "would come out in a costume that looked just like a priest and pretty much ran the whole retreat while [a priest] sat on the side. Each night they did a ritual. The first night we all lit candles. We were told to bathe ourselves in the light. No mention of Jesus being the Light. Then they had us march around until we ended up in a big circle around the perimeter of the Church. It looked like a witches' coven."

The reports came from all over. I didn't pretend to know all that was wrong or right and I didn't disdain the efforts of nuns who meant well and were good in many other ways (better than I), but I did know that we were to follow the Vatican and that evil masquerades itself.

What were Catholics doing involved in something that was expressly cited in the Vatican documents (such as *Jesus Christ, The Bearer of the Water of Life*—which said that "advertising connected with New Age covers a wide range of practices as acupuncture, biofeedback, chiropractic, kinesiology, homeopathy, iridology, massage and various kinds of 'bodywork' such as orgonomy, Feldenkrais, reflexology, Rolfing, polarity massage, therapeutic touch, etcetera, meditation and visualization, nutritional therapies, psychic healing, various kinds of herbal medicine, healing by crystals, metals, music or colors, reincarnation therapies and, finally, twelve-step programs and self-help groups. The source of healing is said to be within ourselves, something we reach when we are in touch with our inner energy or cosmic energy."

There was nothing wrong with meditation. There was nothing wrong—in fact, everything *right*—with trying to heal spiritually or through the foods and herbs that God gave us. What was wrong was conceiving of energies apart from the Holy Spirit. At the same time, it was wrong to throw it

all out (that is, Christian healing) due to a spirit of intellec-
tualism. At LaSalette Mary supposedly said the devil had
"bedimmed" the perceptions of clerics and for sure there
was such an emphasis on the rational, on the philosophical,
and on the physical that mysticism—the larger view—had
fallen by the wayside, even though we were supposed to be
the Mystical Body of Christ. One had to differentiate
between "intelligence" as defined by newfangled, questionable tests (such as the IQ) and wisdom. Of such an intellec-
tual, scientific, and psychological bent were new priests
("new" starting in the Sixties) that any claim of miracles was
met by more skepticism at the local diocese than at the local
secular television station (or newspaper). It seemed counter-
intuitive, but the greatest resistance to claims such as
apparitions and healings or statue phenomena came from
bishops, vicars, and priests who were immersed in rationalism. Obedience was necessary. And many times—perhaps
most times—bishops who rejected alleged miracles were
simply being cautious. The devil could cause "wonders."

But other times it was because priests were of the mind
that miracles had ended with the Resurrection of Christ
(when in fact He had said, *"I tell you the truth, anyone who
believes in Me will do the same works I have done, and even
greater works, because I am going to be with the Father,"*
John 14:12).

Yet miracles there were.

Might there one day be a massive one?

At an alleged site in Spain had been prophecies of a
coming miracle and "illumination," an event that would
cause everyone everywhere to see their sins supernaturally.
According to a visionary there who (as at Fatima) was named
Jacinta, the event would be "seen in the air everywhere in the
world and immediately [would be] transmitted into the interior of our souls. It will last a short time but it will seem like
a long while because of its effect within us. It will be for the

good of our souls and then we'll feel a great love for our heavenly parents and ask forgiveness for all of our sins." It would be, said a second alleged seer, a cosmic happening, "like two stars . . . that crash and make a lot of noise, and a lot of light . . . but they don't fall. It's not going to hurt us but we're going to see it and, in that moment, we're going to see our consciences." Was it related to the 1990 prophecy, which had foreseen the stretch of regional chastisements and in that period also *"a warning that involves not fire from the sky but fear of fire from the sky, and strange loud rumblings," or to the follow-up in 2010 that foretold of a "crescendo of meaning, whereby to each will be shown the imperfection of the past and the need for purification of the future"*?

Fear of fire, but not fire itself. I had never noticed this similarity before. Were they speaking of the same thing? Did Garabandal have credibility after all—despite confusion, despite contradictions among visionaries, despite what may have been an intrusion by the evil one to skew the happenings?

I didn't know. There was concern over previous apparitions in the same region of Spain near Ezkioga that had spread to various nearby villages and had said the same thing: that there would be a warning, a great miracle, a chastisement. This had been stated in the 1930s—three decades *before* Garabandal—by a cadre of seers (at least one of whom had visited Garabandal). The problem was the Church had formally condemned Ezkioga. Were we repeating the prophecies? The illumination sounded like sort of a catastrophe before the "miracle," as a miracle and permanent sign were also mentioned at Medjugorje (along with chastisements). How to discern?

At Medjugorje, however, the secrets involved not a singular warning, but a series of several, and there was no specific mention of an "illumination." According to one visionary, the first warning (at least in her secrets) would be a regional event, a catastrophe that everyone in the world would hear about ("like a dam bursting in Italy"). It would be followed by two more warnings and a "great sign" (exactly the term used at Fatima, instead of "miracle"). In 1981, hundreds of people saw flames erupting on Apparition Hill at Medjugorje but when officials—at the time, Communists—investigated, they found nothing was scorched. Afterward, the Blessed Mother allegedly told the children, *"The fire, seen by the faithful, was of a supernatural character. It is one of the signs, a forerunner of the Great Sign."*

This, said the seers, would occur at the site of apparitions and be "permanent, indestructible, and beautiful."

Exodus 19:18 said, "Now Mount Sinai was all in smoke because the Lord descended upon it in fire; and its smoke ascended like the smoke of a furnace, and the whole mountain quaked violently." Might one of the future happenings be like the pillars of light that led Moses in *Exodus*, or the smoke on Sinai?

As we will later see, the instance of "great smoke" would also figure into an addition to the 1990 predictions.

Let us stay here on the words "pillars" and "light"—the idea of an extraordinary coming luminosity.

Around the world reflections and refractions of light in the shapes of a Cross, Jesus, Mary, and other holy symbols were being photographed constantly. There were Cross formations over land. There were formations over water. There were inexplicable luminosities manifesting on the doors and windows and household items or church articles across America. In Russia, a large pulsing cross-like luminosity that appeared in the sky behind a house was videotaped in broad daylight.

When it was enhanced, it looked like there was a corpus on it.

The same was reported above Tabasco, Mexico—on the same day.

A hoax? Some called it a UFO. Was it natural phenomena (like Saint Elmo's fire, which is caused by electricity in the atmosphere)?

The 1990 prophecy had said two things of interest: that, allegedly, Jesus would return in a *"tower of light"* and also, mysteriously, *"know too that God's Hand will be evident in South America."*

That was ironic because there were reports of crepuscular rays—towering pillars of light—near Palo, Brazil, on December 17, 2012.

It was an atmospheric phenomenon. There had also been reports in Arizona, where it seemed like there were two suns on opposite sides of the sky, along with large pillars of light rising from the horizon—as if there were a sunrise and sunset simultaneously. "This is very mysterious as I have never seen this strange sunset-sunrise at the same time effect before and as of late, I am seeing these quite often," noted an observer on YouTube. "Two suns? This is the third time that I have seen this two sun phenomenon in seven days here in Arizona."

(According to one theory, as quoted in an online encyclopedia, crepuscular rays were "rays of sunlight that appear to radiate from a single point in the sky, specifically, where the sun is. These rays, which stream through gaps in clouds or between other objects, are columns of sunlit air separated by darker cloud-shadowed regions. The name comes from their frequent occurrences during crepuscular hours (those around dawn and dusk), when the contrasts between light and dark are the most obvious."

Precursors?

It brought us to that part of the 2004 addition that said, *"When the huge light is seen, I will act in a way I have not acted before."*

Once the sign came, said the seers, there would be no more doubt that God existed. The seer at Medjugorje who spoke about warnings, Mirjana Dragicević Soldo, said she would tell a priest her first secret ten days before it was to occur—similar to a time frame at Garabandal, where a seer named Conchita said she would announce her secret *eight* days before it occurred. The priest chosen at Medjugorje was a Croatian named Father Petar Ljubičić who recently had been stationed for an extended period of time at Fulda, Germany (precisely where John Paul II had allegedly commented on the third secret) and who after a period of fasting would relay the secret three days before its actual occurrence. He would do the same, he once told an interviewer, before each of her secrets.

By 2013, Father Petar, who was born in 1946, was in his mid-sixties. Obviously, the seer believed her events would occur or at least begin in his lifetime. (The average Croat male lived to be just under seventy, although of course some were older). He speculated that the first two secrets involved Medjugorje itself. "I have a sense and a feeling that this may come very, very soon, but I really don't want to speculate or tell dates about it," he told an interviewer. "You can look at the world today and you will see how urgent it is for us to convert and turn to God . . . Mirjana emphasizes that the time is at hand when the first secret will be revealed. That is why she urges vigilance and prayer in the name of Our Lady."

There was a connection to Fatima, LaSalette, and—again—the idea of penance.

"[The Blessed Mother] not only asks but pleads with everyone to convert, to pray, to fast," said the reputed seer.

"[Non-believers] have no idea what awaits them, and that is why, as their mother, she is in deep anguish for them. It is not enough to just simply pray. It is not enough to just quickly say some prayers so that one can say that they prayed and did their duty. What she wants from us is to pray from the depths of our souls, to converse with God. That is her message. The Blessed Virgin told me that it is necessary to pray a great deal until the first secret is revealed. But in addition to that it is necessary to make sacrifices as much as possible, to help others as much as it is within our abilities, to fast—especially now before the first secret. She stated we are obliged to prepare ourselves."

After the warnings and Great Sign—claimed Medjugorje—would come other secrets that might pertain to Church issues or personal matters of concern only to the seers. At least some of the visionaries said that their final secrets were very severe chastisements—with indications that these events would change the world.

One visionary, in discussing the aftermath, had made reference to "those who are still alive."

We were speaking, as with 1990, about transformation.

A second priest who had been close to the seers felt that after the unfolding of the events in the secrets there would be a "peasant" way of living.

It brought to mind a message in which the Virgin of Medjugorje had said that *"the West has caused civilization to progress, but without God, as if they were their own creators."*

By implication, this was going to change.

Another seer at Medjugorje, Vicka Ivanković, told me that the end of the world, Second Coming, and antichrist were not in her secrets. But she too spoke of monumental coming events.

And who was to say what was in the secrets of the others?

Had not the seer Mirjana Dragicević declined to answer a similar set of questions—saying that speaking of the end times would infringe on her secrets?

One had to wonder if some of it—the sign, or miracle—was related to the prophecies of Saint Maria Faustina, who in the 1930s said before Judgment Day there would be a period of mercy and "a sign in the heavens and over the earth."

Yet, "judgment day" in the view of Vicka and the 1990 messages did not mean the end of the world.

No. Nor even a "barren" one. It did not mean one "depopulated."

But it meant an utter, drastic change in landscape—certainly with proportionate casualties. Mirjana had said her tenth and last secret "was terrible, and nothing can alter it. It will happen." (A previous secret had been somewhat mitigated, it was said.)

To disdain such messages out of hand—as so often occurred—was to risk offending that part of Scripture that said, "Do not quench the Spirit; do not despise prophetic utterances. But examine everything carefully; hold fast to that which is good" [1 *Thessalonians* 5:19-20]. Added in the same part of Scripture was the advice that "as to the times and the epochs, brethren, you have no need of anything to be written to you. For you yourselves know full well that the day of the Lord will come just like a thief in the night. While they are saying, 'Peace and safety!' then destruction will come upon them suddenly like labor pains upon a woman with child, and they will not escape. But you, brethren, are not in darkness, that the day would overtake you like a thief; for you are all sons of light and sons of day. We are not of night nor of darkness; so then let us not sleep as others do, but let us be alert and sober" [1-7].

11

Yet, how dramatic with prophecy could we go?

What was one to make of the seer Mary Loli of Garabandal who said she saw persecution of believers, the Pope in hiding, and then: silence, as the "warning" came, with even planes standing still in the sky.

She didn't say whether she would live to see this—not when I interviewed her—but now, Mary Loli was deceased. There remained a blind man on Long Island who said he was told he'd regain his sight when the Garabandal secrets unfolded. Would he? What would it mean if he didn't?

Garabandal and Medjugorje bore similarities but were also unrelated. There was virtually no discourse between the two. As far as I knew, in the beginning the Medjugorje seers weren't even aware of the Spanish site; they never mentioned it; there was no known communication. In fact the visionaries of Hercegovina, nestled at the beginning in a remote Communist nation, had not even heard of Lourdes or Fatima, although they came to know of them and vice-versa: a member of the Austrian royal family, Archduchess Milona von Habsburg de-Rambures—who had served in Sister

Lucia's convent—said the Fatima seer had prayed for them (aware of the pressures a seer endured).

The mystic Maria Esperanza believed in the apparitions.

So, it appeared, had Mother Teresa—who said she regularly invoked the Madonna there.

But what was one to do with the prophetic indications, if the Church ruled against it?

Unless condemned, they could still be discussed.

But in what context?

It was hard to know what the Church would do. The situation was so fluid that by the time this was published a statement may have been issued. Would Rome declare the huge and growing site an official shrine (it was approaching the size of Fatima), while reserving judgment on the apparitions themselves (saying there was no definitive proof of the supernormal)? Would it reject the apparitions, even condemn them? Or would it accept them, perhaps at least giving the nod to a couple of the seers (least likely, while the apparitions were still ongoing, and while secrets had not yet unfolded to prove themselves). Millions had literally been transformed by the place; hundreds of cardinals and bishops had visited; so had—literally—hundreds of thousands of priests. Countless healings had been reported (many medically documented). It was responsible for more vocations than any other movement or trend in the Church. I had never seen anything affect visitors so powerfully. But the resistance was tangible, as stated by an Anglican priest who had converted to Catholicism and was amazed at the opposition among the many other clergy who had not visited. "My life has been a series of genuine miracles and heavenly visitations," wrote this priest, Father Dwight Longenecker. "Consequently, I am not exactly an answer to prayer for anybody in any hierarchy. Such folks like things to be stable, predictable, by the book . . . and they want to be the only ones offering a Word from Heaven. When I entered the Catholic Church I was shocked to find how many priests loathed Fatima and despised Blessed and now Saint Faustina Kowalska. I was horrified when I heard a bishop say upon hearing of the death of Sister Lucia of Fatima, 'Well, thank God, that's over.' Shepherds should be very careful about what they say. They never know if the sheep are listening. Truly I wasn't surprised by these little bomb-shells. I knew Church history and the life of Christ Himself and understood the sources of such opposition."

Opposition there was, especially when there was the intensity of prophecy: secrets and more secrets.

We knew from Fatima that not everything was contained in them. Seers didn't have the entire picture. Not historically. They received a glimpse. At Fatima, the three secrets spoke of two wars, historic persecution, and a great sign, but nothing of a fantastic pandemic called the Spanish flu that killed fifty to 130 million immediately after the apparitions—including the two youngest seers, Francisco and Jacinta Marto, who succumbed in 1919 and 1920.

God had His prophets—Scripture said He did nothing (major) without informing His servants [*Amos* 3:7]—but to them He revealed only parts of His plan.

And now the prophets were at high dudgeon.

The *"enemy of Creation,"* said the 2010 revelation, was seeking to *"install his spirit as the spirit that conquers for all time."*

It was the end game.

Sister Lucia had also said that.

To "install" meant to establish in an office, a position, a stronghold. It meant to "rule." It was indefinite, as far as time. It meant the devil sought once and for all to make earth a dark place where goodness no longer prevailed.

The overriding spirit would no longer be the Holy Spirit. That was Satan's aim. He sought to degrade us. Before the Garden, there had been no death. Matters were halfway to Heaven. Now they were halfway to somewhere downward. The gravity was carnality, selfishness, worldliness. It was a seesaw. We were taught by Christ to seek always the highest point, the place where there was dignity, the standing that placed us above animals. Most major sins involved degradation. We edged down toward the instinctual. The more denigrated we were, the more we were like creatures of the jungle. That was not to besmirch them. These animals were precious; the 2004 addendum made that plain. It quoted the Lord as saying, *"The smallest of what lives is precious in My sight."* That meant ants. Amoebas. God watched every cilia on every paramecium! He certainly counted the sparrows (*Luke* 12:6). He knew each bacterium. But that didn't mean we were to revert to how animals ate or mated nor how they treated each other. We were to love animals but reject the satanic notion—so pervasive since Darwin, spawned too by the evil of Kant who said not to believe anything you could physically perceive, and Hegel who taught that there were no absolute truths, and Marx who laid the foundation for Communism (and secular humanism)—that *homo sapiens* were simply the most developed line of mammals: soulless, because there *was* no soul, dedicated to themselves, not God.

The notion of "survival of the fittest" made selfishness a virtue and animalism acceptable while religion was an "opiate"—and delusion—of the masses.

That was modernistic thought and the fruit was immorality (along with desperation).

It was stark. It was intense. Witches had been granted religious privilege in the military while churches in Canada and England faced repercussions if their agencies didn't allow adoption by homosexuals or if the churches themselves refused to conduct "same-sex" marriage or if pastors even addressed immorality from the pulpit (which in some areas had become a "hate crime").

It was what was afoot in our time and growing by leaps and bounds no matter who the president was and no matter how loud preachers preached on television. Homosexuals were victims; we celebrated the "filthy" rich; in entertainment, the darker the drama (the more "in your face"), the greater its run on Broadway. *Wicked*! There were "phantoms" everywhere. Was it any surprise that by tradition there was always a light left on backstage for the theatre's resident "ghost"? Was it a coincidence that the new victory sign, the new "thumbs up," the new hand cheer was two fingers raised at concerts and sporting events and anywhere—at rallies, at weddings, at graduations—like the horns of the devil (index and little fingers)?

You could do this, but you couldn't feel right blessing yourself in public.

We were haunted. This was the spirit of antichrist. It was rising. It would precipitate. It wasn't quite there yet. But as the Blessed Mother said, darkness reigned—or was about to. It was a world not just of abortion but of euthanasia, a world in which organs were taken from the dying even before clinical death, a world increasingly based on evil, which was the word "live" spelled backwards. There were "ethicists" who argued that in some instances killing newborns who had birth defects was acceptable.

It was the stuff of the Roman Empire, probably worse. They had infanticide back then (but, curiously, not abortion). It would be a time of upheaval. Little upheavals would spread like flames into regional ones. In time there would be a general uproar. We were seeing the glimmerings of it in Greece and Egypt, in Syria, in American politics. It was a darkening time. We were moving, inexorably—at least for now—into a land of shadows where evil would be the standard. The Light of Jesus was bright in this darkness. But it had to become—and would become—much brighter. An event was in the wings. He was going to be the key part of it. No one knew just how. The 1990 missive said He was going to come in a series of apparitions and towering light. It would be powerful. Some would believe. Most would not. But it would break the grip of evil. Would one call it the Second Coming, or a "manifestation"? The 1990 prophecy called it "the second coming," using lower case. Was that just the way the person who had recorded it wrote or did it mean something less than the Final Coming (which would put it more in conformance with what Vicka said)? *"I will come not as a man of flesh, but like My mother, who already nurses Me and holds Me in her arms, as a light and power,"* He allegedly had told that anonymous recipient back in the original December of 1990 message. *"I will manifest Myself in a series of supernatural events similar to the apparitions but much more powerful. In other words, My second coming will be different than My first, and like My first, it will be spectacular to many but also unknown initially to many, or disbelieved. Yet truly I tell you, the arrogance of the world will have been broken, and so many more than normal will believe."*

That passage became stunningly relevant for believers in Medjugorje when on December 25, 2012—Christmas—the regular monthly message from the apparitions site was delivered for the first time not by Mary, but by *the Infant Jesus,* Who reportedly rose on her lap to say: *"I am your peace. Live My commandments."*

It was true that every Christmas (as well as Easter) the Blessed Mother, resplendent in colorful robes, appeared with the Infant. But this time, said Marija, the Infant stood up on Mary's lap, looked at the seer, and delivered the message in a Voice that was packed with what the visionary, shaken, could only describe as "great authority." Seven simple words. But powerful. Unforgettable. It was nothing less than jolting. For twenty-six years, since 1987, seer Marija Pavlović had been receiving monthly messages that were translated by the local parish and then released to the world, what I calculated to be 311 of them. Never before had it been words from anyone other than the Queen of Peace.

Now it was Jesus Who spoke. Along with Mary, He blessed those present with the Sign of the Cross. "I am still trying to understand what I saw," said Marija, who afterward cried and couldn't sleep that night. "Jesus addressed me as the King of Peace. He was a child but these words were spoken with authority, with a voice that remained strong within me. I heard the Voice of Jesus as a child. It was not the voice of a child of a few hours. I do not know how to say this, a Jesus Who is small, newborn, Who addresses us." She called it a "new moment" for the apparitions and it seemed to be confirmed by what three other visionaries, Ivan, Mirjana, and Jakov Čolo also received that day or on subsequent ones. *"Dear children, accept my messages responsibly and live my messages, because in the living of my messages I desire to lead you to my Son,"* Ivan reported her as saying three days later (December 28). *"All of these years that I have been together with you my finger has been directed toward the Son, towards Jesus. I have a desire to lead all of you to Him. Therefore these days that are upcoming, may your question also be—and I pose this question to you—'What can I do that my heart may be closer to Jesus?' May this question lead you. Say to yourselves, 'What must I leave behind? What must I reject that my heart may be closer to Jesus?' Pray dear children, and I will pray for all of you that your answer in your hearts may be 'Yes, I desire to be closer to Jesus!'"*

What was it? What were His "commandments"?

It was a word used at least sixty-three times in the New Testament and had to do with forgiveness, charity, humility, simplicity; with forsaking anger, helping the poor, remaining away from the seduction of wealth; it had to do with the Sermon on the Mount.

But nowhere was it clearer than the Book of John—particularly chapters 13 through 17, wherein Jesus, at the Last Supper, in language strikingly similar to Medjugorje, stated to His disciples: *"I give you a new commandment:*

"Love one another. As I have loved you, so you must love one another. If you have love for one another, then everyone will know that you are My disciples."

That was reiterated in *Matthew* 22:36-39, which cited a Pharisee interrogating the Lord:

"Teacher, which is the greatest commandment in the Law?"

Jesus replied: "'You shall love the Lord your God with all your heart, and with all your soul, and with all your mind.' This is the greatest and foremost commandment. The second is like it, 'You shall love your neighbor as yourself.'"

It was exactly what was emphasized time and again in near-death experiences: that the main evaluation we faced upon entry into the afterlife was how much we had loved.

His way of addressing the disciples (*"Little children"*) was similar to how Mary had almost always begun those monthly missives (*"Dear children"*). As one observer noted, "The start of the discourse begins: *'My little children, I shall not be with you much longer' (John* 13:33)," noted one observer. "In fact, the whole of the discourse can be viewed as a summary of all that Our Lady has been teaching us these past thirty-one years."

It was also to be noted that in *1 Timothy* 6 it said, "If anyone advocates a different doctrine and does not agree with sound words, those of our Lord Jesus Christ, and with the doctrine conforming to godliness, he is conceited and understands nothing; but he has a morbid interest in controversial questions and disputes about words, out of which arise envy, strife, abusive language, evil suspicions, and constant friction between men of depraved mind and deprived of the truth, who suppose that godliness is a means of gain. But godliness actually is a means of great gain when accompanied by contentment. For we have brought nothing into the world, so we cannot take anything out of it either. If we have food and covering, with these we shall be content. But those who want to get rich fall into temptation and a snare and many foolish and harmful desires which plunge men into ruin and destruction. For the love of money is a root of all sorts of evil, and some by longing for it have wandered away from the faith and pierced themselves with many grieves. But flee from these things, you man of God, and pursue righteousness, godliness, faith, love, perseverance, and gentleness."

Scripture seemed to stand in confirmation, and so did the Pope himself, who on December 21—four days *before* the apparition, in speaking to youth—underscored the idea of peace and the Christ Child, while his Christmas Mass and Christmas Day messages (the *"urbi et orbi"*) kept up this theme.

"May the Child Jesus look graciously on the many peoples who dwell in those lands and, in a special way, upon all those who believe in Him" (Christmas Day, December 25).

"Let us ask the Lord that we may become vigilant for His presence, that we may hear how softly yet insistently He knocks at the door of our being and willing" (Midnight Mass).

"May the birth of the Prince of Peace remind the world where its true happiness lies, and may your heart be filled with hope and joy, for the Savior has been born to us . . ." (Christmas Day).

"So Christ is our peace, and He proclaimed peace to those far away and to those near at hand (*Ephesians* 2:14, 17). How could we now do other than pray to him: Yes, Lord, proclaim peace today to us too, whether we are far away or near at hand," the Holy Father said—very interestingly—in his homily at Midnight Mass, just hours before the apparition.

It was extraordinary because it was nearly as if the Pope had invoked the apparition, and because another Pope—in fact his namesake, Benedict XV—had made a similar, strident plea to Heaven.

"To Mary, then, who is the Mother of Mercy and omnipotent by Grace, let loving and devout appeal go up from every corner of the earth—from noble temples and tiniest temples, from royal palaces and mansions of the rich as from the poorest hut—from every place wherein a faithful soul finds shelter—from blood-drenched plains and seas," Benedict had said in the midst of war and turmoil, on May 5, 1917.

"Let it bear to her the anguished cry of mothers and wives, the wailing of innocent little ones, the signs of every generous heart: that her most tender and benign solicitude may be moved and the peace we ask for be obtained for our agitated world."

Eight days later, Mary had begun appearing at Fatima.

Was the same now occurring with another Pope Benedict—but this time with Jesus breaking through, perhaps even ready to initiate that series of apparitions?

"I will come not as a man of flesh, but like My mother, who already nurses Me and holds Me in her arms, as a light and power," He supposedly had said in 1990, to reiterate.

It was either a special reminder to focus on Jesus or a major turn of events, a new stage, if not both—at this the most famous apparition since Fatima.

Were the apparitions about to end, or suffer?

Was Mary about to depart?

Some noted that in *John,* Christ had also said, *"My children, I shall not be with you very much longer"* and discussed the true peace that He gave as opposed to the peace of the world. *"Peace is what I leave with you; it is My own peace that I give you."*

At Fatima the Infant had appeared with Saint Joseph and the Blessed Mother during the last formal apparition on October 13, 1917 but had not spoken while other visionaries and mystics had seen Him as a youngster, including Saint Faustina Kowalska, who recalled that on May 12, 1935, "in the evening, I just about got into bed, and I fell asleep immediately. Though I fell asleep quickly, I was awakened even more quickly. A little child came and woke me up. The child seemed about a year old, and I was surprised it could speak so well, as children at that age either do not speak or speak very indistinctly. The child was beautiful beyond words and resembled the Child Jesus . . ." He went on to say, *"True greatness is in loving God and in humility."* After a vision of a soul struggling with a hellish afterlife, Faustina said, "I again saw the Child who awakened me. It was of wondrous beauty and repeated these words to me: *'True greatness of the soul is in loving God and in humility.'* I asked the Child, 'How do you know the true greatness of the soul is in loving God and in humility? Only theologians know about such things and you haven't learned the Catechism. So how do you know?' To this He answered, *'I know; I know all things.'"*

Two paragraphs later Faustina—famous for the Divine Mercy devotion—wrote that she "heard these words spoken distinctly and forcefully within my soul: *'You will prepare the world for My final coming.'"*

Now—connected to the reputed Hercegovina apparitions, and to "1990"—this was true drama. As the year 2013 began, Benedict again took to the theme of Christ and "peace"—mentioning that word thirty-one times, including the scriptural admonition that, "We Christians believe that Christ is our true peace" (*Ephesians* 2:14-18)—almost precisely what the Lord allegedly had told the seer in that Christmas apparition.

Was His appearance at Medjugorje a hint that Mary's apparitions there were coming to an end, as He disappeared soon after delivering His message in *John* (during the Last Supper)?

Was He hinting that He was ready to begin His own appearances?

Was He breaking through the veil?

12

There were not many Church-approved apparitions that said He was arriving. At Betania, Esperanza, the stigmatic, had seen a "coming" or manifestation. "It will be very different than what people think," she told me. "He's going to come in silence. People will realize He is among us little by little. His first presentation will be like this, because in those days an innocent person whom He loves a lot will die, an innocent person. This will shock the world, will move the world. Many people will believe. He will disappear for some days and appear again. He will multiply Himself, to assist everyone in their homes, because this will be a definite thing. He will come and knock on every door. And then people will realize it is truly Him."

That also had been indicated at a Church-approved apparition at San Nicolás in Argentina, where Mary had said we are in *"dramatic moments"* and that while it would seem for the moment that Satan was triumphant, this *"will last briefly."* The earth, said Mary, was *"in great danger,"* covered in warning, and the reason was spiritual indifference and the pride of *"sophistication."* These were words coming from an unsophisticated place far away from hubs like Manhattan.

It was also what the 1990 prediction implied, when it said the arrogance of the world (which we can equate with its prince, Satan) would be *"broken."* At Medjugorje, it was believed that the unfolding of the secrets would bring an end to the devil's extended power. Sister Faustina had fore-seen the Second Coming (upper case) and it was a promi-nent theme, again, at Kibeho.

But before the Light, darkness.

Many were those who believed in the concept of three days during which light of any kind would be obliterated. It was not a topic at Church-approved sites, and was discounted by seers at Medjugorje. Yet, some form of dark-ness seemed to be in the cards (if not quite as spectacular as certain mystical nuns, going back to the 1700s, had prophe-sied). A volcano could cause darkness of a sort—closing down photosynthesis. A flare from the sun could cause massive blackouts. We had no idea what kind of surprises the cosmos had in store, but some spoke of "dark matter." The dust from an asteroid: this also would blot out the sun.

But it was more the sense—initially—of the spiritual darkness. There was an ongoing battle. Before any final denouements or during them would be a war and in that war would be *"trials"* that served as *"engagements complete unto themselves."*

That could mean many things and among the possible explanations was that the trials—the chastisements—would include war: military conflict.

It was what one considered when one heard of an engagement. We all knew how battles during the Civil War were often described with that word. Or, it could mean—in the darkness—continued spiritual warfare, at ever-new levels, battles in society, in the home, in the culture. The demons seemed to be coming out of the woodwork. There were so many at each other's throats. Evil twisted words; it was twisting emotions. Little conflicts ballooned instantly into large ones. School kids attacked each other—sometimes with weapons—and ridiculed not just their own but also bus drivers. The new big thing: bullying. There was tension all around, like descent of an energy (or *ascent*, as from the pit). Folks shouted down each other on television, or at political rallies. Raw words were now in common use. I heard them even at a Catholic school play. There was now no discussion; there was confrontation. Half the married folks would divorce. There was remarkable animosity. There was the spirit of umbrage. Everyone was affronted. Everyone took issue. The spirit of anger was—indeed—reaching a "crescendo." In Miami, a demented man who bit the face off a homeless person *growled* (flesh in mouth) when police arrived (and didn't stop until they shot him to death). There was the craze of vampires, of zombies. World leaders insulted each other. Accusations at every level of society were taking constant wing. There was no civil discourse. Crime was down, in many places, but that was largely because there were now 2.2 million men in American jails and prisons. Nearly five million more were on probation or parole. The number in juvenile detention was over eighty thousand. In total, those under correctional supervision nearly equaled the population of the City of New York. Serial killings were now so common that many of them didn't make national news.

There were those school shootings. Newtown, of course, and before that Columbine. Sandwiched between: mass shootings in Oregon, in Aurora, in Arizona. A common thread through a number: the "Gothic" culture, "deathrock," "megadeath," that dark suicidal motif that had begun with rock and escalated past punk and heavy metal into the blatantly diabolic. Video games. Movie violence. The kids were playing the kind of war games they use training actual soldiers—before departing for some place of butchery like Afghanistan. And they had access, our children, to what came close to machine guns. There was rampant use of guns; there was rampant use of drugs—including those prescribed by psychiatrists. The devil had it laid out. In Aurora it had been a theatre showing the premier of *The Dark Knight Rises* that the gunman sprayed with bullets—a demented man who was openly playing out the role of "Joker." On the top of a skyscraper in that Batman movie was a sign that said "Aurora" (as if in premonition) and in another scene in the same movie a map that had the words "Sandy Hook" penciled in large letters (as criminals were shown mapping out a Gotham bombing). Sandy Hook? Aurora? Coincidence? Meanwhile, in the Sandy Hook section of Newtown lived the author of a book that was turned into a hit movie about young people who have to kill other young people (*The Hunger Games*).

Happenstance—or evil synchronicity?

So, yes, undeniably, there was conflict; often, it was spiritual; there were little wars around the globe. There were bombings in the Philippines, and Nigeria. These often targeted Christian churches. The "engagements" seemed to include the precursors of a general persecution—which had been explicitly addressed in the 1990 prediction. But what did the new addition to it mean by *"complete unto themselves"*? Let's revisit the full quote from 2010. *"It is a final battle in which the trials of the future will serve as engagements complete unto themselves. Those who choose to ignore the dynamic of spiritual interaction will find themselves in a very confused state that will lead to more conflict. While love prevails, so does courage, and so does the uncovering of those spirits which now install themselves as guardians for those who have invited into their hearts falsity."* That seemed to mean an assault. It certainly meant war. It could be a dogfight. It could be an invasion. Something "complete" implied that the events, the engagements, would stand on their own, independent of one another. In important aspects, they would be separate. There would be a start and a finish to each. That hinted at a great series of events—social and military—that stood alone and would be seen, eventually, as part of the same picture.

Did it have to be an overt conflict—a battle or war? It did not. An engagement could also mean an "appointment" or "arrangement." It was something scheduled. Thus it could be an appointment with destiny. It could mean the condition of "being in gear," said the dictionary. In the final battle, matters would come—trials—that stood alone, one after another, though perhaps in a gradual manner.

For the 2010 missive had said the *"curtain"* would be drawn *"only slowly"*—and after an initial event. "Drawn" could mean opened *or* closed. Because the prophecy indicated, when the curtain was drawn, that a plan would be revealed, I leaned to the explanation of an opening (not closure): the lifting of a veil or partition. One could consider the beginning of the opening act when the curtain rolls up revealing the feet and legs of actors and the bottom portion of props and gradually, sometimes swiftly, sometimes more deliberately, the entire dramatic configuration—or what the 2010 addition (which said it would be drawn *"only slowly"*)—called the *"entirety of the plan."*

What had been expected, but what had been concealed, would now be revealed, step by step, as are the scenes and characters in a play, though in this one, we too might be on the stage.

Those who ignored these engagements, these battles— the *"dynamic of spiritual interaction"*—would find themselves in a state of confusion, and befuddlement was a first sign of the devil's presence (another was anxiety).

The prophecy was telling us that many people were blind—one might say, most—and this blindness would be detrimental.

It would not be just a failing.

It would have ramifications.

Like clergy, perceptions and intelligence would be— were already—bedimmed.

We were living in a world where the majority headed to the cliffs like lemmings.

There was no opposition to evil.

There was no true uproar when a supermarket supported homosexual activism.

Nor when the magazines on their racks in front of the eyes of our kids at the checkouts displayed gossip and lurid sex and seductive images.

There was no uproar when the National Cathedral in Washington announced that it would allow same-sex marriages.

There was little outrage when cartoonists portrayed the Pope in sexual acts nor when profane Christmas decorations were used (as occurred during the 1990s) at the White House nor when Muslims attacked Catholics during Mass or prepared to behead or hang or beat missionaries nor when major companies forced genetically-modified crops down the collective gullet of the confused, somnolent public nor when the World Health Organization printed instructions on how best to perform various types of abortion nor when the U.S. military halted the use, in an ethics course, of Bible passages. "Lawmakers claim Air Force culture becoming 'hostile' to religion," said a headline on *Fox News*.

But it was okay to be a satanist.

This lack of opposition to evil or failure to see it as evil had allowed it to flourish and it was the flourishing of evil that ran exactly parallel to warnings from Mary on chastisement.

"While love prevails, so does courage, and so does the uncovering of those spirits which now install themselves as guardians for those who have invited into their hearts falsity," said the prophecy.

But we were uncovering nothing. Our society, it seemed, had bought into the view that nothing should be deemed dark. Live and let live. To each his own. We were disengaged from the engagements.

We were lukewarm.

And that was perilous because that meant the Lord would spit us out (*Revelation* 3:16)—that is, those who refused to see evil and who did not even really believe in its existence, which was the *"spiritual dynamic"* mentioned in that missive from 2010.

Didn't they see the devil behind network programming?

Didn't they know he was a man of wealth and taste (on Wall Street)?

Didn't they see him tinkering with "chemical witchcraft" (in labs)?

How many attended church on Sunday but went no further and tended to classify anything supernatural as superstitious (including belief in actual evil)?

As a result, evil would grow. Like mushrooms, like fungus, it loved the dark. There would be more rudeness. There would be more selfishness. There would be less cooperation. On every level, there would be more discord. Fury. It would separate people and regions and nations. This would lead to more conflict. There would be additional potential for military actions. Engagements. Confusion was blindness. Blindness scared people into violence.

One of the synonyms for engagement was "battle," tying together parts of the prophecy *("It is a final battle . . .")*. I will get to scenarios for engagements in due time. In such parlance, in air defense, engagement meant an attack with guns or air-to-air missiles by an interceptor aircraft and so it seemed to be referring—the prophecy—to little battles in a larger war.

13

The war was thus to halt the installation of evil, which brought us back to darkness and the antichrist.

According to Mélanie of LaSalette, a man of perdition would arrive as societal evil grew.

A forerunner of the antichrist would gather with his troops from several nations—shedding blood in an attempt to set himself on high and *"annihilate the worship of God."*

Then would come the antichrist himself, with evil brothers.

"At birth, he will spew out blasphemy," claimed her unapproved LaSalette message (which saw him being born of a "false virgin" who was a Hebrew nun). *"In a word, he will be the devil incarnate. He will scream horribly, he will perform wonders, he will feed on nothing but impurity. He will have brothers who, although not devils incarnate like him, will be children of evil. At the age of twelve, they will draw attention to themselves by the gallant victories they will have won; soon they will each lead armies, aided by the legions of hell."*

Some of this seemed embellished under the influence of previous apocalyptic predictions. Was it speaking literally or, symbolically, of a spirit? *"Incarnate"* meant physical. So of course did an actual birth. He would perform great wonders on earth and in the atmosphere, said her prophecy. Rome would become his *"seat."* His brothers would not be incarnate demons like he but would be *"children of evil."*

"Now is the time; the abyss is opening," said her alleged, unapproved secret. *"Here is the King of kings of darkness, here is the Beast with his subjects, calling himself the savior of the world. He will rise proudly into the air to go to Heaven. He will be smothered by the breath of the Archangel, Saint Michael. He will fall, and the earth, which will have been in a continuous series of evolutions for three days, will open up its fiery bowels; and he will have plunged for eternity with all his followers into the everlasting chasms of hell."*

There would be a series of wars until a final one that would be fought by *"the ten kings of the antichrist."*

They would be *"the only rulers of the world."*

Darkness indeed.

Installed.

Nature would ask for vengeance.

There would be disruptions that sounded like chastisements—severe ones.

"Water and fire will purge the earth and consume all the works of men's pride and all will be renewed," said Mélanie's secret. *"God will be served and glorified."*

Water and fire and *"three days."*

Did LaSalette—this part of LaSalette—confirm the notion of a trial that would involve a preternatural darkness? Did it reflect on those prophecies—so popular, so extreme—that saw three days of trial—an ordeal—during which demons would materialize in a way that was extraordinary?

Just as God punished the Egyptians with three days of darkness (in *Exodus*), so at the end of time, said some, would He visit darkness upon humankind for three days. The faithful would need to barricade themselves in their homes. Blessed candles would provide the only light. Holy Water would be needed for combat. Some said the prophecy went as far back at Saint Hildegard de Bingen in the 1100s. Often quoted was Blessed Anna Maria Taigi (1769-1837), who said, "There shall come over the whole earth an intense darkness lasting three days and three nights. Nothing can be seen, and the air will be laden with pestilence which will claim mainly, but not only, the enemies of religion. It will be impossible to use any man-made lighting during this darkness, except blessed candles. He, who out of curiosity, opens his window to look out, or leaves his home, will fall dead on the spot. During these three days, people should remain in their homes, pray the Rosary, and beg God for mercy. All the enemies of the Church, whether known or unknown, will perish over the whole earth during that universal darkness, with the exception of a few whom God will soon convert. The air shall be infected by demons who will appear under all sorts of hideous forms."

It was a belief that was pervasive among those who were mystically disposed in the Catholic rank and file.

"I had a very interesting dream last night," one man wrote me (on December 31, 2012). " Last night, I awoke at exactly three a.m. after having it. I saw the earth as from a distance, and I saw the Hand of God appear and His Hand was moving around the earth from bottom to top in a circular motion in the same way as the earth rotates. There was a stream or line of clouds which encompassed the earth as His Hand was moving around it. It continued moving around the entire earth until the earth was covered with clouds which caused darkness to cover the entire earth.

Then I was walking and the sky had an orange-red glow to it. This glow was also on the faces of people. As I was walking towards them I was shouting, 'Three days of darkness; Jesus is coming in three days.'"

As I said, this was a widespread belief. The LaSalette missive did not posit three days of darkness. It did mention, however, three days of "a *continuous series of evolutions,*" with the earth opening its *"fiery bowels"*—once Satan was again cast down as he had been cast down before (*Revelation* 12).

A "casting down" recalled not only Scripture but also the statements from Medjugorje that foresaw the breaking of the devil's special hold when events in the first secrets (or at least Mirjana's) took place. Did the antichrist and "darkness" fit together, to be broken by His Light?

The original 1990 prophecy did not see the scenario of the antichrist in quite the same way as Mélanie's alleged secret.

"After [the] breakdown of false society will come persecution of Christians and also a new world order," it had said. *"The antichrist will be on earth trying to affect the new world order. Hardly anyone will notice the extent of his influence until afterwards. He will not be of tremendous visibility until he is accomplished. That is to say, he will not rule, control, and be at all obvious to the world at the peak of his influence. He will not be unlike a figure such as Marx, except his ideas will be more immediate."*

That was fascinating because it indicated the antichrist or an antichrist figure would *"try"* to affect the new world order, which also meant he might not succeed.

There would be a battle. It also meant he would not be the architect of a new world order or at least not the sole force behind it (for if he created it, he would be in control of it from the start).

Thus did 1990 point to a player in the background—not so much the overwhelming dictator envisaged by Mélanie and many others as someone who might be of a scientific or philosophical bent as an adviser or financier or consultant.

The average person might not even know of him.

He might be a philanthropist, an inventor, a banker, an investor. Yes, possibly a writer. But probably more connected.

The notion of his ideas being more *"immediate"* than Marx, however, placed this person in a position of special power (note that it didn't say male or female). The antichrist—or *this* antichrist (*1 John* indicated a number)—would be well-situated.

But he or she would not be obvious. The effects would be powerful but exquisitely subtle, which might mean gradual.

The public would not take notice.

He would be behind the curtain—perhaps the "curtain" that would part at the onset of tribulations. (*"Not until the initial event will the curtain be drawn that reveals the entirety of the plan, and even then, it will be parted only slowly, in the woes of purification."*)

Those tribulations, breaking down modern society, would be what led to a new world order, presumably globalism to bring order in a world of sudden mayhem (including societal uprisings). When Medjugorje claimed that as the secrets unfolded, the special power of Satan would be broken, did this mean a personage of evil, with exceptional power, would exert much of his influence before the breakdown of societies, or simply that once Satan's grasp was busted, he would make a bold, perhaps desperate move, *"trying"* to affect the new world order he may have helped fashion (at the peak of his influence)?

"He will not rule, control, and be at all obvious to the world at the peak of his influence," said 1990.

He would have set things in place.

He would manipulate the system.

The 2010 addition spoke as did Medjugorje about darkness though not "three days" and spiritually it was dark indeed.

Might the antichrist already be in operation (if not physically, in spirit)?

In 1991 I had interviewed a visionary in Ecuador who claimed just such a person was on earth as a young man poised to affect the world through science and the media—which made one think, in retrospect, of the internet (a melding of media with the highest forms of technology).

It also caused one to wonder about other uses of technology that long had been under the suspicion of those who fretted about barcodes, microchips, satellites, security monitors, iris identification, and other devices that in the wrong hands could allow a person or persons exceptional control—or influence. The word *"control"* had been in the 1990 prophecy, but in the negative: as something the antichrist figure would not be able to exercise in an overt manner. Instead, the personage in the locution was *stealth*. Matters would be tended to with great discretion.

In the dark.

It brought to mind various international organizations that were interesting because they interwove and involved leaders in finance, industry, government, business, diplomacy, intelligence agencies, energy (oil), media, academia, politics, science, and all sorts of bureaucracy and convened not only in the United States but in far-flung parts of the world (especially Western Europe) to socialize and discuss pressing matters of the day while, as in the case of one, Bohemian Grove, in California speakers such as George W.

Bush or Henry Kissinger took to the podium, all with a total media blackout.

No reporters were allowed to attend.

This gathering took place over a two-week period every July and those who had attended included former Defense Secretary Donald Rumsfeld, President Bill Clinton, President Jimmy Carter, Alan Greenspan, President Gerald Ford, Newt Gingrich, John Major, David Rockefeller, Henry Ford, Prince Philip, and Vice President Dick Cheney, among others—most of whom were anything but nefarious. But it was bizarre. An incredible array of "important" men would congregate to listen to each other and enjoy entertainment in a secluded area (2,700 acres of redwood) in Monte Rio. It was here, decades ago, that the idea for the Manhattan Project germinated. According to its public-relations department, the Bohemian Grove was started in the 19th century by "five newspapermen, a Shakespearean actor, a vintner and a local merchant" from San Francisco. There were "lectures, music, and delicious food." It had been attended by every Republican president since Hoover. "If I were to choose the speech that gave me the most pleasure and satisfaction in my political career, it would be my Lakeside Speech at the Bohemian Grove in July 1967," wrote Richard Nixon years later. "Because this speech traditionally was off the record it received no publicity at the time. But in many important ways it marked the first milestone on my road to the presidency." Yet there were those bizarre aspects. At one point attendees donned flowing red robes and burned their "cares" in the form of a human effigy in front of a giant, thirty-foot owl that "spoke" to attendees during the mock ritual. For years, Walter Cronkite was the voice.

Was this a small cabal that ruled the West? Was there danger of it and other entities "accomplishing" (there was that word again) the workings of an evil and hidden personage?

Recall the original 1990 prophecy: *"The seat of Satan in America is north of San Francisco."*

Monte Rio—Bohemian Grove—was 53 miles northwest of the Golden Gate Bridge.

It was difficult to see any single organization command global hegemony but there was no denying the prestige of those who attended—ambassadors, defense ministers, presidents!

The owl ceremony may have been intended as a spoof (by most attendees, at any rate), but clandestine photographs of the annual event conveyed a spooky ritual conducted by a mock "high priest." Originally, the ceremony had been set up within the plot of a dramatic performance called the "High Jinks" on the first weekend of the summer encampment (after which the spirit of "Care," slain by the Jinks hero, was solemnly cremated). "The ceremony served as a catharsis for pent-up high spirits," said Wikipedia; the Cremation of Care was separated from the Grove Play in 1913 and moved to the first night to become "an exorcising of the Demon to ensure the success of the ensuing two weeks."

Just for letting off steam—or was there a spirit moving of which members were not fully cognizant? Did they realize how the event could be viewed? How did they rationalize the clandestine nature of it? Could such a setting not serve as the roost for a person of evil influence? There was that incredibly tight secrecy (articles about the place had been killed by major publications) and the fact that a number of the 2,500 or so who attended the July event also found themselves at meetings of organizations such as the Council on Foreign Relations, the Club of Rome, and other groups attached to forces of influence such as the Rockefellers and Rothschilds, who were behind the Bilderberg

Group, which since 1954 sponsored its own annual and equally secretive convocation of bankers, policy architects, and elite. As an author noted, these powerful men "met for the first time under the auspices of the Dutch royal crown and the Rockefeller family at the luxurious Hotel Bilderberg in the small Dutch town of Oosterbeek. For an entire weekend, they debated the future of the world. When it was over, they decided to meet once every year to exchange ideas and analyze international affairs."

Was it a matter of concern?

Noted another commentator: "When such rich and powerful people meet up in secret, with military intelligence managing their security, with hardly a whisper escaping of what goes on inside, people are right to be suspicious. But the true power of Bilderberg comes from the fact that participants are in a bubble, sealed off from reality and the devastating implications on the ground of the black-science economic solutions on the table. No, it's not a 'conspiracy.' The world's leading financiers and foreign policy strategists don't get together at Bilderberg to draw up their 'secret plans for the future.' It's subtler than that. These meetings create an artificial 'consensus' in an attempt to spellbind visiting politicians and other men of influence."

Concern, however, lingered. And if a conspiracy was afoot—a vehicle of *influence*—Bilderberg stood as a prime candidate. Organized each year in a different country and drawing mainly from Western Europe, the U.S., and Canada the group has included the likes not only of the Rockefellers, but Henry Kissinger, Bill Clinton, Gerald Ford, Zbigniew Brzezinski, Alan Greenspan, Timothy Geithner, George Pataki, Dan Quayle, Jeane Kirkpatrick, Bill Gates, Walter Mondale, Alexander Haig, and Donald Rumsfeld (note the overlap). Rumors were that Barack Obama, Mitt Romney, Marco Rubio, Hillary Clinton, and other major political types had attended meetings. Eerily like Bohemian Grove, most of those who belonged to the Bilderberg Group were from financial, industrial, union, educational, or media organizations. Meetings had been attended by representatives from *The New York Times* and major networks. Political affiliation (again, like Bohemian Grove: Democrat, Independent, Republican) seemed not to matter. The annual meeting involved a core Bilderberg committee that each year invited a slew of guests (all told, about 180). There were attendees such as Peggy Noonan, who had been a speechwriter for Reagan. A deeply-rooted Catholic, she hardly qualified as part of a new-world cabal. One could go too far. Many did. Were the Bilderbergers simply a forum to toss around ideas—a super "think-tank"? Perhaps.

But the words of President Woodrow Wilson still resonated, when he had said "there is a power so organized, so subtle, so complete, so pervasive, that they had better not speak above their breath when they speak in condemnation of it." And it had evolved, in some ways, as a shadow government (influencing oil prices and the rise of major politicians), its spin-offs including the Round Table, the Club of Rome, the Trilateral Commission, and the Council on Foreign Relations (which had about four thousand members).

Step by step, these various "tentacles" had influenced major political, economic, and cultural decisions. The Bilderbergers, it was alleged, had long orchestrated a move toward a united European continent (which has partly come to be in the way of the European Union), a Pan-American Union that would start with North American unification (in the idea stage; not yet "accomplished"), and an Asiatic unification. "Since March 2005, without public input and with little public awareness, the United States, Mexico, and Canada have been moving quickly toward establishing a continental resource pact, a North American security perimeter, and common agricultural and other health, safety, and environmental policies," charged one author, Daniel Estulin. "Working groups comprised of government officials and corporate leaders, through secret meetings and formal councils that form *de facto* shadow government, are quietly putting this 'partnership' into action, and, to date, only industry 'stakeholders' have been consulted, usually in private, closed-door meetings. U.S. congressmen and Canadian members of parliament have been kept out of the loop. Clearly, there are two main reasons why an incremental and secretive approach is being used to form the North American Union. First, such a union would be extremely unpopular with the majority of Americans and Canadians and would not be permitted if it were widely publicized. Second, the dissolution of the United States not only violates the U.S. Constitution, it would essentially destroy the U.S. Constitution and the Bill of Rights." Said another: "The Bilderbergers are searching for the age of post-nationalism: when we won't have countries, but rather regions of earth surrounded by Universal value. That is to say, a global economy, one world government (selected rather than elected), and a universal religion. To assure themselves of reaching these objectives, the Bilderbergers focus on a 'greater technical approach and less awareness on behalf of the general public.'"

The spiritual implications were obvious and so were fears that global control could turn into persecution and spawn a personage of evil or anti-religious leader. For the requirements of some prophecies, including LaSalette, to be met, the antichrist had to be someone who performed great wonders (on the earth as well as the atmosphere).

That implied a religious framework.

In this regard I was interested in a rich Canadian named Maurice Strong who had spent decades in quiet but highly influential positions at the United Nations, since 1947 serving six times as undersecretary-general along with

135

membership in the Club of Rome, chairmanship of the Earth Council, a consulting role at the World Bank, and secretary generalship of the Earth Summit—which saw the largest gathering in history of world leaders (for the cause of the environment)—in 1992. Strong was like a prototype: hardly the antichrist himself, but an example of how various segments of society and government, including religion, could be knitted together. Strong reportedly had held meetings with David Rockefeller and Baron Edmond de Rothschild and critics asserted that programs he pursued would allow a handful of international bankers to control massive tracts of land in the name of conservation, fears that seemed bolstered—in 1990—when in an interview, Strong discussed the plot of a novel he wanted to write in which a group of world leaders, convinced the West would not clean up its environmental act, formed a secret cabal to bring about a financial panic. "World events do not occur by accident," former British defense minister Denis Healey had once said. "They are made to happen, whether it is to do with national issues or commerce; and most of them are staged and managed by those who hold the purse strings."

On the religious front, Strong had chaired a meeting of two thousand representatives from the world's religions and his wife Hanne engineered a U.N.-based effort called the Environmental Sabbath project to disseminate spiritual messages and sermons based on the ecology to thousands of churches.

Abuse of nature played a key part in how mankind had strayed. This was God's Creation that was in many ways on the verge of ruin. But using ecology in a pagan way raised alarm. The Strongs owned a massive tract of land in Colorado with Buddhists, Hindu masters, channelers, monks, priests, retired hippies, psychics, crystals, a shrine to the earth mother, astrologers, Indian ritualists, shamans, yogis, and a Carmelite monastery on it (in the San Luis

Valley below the splendiferous mountains called *Sangre de Cristo* for "Blood of Christ"). "From the fall of 1966 through the spring of 1970 there were hundreds of unidentified flying object sightings and many of the first documented cases of unusual animal deaths ever reported," noted one website dedicated to the valley. "During peak 'UFO' sighting waves in the late 1960s dozens of cars would literally 'line the roads' watching the amazing aerial displays of unknown lights as they cavorted around the sky above the Great Sand Dunes/Dry Lakes area." The goal, said one brochure, was an elite community to provide "renewal and training for teachers and leaders who in turn are able to carry their message to many others around the globe."

There in southern Colorado an hour from Alamosa a spiritual community had thusly sprouted near what the Indians had called the "Sacred Mountain of the East" and the "place of emergence."

14

Unity was good when it was founded on love and Christian principles but something else when it sought to control.

That was precisely what seemed to be afoot in the world, whether or not Bohemian Grove or the Bilderbergs played a central part in it.

There was a spirit moving, the inclination to control an occult tendency—the reason, in fact, for witchcraft. There were hints of it at the United Nations: paganism. You could *feel* it praying a Rosary in the lobby (as I once had). Besides its support for global birth control, its issuance of brochures on how to do abortions (through its World Health Organization), and its proclivity for a united religion, there was concern that among loosely affiliated organizations that consulted U.N. members (known as "non-governing agencies") was a deep and dark group called Lucis Trust. The organization had offices in Manhattan, London, and Geneva, which reeked not just of globalism but by its own reckoning had been formed in 1920 by Alice Bailey (and husband). Among Bailey's books: *Letters on Occult Meditation, A Treatise on White Magic, Esoteric Astrology,* and *Discipleship in the New Age.* Worse yet, she had taken her creed from

Madame Helen Blavatsky, one of history's most notorious occultists (author of *The Secret Doctrine* and founder of Theosophy). This was no ordinary psychic group; it had leverage of the U.N.; and it made no secret that it sought to encourage a new world order (from a spiritual perspective). It was the finance arm of organizations that descended from Bailey, including "World Goodwill," the "Arcane School," and "Triangles"—which was founded in 1937 as a network of spiritual cells whose members pray a "Great Invocation" on the night of a full moon. The "invocation" was used as the opening prayer for that Earth Summit in 1992. Through World Goodwill, Lucis initiated programs to develop a unified world. Every week it meditated in an effort to send energy and "strengthen human consciousness," announcing one event as taking place "at the Church Center, 777 United Nations Plaza—12th Floor from 5:30-7:30 p.m." "Goodwill is the touchstone that will transform the world," boasted Lucis Trust, which was located on the twentieth-fourth floor of a building at 120 Wall Street. Until 1922, when it decided that its image was suffering, Lucis Trust also had a publishing branch called "Lucifer Publishing." "Many religions believe in a World Teacher or Savior, knowing him under such names as the Christ, the Lord Maitreya, the Imam Mahdi, the Bodhisattva, and the Messiah, and these terms are used in some of the Christian, Hindu, Muslim, Buddhist and Jewish versions of the Great Invocation," said the Lucis website, by way of explaining its unifying principle.

One day would a personage of exceptional "influence" rise from a similar, hidden group?

Another group spawned by Theosophy represented the six great faiths with the mural of a six-pointed star made of two interlocking triangles connected by a serpent.

One could posit any number of ways for the rise of an antichrist. There were movements in the direction of globalism. Most seemed good—"beneficial"—on the surface. Most were not occult. By all odds, this was a conspiracy orchestrated not by a single human cabal but by spirit forces that used people from every walk, often well-meaning folks who did not realize or believe the larger picture.

To see that the world was becoming "as one," one had only to watch kids wearing American t-shirts as they played outside of African huts or go to China and spots signs for McDonald's and Kentucky Fried Chicken or watch a computer boot up with the Apple or Windows or Facebook symbol.

The greatest concern, after global spiritual meddling, was in the areas of technology, food, and health. There were diverse issues, from international finance and commerce (banks were already global, as were the large corporations) to farming and medicine. Philanthropists believed they were helping mankind by perpetuating a united front making birth control, abortion services, genetically-engineered crops, and vaccinations globally available. Through a foundation he had set up with wife Melinda, William Gates of Microsoft sought to reduce population density, expand educational resources, improve hygiene, and save lives by providing vaccines—on the surface, noble aspirations. In 2012 he met in New York with David Rockefeller, Warren Buffet, Michael Bloomberg, George Soros, Oprah Winfrey, and Ted Turner (a little billionaires' club) for a meeting at which population control topped the agenda, a cause Melinda, who took direct issue with the Vatican over the matter, said was her life mission as she and Bill funded organizations such as Planned Parenthood, which had been founded by the anti-Catholic eugenicist, Margaret Sanger, who also had occult beliefs, some based on Blavatsky.

"As 'the most active occult group from the 1880s to the 1920s,' the Theosophical Society exercised a profound influence on what was to become the New Age Movement," noted one writer, Jameson Taylor. "After moving to London in 1887, Helena Blavatsky made the acquaintance of Dr. William Wynn Westcott, a freemason and Rosicrucian. A year later, Westcott co-founded the Hermetic Order of the Golden Dawn as a 'magical fraternity' devoted to preserving the secrets of the 'Western Esoteric Tradition' and 'dedicated to the philosophical, spiritual, and psychic evolution of humanity.'"

A spirit moved.

Most involved were not aware of it.

Although well-meaning, some feared that Gates, Buffet, and others who were super-rich might fall into the temptation of promoting mandatory birth control or even using vaccinations to both prevent disease and cause infertility—in effect, killing two birds with one biotechnological stone.

Those fears only grew all the more shrill when during a talk on population growth in 2010 Gates said, "The world today has 6.8 billion people. That's heading up to about nine billion. Now if we do a really great job on new vaccines, health care, reproductive health services, we could lower that [number of nine billion] by perhaps ten or fifteen percent."

"If we do a great job with vaccines *we can* lower [population]"?

Back in the early 1990s, according to another investigative author, F. William Engdahl, the World Health Organization oversaw massive, Rockefeller-funded vaccination campaigns against tetanus in Nicaragua, Mexico, and the Philippines. Suspicious because the vaccine included something called hCG (a hormone critical in maintaining a pregnancy), *Comite Pro Vida de Mexico,* a Roman Catholic lay organization, launched an investigation and found, according to Engdahl, that when combined with a tetanus vaccine, *the hormone caused a woman's body to turn against both tetanus and the crucial hormone*, rendering the woman incapable of maintaining an unborn child. The vaccine had been given only to women of child-bearing age, none of whom were told they were being injected with an abortion agent along with a vaccination (neither men nor children were vaccinated).

That charitable organizations funded by Bilderberg-type elite (Rockefellers had always been strong members) and overseen by the U.N. would allegedly insert a contraceptive or abortifacients into the bodies of unknowing humans was sobering.

Would Gates head in the same direction?

Could he be excused for pondering such questions, particularly in light of how intrusive Microsoft could be— all but forcing software updates and even *restarting* computers without permission, patching files silently, even when auto-updates had been disabled? Translation: it took control of personal property. Nor was it just Microsoft. There was Facebook, with information on a billion subscribers, and Google, which could view your house via satellite or with a street view. As for the government, it had the capability of monitoring e-mails, tracing every internet search, reading computer keystrokes, tracking cell-phone users, infiltrating Wi-Fi systems, or even taking over the microphone of a smartphone to listen in on conversations. The National Security Agency already had upwards of thirty thousand employees, most specializing in high technology. Potentially more worrisome was the idea of implanted "microchips," the miniscule silicone bits that could be inserted under the skin to hold emergency medical information in those who suffered dangerous conditions and might not be conscious to let responders know about their ailments. That seemed benign—and even beneficial— enough; some already had them inserted, while in many parts of the country cats and dogs were implanted with microchips along with farm animals to provide identification in the event they strayed. Municipalities wanted to mandate them on certain pets. They were widely used to track the migrations of wildlife. But it was this idea of tracking that was the main objection, the concern such a microchip not only could be programmed with information but also engineered to send signals to a satellite and allow officials to track a person's whereabouts.

Already, India had a system that was issuing biometric identification cards to every one of its 1.2 billion people, and in the U.S., passports now bore a microchip. Such technology nudged dangerously close to the point where a nefarious world leader could keep track of and thus control entire populations, perhaps even through new health-care programs.

The task was differentiating the paranoid from the legitimate. The plots were claimed everywhere from contraception, abortion, flu outbreaks, "chem-trails," and vaccinations, to genetic modification, health-care reform, sterilization programs, electromagnetic research, and manipulation of agriculture.

This much, however, could be known: for decades, low-key, even secret elements of elite society had been planning myriad ways of controlling and diminishing the number of humans populating a "stressed" planet. That was documented by Engdahl in an eye-opening book called *Seeds of Destruction,* which detailed an incredible memorandum issued as a top secret federal policy proposal under President Richard Nixon in April of 1974 with the title "Implications of Worldwide Population Growth for U.S. Security and Overseas Interests." Known also as National Security Study Memorandum 200, or "NSSM 200," it was made official U.S. policy under President Gerald Ford. The memo—which was kept secret for fifteen years (until organizations affiliated with the Catholic Church forced its declassification)—was commissioned by Nixon on the recommendation of John D. Rockefeller III and was written by Bilderberg regular and then-Secretary of State and National Security Advisor Henry Kissinger, who had extremely strong ties to the Rockefellers going back to the 1950s, at various junctures working for them.

Why the scope and implications of this memorandum as well as Rockefeller involvement in eugenics had never created a controversy of international magnitude was mysterious, for the Rockefeller studies had a profound influence on many presidents and could be seen as the fountainhead for catchphrases such as "freedom of choice," "sex education," and "sustainable development"—listing as the aforementioned study did the "right of the individual couple to determine freely and responsibly their number and spacing of children and to have information, education, and means to do so."

Kissinger had argued that global population should be reduced by five hundred million and that the food supply should be controlled by the United States, asserted Engdahl, who claimed the memo outlined a strategy of promoting fertility control under the rubric of "family planning" and of hiding it in foreign aid programs. He said there already had been sterilizations carried out by organizations such as the Family Health International and International Planned Parenthood Federation under the direction of the U.S. Agency for International Development. "The secret Kissinger plan was implemented immediately," he wrote. "The thirteen priority countries for population reduction were to undergo drastic changes in their affairs over the following thirty years. Most would not even be aware of what was happening. The Brazilian government [for example] was shocked to find that an estimated forty-four percent of all Brazilian women aged between fourteen and 55 had been permanently sterilized. Most of the older women had been sterilized when the program began in the mid-1970s."

The thirteen priority countries: India, Pakistan, Indonesia, Thailand, the Philippines, Turkey, Egypt, Mexico, Ethiopia, and Colombia, as well as Brazil.

It was shocking to realize how many high-ranking officials had come from the Rockefeller Foundation or linked organizations and the extent to which such hidden elements sought global population reduction due to fears that a large population would consume valuable natural resources and upset the balance of power and wealth. Instead, the Rockefellers, and others of their ilk, says Engdahl, sought to create a new order in a less populous world. Rockefeller programs have been connected to research leading to everything from the intrauterine device to the abortion pill RU-486.

One thus saw why many grew antsy when new vaccines were introduced (by global pharmaceutical companies), or when there were outbreaks of something such as swine flu (with new DNA components).

In fact, some were concerned that certain vaccines might cause the very illnesses they sought to prevent, or would harm recipients with unhealthy additives such as mercury (which many believed had led to the increased rates of autism). There were cases, according to W.H.O., where pharmaceutical companies had inserted live (not just immunity-provoking, inactive) viruses in vaccines to speed approval of vaccinations for the virus they released—into the population—in low doses. Worse, many vaccines originated in stem-cell lines that were derived from aborted fetal tissue.

Were fears overextended? Was there paranoia? "I have written about the swine flu pandemic on various websites, and had an article published in July in the Vatican news-paper, *L'Osservatore Romano*, on the subject," one doctor, Brian Kopp, from Pennsylvania, wrote me. "There is a tremendous amount of disinformation about this flu as well as about vaccines being circulated online. Most of it comes from well-meaning, but poorly informed individuals. Some of it comes from groups that are very much opposed to everything we believe as Catholics. I believe that Catholics online without a medical/scientific background to evaluate all the rumors and stories need concrete guidance and assis-tance in sorting fact from fiction, as well as a resource that is unbiased for or against vaccines. There is an aspect of this that relates directly to our Catholic witness. If we as Catholics accept uncritically every negative report about this pandemic, and/or spread or forward messages that are irrational or unsupported by scientific evidence, it dimin-ishes our credibility as Catholics, and could jeopardize the souls of those who might otherwise accept the Gospel and come into the Church."

Point well made. But was it farfetched to worry that something like a flu bug or bio-warfare agent might be unleashed one day on the unknowing masses?

There was no reason to believe that any group had engi-neered swine flu as part of a secret policy and one had to be cautious not to fall into a conspiratorial mindset. Still, fears were understandable in light of certain researchers. "One of the more prominent members of the American Eugenics Society in the early 1920s was Dr. Paul Bowman Popenoe, a U.S. Army venereal disease specialist from World War One, who wrote a textbook entitled *Applied Eugenics*," wrote Engdahl. "In sum, Popenoe said, 'The first method which presents itself is execution . . . Its value in keeping up the standard of the race should not be underestimated.' He went on to eloquently advocate the 'destruction of the individual by some adverse feature of the environment, such as excessive cold, or by bacteria or by bodily deficiency.'" Estulin claimed that the elite inner circle of the Bilderberg Group still advocated a modern kind of eugenics and had the notion of one day reducing the world's population by eighty percent, as called for by the 1974 United Nations' "Assessment on Biodiversity."

Nor did it allay fears when, in 2006, upon receiving a prestigious award, an "eminent" professor at the University of Texas endorsed reduction of the human population by ninety percent, perhaps using a deadly airborne germ such as ebola (the deadly African hemorrhagic disease). Meanwhile, England's Prince Philip, another key participant in groups such as the Bilderbergers, had said, even before that, in 1988, that if there were such a thing as reincarnation, he wished he could come back as a virus "in order to contribute something to solve overpopulation."

I wanted to know more about that.

15

And I wanted to know about the Georgia Guidestones.

About ninety-three miles from Atlanta, in a rural area of rolling pastures, near a town called Elberton, were six upright slabs of granite that stood like a small version of Stonehenge. Etched on them were messages to the future.

They mysteriously alluded to the belief by whoever had built them that the world was headed for a catastrophe—in some ways, the kind of calamities inferred by the 2010 prophecy, as well as the earlier ones.

The stones, fewer in number than the megaliths at Stonehenge (though taller), were built indestructibly and had been designed in an exquisitely astronomical formation such that the North Star was always visible through the alignment of a hole while the sun poured through other openings at the equinox or solstice and at noon each day through yet another aperture (this in the capstone) illuminating the day of the year on a central column.

But it was those words etched on the uprights that gathered the most attention. For on that capstone—in classical Greek, hieroglyphics, Babylonian cuneiform, and Sanskrit—the letters said, "Let These Be Guidestones to Reason" and just below, on the uprights themselves, were messages that seemed aimed at future readers (or perhaps one should say survivors):

—"Maintain humanity under 500,000,000 in perpetual balance with nature"

—"Guide reproduction wisely—improving fitness and diversity"

—"Rule passion—faith—tradition—and all things with tempered reason"

—"Protect people and nations with fair laws and just courts. Let all nations rule internally resolving external disputes in a world court. Avoid petty laws and useless officials"

—"Balance personal rights with social duties"

—"Prize truth—beauty—love—seeking harmony with the infinite"

—"Be not a cancer on the earth—leave room for nature"

These messages were in English, Spanish, Arabic, Chinese, Hebrew, Russian, Hindi, and Swahili.

Just west of the stones was a plaque set in the ground above a time capsule that was buried six feet below. It implied that it was meant for the ages and conjured the image of future stragglers coming upon the monument as they roamed a ruined or transformed countryside. The very fact that the message was in so many languages further hinted that those who happened upon them might not be American.

Or was it just a call to global unity?

Whatever the intent, the messages recalled aforementioned elite who wanted to winnow down the populace (which the stones said could be a "cancer on the planet") and create world government (at least judicially). Who had put these stones there? Was it someone tied to a secret global group or just a single eccentric?

All we knew was that in 1979 a neatly attired and well-educated man who went by the pseudonym of Robert C. Christian had entered Elberton and approached Joe H. Fendley, president of the Elberton Granite Finishing Company, saying he represented an unnamed group that wanted to erect a monument, the designs of which he proceeded to spell out. When the odd plan was met with skepticism at the granite works, "Christian" sought the assistance of a local banker, Wyatt Martin, president of Granite City Bank, who became his intermediary and the only one allowed to know Christian's true name, though not the group he represented.

According to a plaque that was engraved at the site, Christian insisted that the banker sign a confidentiality agreement "for perpetuity," saying he and his group "wished to remain anonymous forever." His first down payment was $10,000 for a structure that cost in the six figures, a payment that had convinced Fendley he was serious. He never blinked at costs. He told the banker his group had been planning the project for two decades.

The monuments had been finished in 1980 as four hundred locals looked on (no one knows if Christian—who said he had chosen that pseudonym because that was his faith—was present and hidden among the crowd at the dedication). During planning and other meetings with Martin he had arrived from various airports and wired money from different banks. He chose Elberton, it was said, because it had a mild climate, excellent granite, and sentimental value (his great-grandmother had been a native Georgian). Martin believed that "Christian" had died around the time of the September 11 attacks, estimating that he would have been in his eighties at that time, when communication between the two stopped. "He made it clear that he was very serious about secrecy," Martin told a magazine, while a brochure on the monument issued by the granite company explained that Christian was spokesman for "a small group of perhaps half-a-dozen people who believe in God and country seeking to erect a monument to help in some way to improve this world and this world's people." Christian described himself as a "patriotic American" in every sense of the word. "It is very probable that humankind now possesses the knowledge needed to establish an effective world government," the group was quoted as saying. "In some way that knowledge must be widely seeded in the consciousness of all mankind. Very soon the hearts of our human family must be touched and warmed so we will welcome a global rule of reason. We are entering a critical era. Population pressures will soon create political and economic crises throughout the world. These will make more difficult and at the same time more needed the building of a rational world society. The approaching crisis may make mankind willing to accept a system of world law that will stress the responsibility of individual nations in managing internal affairs, and which will assist them in the peaceful management of external frictions.

"We, the sponsors of the Georgia Guidestones, are a small group of Americans who wish to focus attention on problems central to the present quandary of humanity. We have chosen to remain anonymous in order to avoid debate and contention which might confuse our meaning, and which might delay a considered review of our thoughts. The celestial alignments of the stones symbolize the need for humanity to be square with external principles which are manifest in our own nature, and the universe around us. We must live in harmony with the infinite. We profess no Divine inspiration beyond that which can be found in all human minds."

Some speculated that R. C. Christian played on "Roman Catholic," but more convincing were those who argued there was a link between the name and an ancient occult school of thought called "Rosicrucianism." In its modern form, Rosicrucianism seemed to have been contrived as a secret philosophical society by a late medieval German named Christian Rosenkreuz (note that his initials, if reversed, would be "R. C."; he also was known, in fact, as "Frater C.R.C" and as Rosicrucianism's "Christian Father"). Membership had included mathematicians, natural philosophers, alchemists, and astronomers—with a decidedly Masonic ring. "During Rosenkreuz's lifetime, the Order was said to consist of no more than eight members, each a doctor and a sworn bachelor," noted Wikipedia. "Each member undertook an oath to heal the sick without payment, to maintain a secret fellowship, and to find a replacement for himself before he died." Rosicrucianism, it said, "held a doctrine or theology 'built on esoteric truths of the ancient past' which, 'concealed from the average man, provide insight into nature, the physical universe and the spiritual realm. Between 1607 and 1616, two anonymous manifestos were published by this group and promoted a 'universal reformation of mankind.'"

Some claimed Rosicrucianism was in fact the basis for Freemasonry and that only Rosicrucians knew the meaning of secret masonic symbols. Rosicrucians, whose magazine was called *New Age*, also had been linked to an occult group known as the Golden Dawn.

16

It was hard to discern but from any secret milieu could rise a person of undue influence who could not be tied to any one group and was based on no single organization. The spirit of globalization under the umbrella of secular humanism was a spirit that arched across the fields of science, economics, law enforcement, banking, commerce, manufacture, media, health care, environmentalism, retail, transportation, biotechnology, agriculture, human rights, government, the judiciary, religion, and—supremely—the internet. When one called an American company now, one got *India*.

There were certainly some good—and Christian—aspects to unity. Christ wanted us to be brothers. He wanted all people to share in the fruits of the world. He wanted the well-to-do to look after the desolate. He was against racism. He was against ethnicity. Above all, He had preached love.

The question was not whether unity was good but how (and by whom) unity would be fashioned.

Right now, when not ecological, or military, it was energized by mammon.

Materialists were in charge. There was no spiritual underpinning, at least not a Christian one.

And so, yes, one had to be concerned that Satan would come here too as an "angel of light."

It was difficult to buy the notion that a single cabal like the Masons could orchestrate it all (that theory was too easy), but that there was a dark force was symbolized by an odd and strangely low black cloud that I watched hover (on an otherwise cloudless day) over the monument.

Across the road from the monuments was a house owned by an impoverished 43-year-old grandmother who said she had often seen strange lights at night flashing in the middle of the monuments (which sounded like rituals) and eerie whirlwinds of hay.

It was well known that occultists had conducted ceremonies there; a witch and warlock were even married at the monuments.

So it was interesting why something that was ostensibly innocuous and governmental had such an aura and at the same time how the "guidestones" interwove with other monuments around the world such as Gizeh, Stonehenge, and Aztec pyramids, along with the practices of ancient European druids, as well as symbols at places such as the massive new airport near Denver, where uncanny artwork seemed to be the order of the day.

Mostly, it seemed more like a clumsy attempt at the *avant garde* than a hidden message, but, again, a spirit was moving. There was a time capsule here and also a capstone with the classic Masonic symbols of square and compass on it and the words, "New World Airport Commission." That, it was explained, was simply the way a local group of businessmen viewed it: a new, "world-class" airport and city (nothing esoteric). Onlookers, however, had fretted over airport murals showing, for example, three females—an

African, a Native American, and a blonde girl—dead in coffins, the girl with a Star of David and Bible on her chest. Another depicted a future calamity that involved a line of mourning women in rags with dead babies and a towering, Darth Vader-like figure brandishing a massive sword that stabbed the back end of a dove (while in his other arm is a machine gun). There was fire: a burning city. Why was there fire? Why coffins? And why was the airport so far from downtown Denver and so large—far bigger than was currently warranted?

Did the government plan to use it as the major western staging area if an apocalypse or civil war erupted?

At the front of the airport, again strangely, was a horse with eerie, glowing red eyes.

That hardly meant that the antichrist was taking flight nor that there was conscious planning behind all the oddities (again, it was more the spirit), but it made me think back to the concept of "illuminati." These, it was said, were *agenturs* who were "well-bred," educated, and trained for placement behind the scenes at all levels of government. From those spots, it was feared, they would fashion—and control—governmental decisions. It was further claimed that they had been launched back in 1776 by a Jesuit-trained Bavarian law professor named Adam Weishaupt, who was initiated by a Masonic lodge in Munich and sought a project of "illumination" (at the behest of the German banker Mayer Amschel Rothschild) to enlighten the societies of men through "reason," dispelling the "clouds of superstition and of prejudice" (read: the Christian faith) and creating a new world order (one that would rid mankind of governments, family, organized religion, patriotism, and inheritance.)

Initially membership in the formal organization called Illuminati had been just a handful of highly secretive men, but reportedly it soon branched into a covert organization with "cells" that were largely kept from communicating with each other as it sought to shape the outcomes of history.

These had been folks, one may ascertain, who certainly sought to exert influence (as opposed to raw power), men who would not be observed on the world stage (at least not in public) at the height of that influence, just as the 1990 message described: until they were *"accomplished."* That brought to mind the Bilderbergs and Bohemian Grove and indeed "Bohemia" bordered Bavaria, a German state, in Central Europe. (*"As for the antichrist, remember Europe, and especially Central Europe,"* said the 1990 prophecy).

Were they—these bankers, these officials, these industrialists—the modern version of "illuminati" (though no longer belonging to a series of actual cells)?

Weishaupt and his co-conspirators, it was said, had established a network of agents around Europe that infiltrated loci of power. Their final goals remained enigmatic. The order had branches in most European countries and during one ten-year period about two thousand members (about the same, ironically, as the annual Bohemian Grove extravaganza). Fascinating it was that the famed German stigmatic and mystic Blessed Anne Emmerich, in the first of two thick volumes on her life, *The Life and Revelations of Anne Catherine Emmerich,* was quoted as saying on page 405, "I always see these 'Illuminati' in a certain connection with the coming of antichrist. For, by their secrets, by their injustice, they forward the accomplishment of that mystery of iniquity."

Whether or not there were modern groups with a direct lineage from Weishaupt's "Illuminati," it showed the proclivity through centuries for clandestine elites to affect (or *try* to affect) the workings, education, and finances of mankind. Some accused the Rosicrucians of being "illuminati" and in fact a famous Scottish scientist named John

Robison wrote toward the end of his life about the way in which Illuminati had infiltrated Masonry, using its lodges for cover. "The Association," as he called it, "was abolished in 1786 by the Elector of Bavaria, but revived immediately after, under another name, and in a different form, all over Germany. It was again detected, and has spread into all the countries of Europe. It took its first rise among the Freemasons, but is totally different from Freemasonry. It was not, however, the mere protection gained by the secrecy of the lodges that gave occasion to it, but it arose naturally from the corruptions that had gradually crept into that fraternity, the violence of the party-spirit which pervaded it, and from the total uncertainty and darkness that hang over the whole of that mysterious Association." In a treatise called "Proofs of a Conspiracy Against All the Religions and Governments of Europe Carried On in the Secret Meetings of Freemasons, Illuminati, and Reading Societies," Robison claimed that "their real intention was to abolish all religion, overturn every government, and make the world a general plunder and a wreck" so the elite "might rule the world with uncontrollable power"—which again sounded like the 1990 prophecy.

He and others blamed the Illuminati's influence for a number of major historical events including the French Revolution (during which Catholic churches were plundered without mercy).

No doubt, too, they had a hand in furthering the "age of reason." The illuminati, said another defector, were "thousands of conspiracies operating in parallel."

Again, it was a *spirit*. "In June of 1991 David Rockefeller reportedly said, 'We are grateful to the directors of the *Washington Post*, *The New York Times*, *Time* magazine, and the other directors of the national and international press who for the last almost forty years have attended our meetings and have respected their promises to be discreet,'" noted a Catholic film producer from England. "'It would have been impossible for us to develop our plan for the world if we had been subjected to the full glare of publicity during those years. The world of today, however, is much more sophisticated and better prepared to march on to a One World Government.'"

One goal: controlling banks, petroleum, gold, diamonds, and other raw materials, with a population reduction to below one billion within the next two to three generations—"'culling the human herd' in the interest of retaining their own global power and the feudal system upon which it is based," charged another conspiracy buff (for our discernment).

While there was little doubt that such interests had been attempting to unite the world economy behind the scenes, and no doubt that secretive groups had alarming influence, the question was how far one could go with theories and whether the antichrist mentioned in the 1990 prophecy would come from any specific milieu or simply orchestrate groups like the Bilderbergs without their knowing it.

He would exert influence under the radar of humans.

He would be a mystery to everyone.

Yet somehow, he would be in our midst. He would use the new world order they had so arduously and naively formulated.

Was the Dark One already roaming the earth? There were now twenty-seven countries in the European Union and they included all but Switzerland and Serbia, when it came to Central Europe. Austria, Germany, Czechoslovakia, Hungary, Liechenstein, Poland, Slovakia, and Slovenia were often defined as "Central Europe." Some also considered it to include Croatia, Serbia, and Romania. On the edge of *that* was Bosnia-Hercegovina—where Medjugorje was. This part of the world had not only been crucial to the past but would be critical in the future, with indecipherable ways. Was something ready to rise from there and take advantage of what unity had been developed across the continent of Europe as well as the crises it now faced, and would face in the future, as matters reached that "crescendo"?

17

"While love prevails, so does courage, and so does the uncovering of those spirits which now install themselves as guardians for those who have invited into their hearts falsity," said the 2010 addition. *"The angels stand ready to assist those who unleash power with humility and belief. Only those in union with God will be able to see in the darkness which so many expected and that already is upon the earth."*

What was formerly concealed would now show itself—themselves.

The rituals would break out into the open—as during Hollywood awards, as during halftime at the Super Bowl.

In an ad for Mercedes-Benz during football playoffs was that song *Sympathy for the Devil* ("please allow me to introduce myself, I'm a man of wealth and taste") playing in the background.

Right after that had come an inaugural address that trumpeted a riot in New York ("Stonewall") that had occurred at a Mafia-run gay bar as having sparked the homosexual movement—which was likened to the cause of civil rights.

At the same time newspapers in Los Angeles and Sydney, Australia, were beaming and brimming with news that Catholic cardinals were being brought to public scrutiny (one before a government panel).

If it seemed odd that a feeling of the occult would touch the power elite as well as the field of entertainment—that originators of the "new world order" would so often seem tainted by a spiritual and not just political darkness—this was because the spirit of control was the spirit behind witchcraft: wanting to manipulate others, as witches tried to do through spells (*santeria*) or drugs (*pharmakeia*). Said the great expert on deliverance, Derek Prince: "Witchcraft is anything that takes the place of the Holy Spirit for control. It always goes for control and manipulation."

And so it was. When it was in our own lives, we needed to root it out.

It was burbling to the surface across the societal spectra.

As for governmental control, it was to the point where Homeland Security could use a laser to tell what you had recently eaten from fifty yards away.

And that was nothing compared to the supernatural manipulation.

As the 2010 prophecy warned, *"Only those in union with God will be able to see in the darkness which so many expected and that already is upon the earth."*

There was increasing evidence that the assassination of JFK had been by a top-secret band of intelligence operatives who may have used sophisticated psychological techniques back in the Sixties. There was no telling what they were concocting now.

Evil spirits were installing themselves and increasing the authority of those who sought yet greater wealth and control, as well as installing themselves as lords over a general public that through negligence (and indifference) had allowed darkness to prevail.

That meant all of us.

There was a general onslaught of darkness that eventually would precipitate an antichrist. Evil spirits were being allowed to take over and those who ignored their workings (the *"dynamic of spiritual interaction"*) would find themselves in a very confused state (stated the prophecy) because a first goal of demons was to cause confusion (along with anxiety).

That dovetailed with a part later in the prophetic word whereby it warned that *"the dark spirits are now allowed to materialize in full due to the pretense and aspirations of man."*

There were those who expected the antichrist to rise in the Muslim world (from Egypt or Turkey, from Syria, from Iran, where leaders publicly expected the end-times and a "Mahdi"). LaSalette, had gone more dramatic still, claiming (to recount) that *"the Antichrist will be born of a Hebrew nun, a false virgin who will communicate with the old serpent, the master of impurity, his father will be B* [this letter left unexplained]. *At birth, he will spew out blasphemy; he will have teeth; in a word, he will be the devil incarnate. He will scream horribly, he will perform wonders, he will feed on nothing but impurity. He will have brothers who. although not devils incarnate like him, will be children of evil. At the age of twelve, they will draw attention to themselves by the gallant victories they will have won; soon they will each lead armies, aided by the legions of hell."* In the fourteenth century, St. John of the Cleft Rock had stated, "It is said that twenty centuries after the Incarnation of the Word, the Beast in its turn shall become man. About the year 2000 A.D., Antichrist will reveal himself to the world."

As Archbishop Fulton John Sheen had once said, "We do know that at the end of time, when the great conflict between the forces of good and evil takes place, Satan will appear without the Cross, as the Great Philanthropist and

Social Reformer to become the final temptation of mankind."

A former prime minister who had gained international prominence when he was elected chairman of the first session of the U.N.'s General Assembly had even called for such a reformer, saying, chillingly, many years back (in Belgium, in Central Europe), "We do not want another committee, we have too many already. What we want is a man of sufficient stature to hold the allegiance of all people, and to lift us out of the economic morass in which we are sinking. Send us such a man and be he God or the Devil, we will receive him."

So it seemed that the atmosphere was ripe.

Were we speaking of a minor one, perhaps even a false pope—an *antichristus misticusi*—or a final "beast," the *Antichristus magnus*?

Everywhere, said LaSalette, there would be "darkness" (just as 2010 used that same term) and *"extraordinary wonders."*

Let's focus on that. For there were marvels—supernatural wonders—everywhere one turned.

Actually, one had only to turn on the television to the shows on "ghost-hunters" and orb lights, poltergeists, and apparitions (unholy ones), which seemed now to be coming out of the woodwork.

No doubt, a veil was lifting.

Or, there were the shows on "UFOs," for they too were being spotted all over, and to our peril. For the UFO phenomenon showed many signs of a deception by the evil one. Such objects, which first came to large public notice at Mount Rainier, Washington, in 1947, often appeared over old Indian burial mounds like the Allagash in Maine and Apache-Sitgreaves National Park in Arizona or in forests where witches did rituals.

While there was certainly the chance that extraterrestrials existed (and also that a good number were hoaxes or delusions), most brought to mind what Indians had called "spirit lights." One might also say: "shape-shifters."

Few knew they likewise had been prominent in medieval Europe during the "Black Death."

In one case a bishop had exorcised a luminosity that hung over a town in Italy (it immediately dissipated).

Even a government report in Britain noted there were "historically significant ties to UFOs and disasters."

And now they seemed everywhere. There were the strange lights along with "crop circles" and reports of "alien" abduction and the reason to suspect a demonic root was that aliens were portrayed as slanty-eyed creatures bearing similarity to antique voodoo statues.

They often haunted families for generations and sometimes departed with the odor of sulfur; they left "abductees" in a state of fear. In some cases, they left bruise or claw marks. Those who encountered such "creatures" had been known to commit suicide—haunted by such entities. Others "channeled" them as mediums channeled spirits. Or, those who encountered aliens suddenly developed psychic "gifts." Poltergeist activity frequently erupted in homes where aliens visited. Indeed, the director of that movie said he was frightened at the strange occurrences in the crew's hotel during the filming of the movie. As Father Gabriele Amorth, the famed Rome exorcist, had said: "Demons occupy a house and appear in electrical goods. Let's not forget that Satan and his followers have immense powers. It is normal for domestic appliances to be involved and for demons [to] make their presence known via electricity." (See too *Close Encounters of the Third Kind* and the appliances going haywire).

One had to remember that Scripture had referred to Satan as "prince of the power of the air" and could also cite

LaSalette and that (alleged) prophecy of *"astonishing wonders [that] will take place on the earth and in the air."*

Sometimes, it seemed like the Nephilim (see *Genesis* 6:4).

There were even those who feared UFOs were a deception that could lead to establishment of an antichrist as nations grappled to deal with an "extraterrestrial" disclosure that as one writer fretted *"will be the catalyst that unites the world under the one-world leader, the antichrist. He will be the leader of the one-world government, one religion, and one economy. People need to understand all of this now so that when the curtain is unveiled, they already have made their choice about which God to serve."*

Through the centuries deceiving spirits had come in accordance with the culture as fairies, leprechauns, gnomes, wood nymphs; now, in the space age, in at least some instances, they came as outer spacemen. Hollywood had literally set the stage with *Close Encounters, Star Wars,* which portrayed extraterrestrials (Yoda, ET) as almost cuddly. They had come to stop us from destroying ourselves. We were to embrace them. One problem: it smacked of New Age globalism. Another: if they were physical, why had they never left any evidence? Some claimed they had, in New Mexico, at Roswell. But there were major questions about that claim, evidence of aerial experiments at an Air Force base not too distant that had gone awry and would explain the wreckage. The argument was long; it was convoluted. Suffice it to say that with so many hundreds of thousands of reports, many by reliable witnesses (including Jimmy Carter and Ronald Reagan, not to mention the family of Elvis Presley), it seemed peculiar that there was so little and perhaps *no* physical evidence. When Elvis was born on January 8, 1935, at 3:30 a.m. in Tupelo, Mississippi, recounted one author, "a mysterious blue UFO shone over the house from above at the exact moment that Elvis made his grand entrance into the world." The account was attributed to Elvis's father, Vernon. A twin brother was born stillborn. In his library was Blavatsky's dark classic *The Secret Doctrine* and on Elvis's jumpsuits, noted the author, were ancient Mayan and Native American symbols. Such symbols were also associated with Greek and Egyptian mythology and have been reported in a famous "UFO" abduction case (whereby the person was temporarily taken out of our reality by extraterrestrials). Other famed musicians who claimed to have encountered UFOs included Jimi Hendrix and John Lennon. UFOs were seen at Woodstock and other major counterculture happenings. Was it just drugs? Between one and twelve million claimed to be "abductees." Said document compiled by the Library of Congress for the Air Force Office of Scientific Research in 1969 that was entitled *UFOs and Related Subjects: An Annotated Bibliography,* "A large part of the available UFO literature is closely linked with mysticism and the metaphysical. It deals with subjects like mental telepathy, automatic writing, and invisible entities as well as phenomena like poltergeist [ghost] manifestations and possession. Many of the UFO reports now being published in the popular press recount alleged incidents that are strikingly similar to demonic possession and psychic phenomena."

Insanity? Fantasy? "The fruit of it is very obvious," charged Guy Malone, who started a ministry called Alien Resistance. "Anybody who is a contactee or abductee—all of their testimonies include stories where these beings are telling them spiritual 'truths'—such as, 'you are god' and 'we're spirit guides here to help mankind evolve into utopia.' So simply, without even looking at the Bible for a doctrinal position, the fruit points it out as deceiving spirits, the doctrine of demons, as *Timothy* said to expect [*2 Timothy*: 3:1-17]."

Or as Saint Augustine once noted, "what men can do with real colors and substances the demons can very easily do by showing unreal forms."

That was relevant because UFOs were also tied to ever-increasing sightings of strange beasts: abominable snowmen, the skunk ape, mothman. Here too was often an occult underpinning. Why would a man-ape leave behind— as was also true here—the sulfur smell or something comparably pungent? How could so many be spotted—again like "UFOs"—without leaving final physical evidence (though some did claim the discovery of hair)? In the case of mothman, who was first spotted in West Virginia, in 1966, the description was of a winged, red-eyed "man" who appeared just before a massive bridge collapse (which killed forty-six). Why would UFOs be spotted where bigfoot was— if both were not part of the same deception (at least in many cases)?

How brilliant it seemed, the part of the 2010 message that urged *"the uncovering of those spirits which now install themselves as guardians for those who have invited into their hearts falsity"* and said that *"only those in union with God will be able to see in the darkness which so many expected and that already is upon the earth"* while adding that *"the dark spirits are now allowed to materialize in full due to the pretense and aspirations of man."*

The world was not only stranger than we imagined but stranger than we could imagine, stranger than science. And deceptive. Deception was in the wind. Discerning phenomena had to be weighed against paranoia. A veil had been drawn back or thinned. More was coming. It was why Holy Water was so important, along with Blessed Salt, and the Holy Face of Jesus. These were potent against the intrusion of spirits that sought to present themselves as *"guardians"* and as the veil thinned, there were the constant reports of haunted celebrities, of ghosts caught by security cameras, of graveyard lights, so many "ghosts" that in Indiana there was even a real estate agent who specialized in selling haunted houses. Necromancy was common. Spirit mediums had become celebrities, performing on TV. All it took to attend a séance was now the click on the remote control or an internet button. This focus on the netherworld was pronounced in computer games. Hidden in many was a wizard or a witch or at the least symbols of paganism. Sometimes, there was also the pentagram—but only once a youngster got deep into these obsessive, addictive games. So was there an occult touch to card games and certainly to books such as Harry Potter and these items opened a porthole to magic—the devil's version of the Holy Spirit; one day, along with the almost countless other forms of societal evil, it would energize—would precipitate—a personage of evil. For years, the notion of a savior and wonderworker known as "Maitreya" had gathered a cult following, with many pointing to this looming "person" as antichrist. There were many eyes too on the Mideast. But again: it seemed unlikely that such an entity would be identified except in retrospect, once he was *"accomplished."* As one pastor pointed out, *Revelation* 13 spoke about spiritually dark times, the tribulation period, when "Satan's son" would emerge on the scene, "the man of perdition, the man of sin, the beast, best known as the antichrist, the most evil man who ever lived, history's vilest embodiment of sin and rebellion," and would have with him his "devilish worship leader, a religious guru, the false prophet," referred to, in *Revelation*, as the "second beast." He would be given power to give breath to the image of the first beast, and would kill those who didn't want to worship him. Like many, the pastor, an evangelical, feared this would come after formation of some kind of "banking union" that would control the populace through technological identification, perhaps a barcode-like chip— "mark of the beast"—that was implanted, leading to a sort of financial worship. The 1990 message asserted that *"soon the world will not be the world you know,"* not a barren world, or one depopulated, but *"the end of your technological era."* Many inventions of mankind would be broken down, and there would be a life of peasantry (*"everywhere"*).

It was after this breakdown that the antichrist would operate, along with a persecution. Before Christ would come an antichrist. This suggested that massive events—chastisements far larger than the warnings already seen in the way of hurricanes and quakes and tsunamis—would occur before the antichrist exerted his greatest influence or at least accomplished his central goals. One can imagine that the template for a new world order so assiduously developed for several centuries now would finally be able to take control of a decimated set of societies. Destruction would pave the way to authority by a small number with global authority as humans struggled to reorganize. They would seem "benevolent." Whoever or whatever group was most organized would be equipped to fill the economic and political vacuum in re-establishing order as well as an infrastructure. One can imagine the systems of communications and transportation in a state of disarray or largely non-existent after a large disaster. It took the collapse of just two towers in New York to bring transportation across the United States to a screeching halt for a week. What would happen if an event occurred that affected many more buildings and perhaps in more than one large metropolitan area? And what would happen if that was followed by a second and even a third major event—whether natural, terrorist, or military? We were talking very big. "Huge." An asteroid or a solar flare had the capability of bringing down the entire electrical grid, as did an airborne electronic pulse by a sophisticated enemy country. Similar effects could be achieved, of course, by a simple, slow-grinding but massive economic implosion. A relentless depression. Or, epidemics. A disease like swine flu, bird influenza, hemorrhagic viruses (such as ebola), or most likely something entirely new and reconfigured would cause panic and the same kind of decimation as an instant cataclysm. The need for order—in the wake of that breakdown (which might kill leaders, destroy the communication grid, and totally disrupt the transportation of goods, particularly food and gasoline)—would be paramount. The prophecy explicitly stated that it was *"not speaking of a barren world, or one depopulated,"* but a greatly disrupted one.

And so the question became: in paving the way for a nefarious personage, what would a world after chastisements, or at least initial events, look like?

When something was not barren, it meant that it was not altogether desolate, that it could still be fertile, that there could be reproduction. But it would be *changed*. Frustrating it was to peer further into the fascinating prophetic verbiage for in stating that the world would not be barren the prophecy could have been saying, on the one hand, that there would be no great desolation, or that while there was desolation—the land, the world—would not be "dead"; this was also true of the word *"depopulated,"* one definition of which said it meant "having lost inhabitants by war or epidemic"; and so one could view the coming events with the idea that there would *not* be a huge loss of human life.

But "depopulated" also meant "uninhabited"—no longer lived in—and that certainly left the door open for great regions of destruction and a massive reduction in the number of people if not obliteration: there would still be people around and they would be able to reproduce (as well as till the soil). It was a flip of the coin. Whichever definition one favored, it was saying that the world was not going to end; it was going to change. And when it changed, the change would be radical and would open the way for persecution and an antichrist.

The original 1990 prophecy followed that with a new paragraph describing an appearance—a towering manifestation or "coming"—of Jesus. There was the implication that this would defeat the antichrist. Here we had Mélanie at LaSalette saying that he would be defeated by the "breath" of the Archangel Michael. In Scripture, Christ's arrival comes and the devil and his prophet are cast into a lake of fire. "Immediately after the tribulation of those days shall the sun be darkened, and the moon shall not give her light, and the stars shall fall from heaven, and the powers of the heavens shall be shaken: And then shall appear the sign of the Son of man in Heaven: and then shall all the tribes of the earth mourn, and they shall see the Son of man coming in the clouds of Heaven with power and great glory" said *Matthew* 24:29-30.

The darkness would come *after* major chastisements, or as part of the final ones.

But let's stay on this issue of depopulation.

Once more, Fatima came into play. The flu that killed those two seers just a couple of years after the apparitions (and may have originated from American troops who were traveling to Europe) had a death toll of between fifty and one hundred and thirty million from the U.S. to Europe to the Arctic and even remote Pacific islands.

Today, with more than seven billion people in the world, such a toll, at the same percent (three to eight), would have been tallied at 210 to 546 million. Moreover, during the Spanish flu (as it was known) twenty-seven percent of the public—in today's numbers, two billion—had been infected.

These were astonishing numbers and though we seldom think of the "Fatima" epidemic, it may well have killed more than did World War Two.

When one went back to the medieval bubonic plague, one was talking about a disease that had killed a quarter to a half of Christian Europe: perhaps twenty-five to fifty million.

Might something like that precede a new world order as countrysides turned bleak but not entirely barren (or depopulated)? Is *this* the kind of landscape envisioned by those who erected the Georgia stones?

Such a massive loss of life would seem to come under the category of a "depopulation," and thus the 1990 prophecy did not seem to be referring to an event or events of that magnitude leading *up* to the antichrist.

But something was coming to cause phenomenal change.

Antibiotic-resistant bacteria?

It would be "the end" of the "technological era." And here is where the son of perdition would step in.

He would be a bit like Marx.

He would be behind the scenes.

After this breakdown of false society would come persecution of Christians. The antichrist would be on earth trying to affect the new world order. Hardly anyone would notice the extent of his influence until afterwards. He would not be of tremendous visibility until he was accomplished. That was to say, he would not rule, control, and be at all obvious to the world at the peak of his influence. He would not be unlike a figure such as Marx, except his ideas would be more immediate.

18

We knew only that the *"arrogance of the world,"* which was the spirit of pride, would be *"broken"* (which sounded like great coming tumult).

It might no longer be a world with cars or television or planes, since, allegedly, in 1990, Jesus had said He would not come into *"such"* a world in such a way.

Something was coming that was not just huge, but huge, huge, huge. Hurricane Sandy had been "big." So was the quake in Los Angeles, shortly after the 1990 prophecy. Hurricane Katrina and September 11 were in a higher category. They had been *"very* big." But we were staring down the barrel of something not just one but perhaps several magnitudes more intense.

Might it be something like a larger, much larger, version of 9/11?

In the 1990 prophecy had been the warning not to go to New York for twelve years because it was under an *"evil cloud"* and *"the pride there will be broken."*

It was just short of twelve years later that the World Trade Center had fallen.

When the Trade Center collapsed, the running theme in comments by shocked New Yorkers was that those two buildings had been the city's "pride."

There were other signs, on September 11, and they evaded the vast majority of Americans—while foretelling the future of their country.

Few knew that America's first president, George Washington, had stood at St. Paul's Episcopal Chapel near what is now Wall Street and along with the first Congress and cabinet, prayed for the consecration and future protection of the nation on his very day of Inauguration in 1789.

At the time, the church had owned many surrounding acres, including watery property across the way that would later be landfilled—and was to be the site for construction of the World Trade Center.

In other words, on his first day of office, the nation's first president had stood on property that included what would become infamous as "ground zero"!

And that was just the start of it. Washington's inauguration itself had taken place in Federal Hall, which was in the heart of Wall Street. That structure saw cracks in its foundation widen to an unnerving degree when the towers fell (causing a magnitude–6.2 tremor).

The chapel of Saint Paul itself was one of the very few proximate buildings to survive—and did so virtually unscathed, but for a broken window; some believed it was because a large sycamore, which fell during the collapse, had shielded it.

The sycamore was found toppled over with a brick tangled in its roots, which was seen as another sign.

For in *Isaiah* 9:10 is the passage, *"The bricks have fallen, but we will rebuild with hewn stone. The sycamores have been cut down, but we will plant cedars in their place."*

The words were in reference to the defiance of ancient Israel in the face of the attacks by Assyrians.

Assyrian descendants were thought to include members of Al Qaeda. Their blood may have flowed in the terrorists' veins. Moreover, Assyrians had been based in *Iraq*—one of two nations America attacked in defiance of and in retaliation for September 11.

The ancient attacks on Israel were seen as chastisements from God. Its "hedge" of protection—its "wall" (as in Wall Street, which once ran along a wall)—had been removed.

Now, in 2001, "bricks" had certainly fallen. The modern version of them was steel and glass—although, symbolically, and incredibly, there was that brick in the roots of the St. Paul's sycamore, which since has been bronzed as an icon of 9/11.

After the attacks, politician after politician defiantly vowed to rebuild and even quoted *Isaiah* 9:10 (though not in its proper context!).

This was all pointed out by author Jonathan Cahn in a brilliant bestseller called *The Harbinger* that further documented how—as in ancient Israel—Americans sought a "hewn" stone—which meant a stone from a quarry—as the cornerstone for the new "Freedom Tower" that would rise in the place of the destroyed structures. It was a "gazit" stone that weighed twenty tons from a quarry in the Adirondacks.

If *that* wasn't enough, there was also a fact that a type of cedar tree—named the "Tree of Hope"—was planted in the sycamore's place. *"The bricks have fallen, but we will rebuild with hewn stone. The sycamores have been cut down, but we will plant cedars in their place."*

No lesson had been learned. There was only defiance. We were cursing ourselves. As in ancient Israel, this presaged further attacks.

Instead of evaluating the terror from a moral and introspective viewpoint, from a spiritual perspective, America almost immediately set about declaring war in Afghanistan and Iraq and like ancient Israel vowed to rebuild bigger than before. The wars would cost five trillion dollars, hundreds of thousands of lives (the majority of them children, women, and male civilians), and the sympathy of most of the world, which recoiled at the militarism. More American lives were lost in those wars, moreover, than during the original attacks of September 11; meanwhile, tens of thousands of young Americans would return missing limbs and their mental balance. The symbolism was astounding. America's ground of consecration was Ground Zero! When there was no other way to get through to us, noted the author, God lifted His hedge of protection—as He did in ancient Israel (allowing enemies to enter). Noted a commentary on the *Isaiah* passage: "That which God designs, in smiting us, is to turn us to himself and to set us seeking Him; and if this point be not gained by lesser judgments, greater may be expected."

As time passed, it appeared as if life was gradually returning to normal, noted the narrative on Isaiah and Israel. "There was a respite, peace. With each passing year, it seemed as if the danger was farther behind them. But it was an illusion. The problem and the danger only increased. It was a period of grace, given to them in mercy, that they might change their course and avert the judgment. But if not, then a greater judgment would come, and that final breaching of their walls would be remembered as the harbinger that was the beginning of their fall. These were their most critical days."

The attack was thus a harbinger *and* a judgment—the culmination of warning and chastisement. In fact, noted Cahn, 9/11 was followed seven years to the week by the beginnings of the collapse of the financial markets. In Scripture, the seventh year is called the "Shemitah." Credit is cancelled and debt is wiped away—as so many debts had to be cancelled in 2008, when the greatest financial crisis since the Great Depression occurred, right there near Ground Zero and at another spot (Federal Hall) that figured into Washington's inauguration. It was seven years after 9/11 that this neighborhood experienced the greatest single-day stock market crash (point-wise): September 29, 2008, precisely the twenty-ninth day of Elul, as it was known in ancient times— the critical and crowning day of the Hebrew Shemitah. How many—how *many*—times were "towers" mentioned by Scripture in reference to chastisement? Even causing a small quake!

"Here on Wall Street, George Washington took the oath of office as our first President, and this site was home to the first Congress, Supreme Court, and Executive Branch offices," says a government website about Federal Hall. "The current structure, a Customs House, later served as part of the U.S. Sub-Treasury. Now, the building serves as a museum and memorial to our first President and the beginnings of the United States of America."

Now too, there was an idol—the statue of a golden calf—on Wall Street.

The critical question was whether we'd learned from the Wall Street crash and if not—if the market went higher than ever (which it now had, as if in further, unyielding defiance)—what might happen next.

In my own reckoning, the number seven once more seemed involved.

According to Scripture (*Leviticus* 26:18-21), the Lord had said, "If also after these things you do not obey Me, then I will punish you seven times more for your sins. I will also break down your pride of power; I will also make your sky like iron and your earth like bronze. Your strength will be spent uselessly, for your land will not yield its produce and the trees of the land will not yield their fruit. If then, you act with hostility against Me and are unwilling to obey Me, I will increase the plague on you seven times according to your sins."

This—in light of the 1990 prophecy—was nothing less than astounding.

Huge, huge, huge.

For there were strains of the very same language—even though the receiver of the alleged message had never read this part of the Bible.

There was the phrase, "I will also break down your pride of power . . ."

In speaking of New York, the 1990 prophecy had said that *"the pride there will be broken."*

There was the word "stand."

"The very artifice of your societies is false and against the accordance of God's Will," said the original communication. *"This artifice shall not last.*

"Your very conceptions of happiness and comforts are a great evil and falsity.

"They will not stand" [emphasis added].

It was an explicit description of the land reduced to a crisis state—perhaps not permanently barren, but barren for a period, for an excruciating period, however short a time it might be.

A sky like iron. This indicated clouds, or smoke, some form of cover or darkness.

Storms? A volcano? A completely unanticipated cosmic phenomenon?

The trees would be fruitless. As at LaSalette, there would be crop shortages, followed, one might presume, by famine (and disease born of weakened bodies), as occurred in France and Ireland right after LaSalette. For the year before that apparition, there had been substantial problems—a blight—with the potatoes. About a quarter were bad. The Blessed Mother in 1846 had warned that if matters continued it would get worse. It did. Immediately after, seventy-five percent of the crop failed. In Ireland, a million would die; in France—in the region of LaSalette—ten thousand.

But back to the number "seven": It was seven years after September 11 that the financial collapse had begun. Was that seven times the disaster of 9/11 (at least, economically)? It was, when one considered that the entire world, and nations such as Greece, Spain, and Ireland, not to mention the deepest recession since the Great Depression in America (though there was plenty of more room for more descent).

This crisis—based on Wall Street greed—cost American homeowners an estimated $17 trillion.

That was three times the war costs after 9/11 and didn't touch the damage to banks, financial institutes, stockholders, and other nations.

One might guess it was at least a sevenfold augmentation.

Part of the reason for the loose credit that caused the collapse originated, in fact, with federal actions to make credit easier in the *wake* of 9/11. We see how it all connected. And now—if we didn't respond to the 2008 warning/chastisement as we should—one seven times greater yet was in the wings.

A "plague" would be loosed. Might one take it literally? In looking at "seven," one also had to note in *Proverbs* where it was prescribed that when a thief was caught, he pay seven times what he stole; in *Matthew* (12:40-49) the Lord spoke of seven spirits coming upon those in a wicked generation; in *Genesis* 4:24 it said: "If Cain is avenged seven-fold, then Lamech seventy-sevenfold"—which meant a vastly magnified situation.

Several years after the financial debacle, in 2011, a highly unusual quake centered near Richmond, Virginia, was not only felt all the way to Washington and New York *but badly cracked* the Washington Monument—so badly that it was closed for nearly two years.

Meanwhile, when Hurricane Sandy struck a bit more than a year subsequently, it damaged Liberty Island such that the Statue of *Liberty* had to be closed for months.

In the span of a few years, Federal Hall and the Washington Monument had incurred structural cracks and the nation's great symbolic statue was closed when the pier and park surrounding it—at the nation's entrance—were overcome (with thrashing waves).

Meanwhile, a building across the way from the Twin Towers that was used by the City of New York as its emergency management center because it was on a rise that allowed an entrance on one side to be a couple stories above the rest of the area in the event of storm surge, and had been reinforced to prevent its collapse in the event of a quake, had come tumbling down a few hours after the two skyscrapers on 9/11/01.

New York's vaunted emergency management center—set to handle crises—itself had been destroyed.

I had visited there. I had interviewed officials on potential future disasters. They spoke much about the possible use of toxins by terrorists and also the danger of hurricanes and the threat of quakes but none could have guessed that the future event was across the street from them!

Now, their "indestructible" headquarters had been obliterated—collapsed from the reverberations of the other two buildings.

19

There was the possibility—only a possibility, but a possibility—that in Scripture could be found a general framework for chastisement and perhaps a timetable.

Here we read *Isaiah* 7: 7-9: "Thus says the Lord: This shall not stand, it shall not be! Damascus is the capital of Aram, and Rezin is the head of Damascus; Samaria is the capital of Ephraim, and Remaliah's son the head of Samaria. But within sixty years and five, Ephraim shall be crushed, no longer a nation. Unless your faith is firm you shall not be firm!"

There was the verb "stand" again.

And here was a possible time-frame—one that involved the number seven again, for sixty-five plus five was seventy; there was the temptation to add that number to the 1990 prophecy and come up with 2060.

By that time, would our nation—our modern world—be radically changed? (Or sooner?)

There was also *2 Chronicles* 36:21: "Until the land has retrieved its lost Sabbaths, during all the time it lies waste it shall have rest while seventy years are fulfilled."

In that potato famine forecast at LaSalette—caused in part due to irreverence and violation of the Sabbath—there had been a million dead with children trembling and dying in their mothers' arms; and throughout history there had been further blight and other crop failures as now in North America and Australia and so many other places were crop failures due to extremes: drought or flooding. There had been many "mega-droughts" affecting a third or more of America—and lasting decades. Climatologists had marshaled evidence showing that some prehistoric droughts lasted centuries (even a thousand or more years) and afflicted massive territories. Analyses of tree rings revealed that a great drought occurred a thousand years ago and lasted two centuries, followed by a "little ice age." And even further back in time, there may have been droughts that persisted for longer yet and devastated populations.

"I gave you six days to work, I kept the seventh for myself, and no one wishes to grant it to me," said Our Lady of LaSalette. *"This is what weighs down the arm of my Son. If the harvest is spoiled, it is only because of the rest of you. I made you see this last year with the potatoes; you took little account of this. It was quite the opposite when you found bad potatoes; you swore oaths, and you included the Name of my Son. They will continue to go bad; at Christmas there will be none left. A great famine will come. Before the famine comes, children under the age of seven will begin to tremble and will die in the arms of those who hold them."*

As several historians noted about France just before the potato famine, "Lower class non-work activities shifted from the religious to the secular. Church attendance among the lower class in Paris declined during the nineteenth century as churches were not constructed or expanded quickly enough to accommodate the growing population. The lower class turned from worship to indulge in leisure activities: seeing popular theatre and vaudeville shows, dating and drinking in beer halls, dancing in music halls, and spectating and gambling at sporting events (horse racing and soccer were the most popular sports). Many lower class individuals became literate primarily to read the racing forms.

"Some upper-working class families were wealthy enough to visit the countryside for short periods; some vacationed for a weekend, week or month. They rented small homes or stayed in country inns. With the expansion of the railway system and increased competition between the rail companies and horse drawn trolleys, train fares declined, and day travel became more affordable for the lower class."

As the Industrial Revolution took hold, there was the break-up of families.

There was dehumanization.

This was caused by mass production.

And it would greatly figure (as we will see) into the prophecies.

Religion was replaced by entertainment.

This went even to that apparition in Wisconsin.

There—before the massive fire—Adele had been told, *"Make a general confession and offer Communion for the conversion of sinners . . . Gather the children in this wild country and teach them what they should know for salvation . . . Teach them their catechism, how to sign themselves with the sign of the Cross, and how to approach the sacraments; that is what I wish you to do. Go and fear nothing."*

Blasphemy? Violation of the sabbath?

The modern world made the France and Wisconsin of the 1800s look devout.

A video showing a Crucifix with ants crawling all over it had been displayed at the Smithsonian National Portrait Gallery. At one abortion clinic, a rubber chicken was hung on a Cross to mock the protesting Christians. No wonder lightning darned the skies of the nation's capital, no wonder towers tumbled, no wonder there were cracks. And darning it was. I saw startling photographs of storms over D.C. and New York, bolts striking between the Jefferson Memorial and the Washington Monument (between which was the Bureau of Public Debt).

Damaged too—seriously—had been National Cathedral.

Throughout the Bible, defiance was met by worse judgment.

And so the trumpet sounded. A photographer had encountered the sound of one as he approached a police barricade in the eerie quiet of lower Manhattan after September 11 and spotted a strange trumpeter illuminated by shafts of light caused by the smoke and dust beyond the barrier—a fellow playing eerie music. When the photographer tried to snap a picture, his camera mysteriously jammed.

Was it an angel?

For decades there had been reports of strangers who were encountered as hitch-hikers and would tell the driver that Jesus was coming.

In *Revelation* (8:7) a trumpet is used by angels to announce purification. Now, people around the world were hearing a "trumpet"—not from any person, not from any mysterious strangers, but from the ground and air and sky around them: unusual reverberations that had some of the same qualities of a horn, perhaps an ancient shofar. Starting in 2011, loud, mysterious sounds began to be reported first across Eastern Europe (Kiev, Ukraine) and then other parts of the world, just about every part.

At times they seemed to be coming from the ground— an unnerving, humming, rumbling quality—while in other instances it was more like the low echoing resonance (from baritone to bass, with a sighing chorus) of some sort of gigantic musical device, not so much playing—trumpeting—as moaning.

Strange exterior sounds, in dozens of cities; it was a rash that swept across YouTube as folks recorded sounds that did seem inexplicable or perhaps better said *unnerving.*

There was an unsettling quality to them, some sounding similar to factory machinery and others like distant traffic—even in the middle of a remote Canadian forest. A throbbing vibrating rumbling noise that reached a peak and settled down and reached another crescendo and couldn't be pinpointed to anywhere.

The sky was sounding. The earth was groaning. Had Maria Esperanza been correct—was there something very deep, right down there at the core, far beyond the purview of seismologists, that was "out of balance"? Or was this a supernatural sound? A warning? In Slovakia it was like a distant bass drum, in London a heavy buzzing screech, in Saskatoon metallic and yet jungle-like echoes, in Cambridge an otherworldly resonance, in Illinois an eerie low-banshee sound, in Massachusetts a disconcerting horn-like nearly trumpet sound, in the Pine Barrens of New Jersey a low tuba-like noise. Often, mostly, the quality of rumbling—tremors. In some cases, animals reacted; car alarms went off; sometimes it brought to mind the sounds from the spaceship in *Close Encounters* (or the opening occult sounds in *Star Wars).*

While they spanned the entire Western hemisphere, they seemed especially frequent from the Mid-Atlantic states in the U.S. up through Michigan and Illinois before heading into Canada.

Noted a blogger: "All over the world, people are experiencing strange music and noise from the earth and the firmament above. Sometimes, it comes from the sky as droning trumpets that sound notes in the lower to middle registers, but are nevertheless musical in nature. Invariably, as they moan out their somber blasts, people are swept into a state of emotion. Some reports have them thinking of the end of the world. Others tell of various listeners swept into a state of foreboding.

"That's not all. There are growing numbers of reports on sounds of an entirely different type. These are explosions that come without any warning, are heard for a few days, then fall silent once again. Sometimes, they appear to come from underground. Often, they seem to come from just outside a living room or bedroom wall, reported to resemble the sound that might result from the head-on crash of two speeding locomotives. They come at so high a volume that they should be heard over long distances. But this is not always the case.

"Furthermore, though unbelievably loud to the imme-diate hearers they seldom, if ever, register traces on local seismographs. Imagine a thud, a roar, and the clanking of metal at unbelievably high volume. Residents rush outside, but discover nothing out of the ordinary, nothing at all. This is an emerging mystery. But it is far more than a simple mystery; it portends a threat of some sort."

The mysterious sounds had one thing in common: Sooner or later, listeners reported that they found them-selves contemplating things supernatural.

In Clintonville, Wisconsin—not far from the shrine dedicated to that apparition in Champion—police received hundreds of calls one week from citizens awakened by noises that they said seemed to be coming from under the earth. "At times, they said, it was like someone banging on the pipes in the basement, while at other times it was so loud that windows rattled and the ground jolted," reported *The New York Times.* "City officials in this small town about an hour west of Green Bay believe there is no physical threat to residents and note that no major damage has occurred to property. But night after night of the same quake-like eruptions has inspired a local obsession—driven by fear and fascination—to pinpoint the cause. But almost a week since it started, there is still no complete explanation for why Clintonville, population about 4,600, is booming."

Verda Schultz, 47, thought someone was slamming car doors outside her house, reported the newspaper, but when she got up to yell at the person, she noticed that all the people in her neighborhood were already gathering on the street in their pajamas. "There's something radically wrong with this earth," she said, noting that her horses and dog had been acting oddly.

Some experts attributed it to "microquakes," and indeed seismic monitors picked up a magnitude-1.5.

Others argued that it was far more than a single, simple quake.

"Just wanted to tell you I've heard them too!" a woman named Lisa in Eau Claire, Wisconsin, wrote me. "I have an older horse who has been acting very strangely the last several weeks; standing at the end of her pasture near the fence and staring at the southeast sky. She's been worrying me because she won't even come to the barn to eat; I have to practically drag her with the lead. Then she'll eat as normal but suddenly will run back to her spot at the end of her pasture and stand and look. We do have coyotes around and she has always been interested in them so I thought it was either that or maybe she's getting senile, but two Saturday's ago I was out with her doing chores and was about to put her on a lead to 'drag' her back to the barn when suddenly I heard huge booms from the area she was watching. These weren't gunshots or anything I could identify (as I hear those a lot too around our farm). The direction she is looking there is only farmland and steep wooded hills for several miles and the noise actually sounded like it was close, almost surrounding us, very loud and scary. I ran back to get my cell and record a video but by the time I got to it the sounds were done. After they ended the horse calmly turned away and walked back to the barn where she ate and acted normal. Every morning and evening when I come to take care of her, I find her standing in the same place staring at the sky to the southeast."

Right after Hurricane Sandy, what a newspaper described as "a mysterious boom" shook a New Jersey community. In Canada, a "mysterious hum" was plaguing Windsor. In January of 2013, loud "explosions" or resonations were reported in North Hollywood, California, and Salem, Massachusetts, and South Carolina and Utah, where checks with seismologists, an Air Force base, an artillery training ground, and rocket manufacturer offered no clues.

Were such sounds a form of hoax or mass cyber (YouTube) hysteria? "Or could these sounds from all over the world be the Lord roaring from Heaven, since He has a controversy with the nations?" another asked. "Just throwing it out there for discernment (*Jeremiah*), 30: 'Therefore you shall prophesy against them all these words, and you shall say to them, "The Lord will roar from on high and utter His voice from His holy habitation; He will roar mightily against His fold. He will shout like those who tread the grapes, against all the inhabitants of the earth," 31: A clamor has come to the end of the earth, because the Lord has a controversy with the nations. He is entering into judgment with all flesh; as for the wicked, He has given them to the sword,' declares the Lord. 32: Thus says the Lord of hosts, "Behold, evil is going forth from nation to nation, and a great storm is being stirred up from the remotest parts of the earth."

"For the last two nights of heavy rain in Atlanta there has been constant rumble and low roar punctuated by heavier booms of thunder," said a witness. "It's like being at a railroad crossing of a never ending heavy trailer loads with periodic crashes and splashes of lightning. It is non-stop. One friend described it as coming from the bowels of the earth not from the sky."

"I haven't heard the rumblings in the real world myself but about six to eight years ago, when I was in a difficult personal situation, I had some time praying and fasting and one day I saw something like a dream or vision," added another, from Germany. "In my mind I was told it was two years ahead, shortly after the new year would begin and then I saw the horizon and heard a loud rumbling—which was like shaking the whole earth. I immediately thought of the thunder which is described in some forecasts as coming in the end times before three dark days—although it was not exactly like a thunder but more a great rumbling. I was shocked and thought: Why do you worry about earthly things? From that day on I expected something special to come. I was not afraid or worried but sometimes thought of it. Nothing happened, so I assumed: Maybe God has heard the prayers of His people."

There was more a sense, however, of the ominous. The potential supernatural dimension was indicated in legends attached to Moodus, Connecticut, where inexplicable rumblings went back to Indians who believed a "god" was angered at local witches and created a wind that caused the distant rumblings and blew the witches from their caves. Moodus meant "Place of Bad Noises" and it reminded me of the Indian word *"huracan,"* from which we get "hurricane."

That meant "evil wind."

In Scripture it said: "Listen closely to the thunder of His voice, and the rumbling that goes out from His mouth" (*Job*

37:1-3). "Then the Spirit lifted me up, and I heard a great rumbling sound behind me, 'Blessed be the glory of the Lord in His place,'" said *Ezekiel* 3. "And I heard the sound of the wings of the living beings touching one another and the sound of the wheels beside them, even a great rumbling sound." Added *Revelation* 8: "Then the angel took the censer, filled it with fire from the altar, and hurled it on the earth; and there came peals of thunder, rumblings, flashes of lightning and an earthquake."

The rumblings in *Revelation* were connected with the opening of God's temple and that's what one pondered: if the manifestations—whether heard at a physical or spiritual level—symbolized a great spiritual shift.

Or a tectonic one.

It certainly was a time of quakes and sometimes strange ones. Since 1990, or perhaps one might say 1989 (when San Francisco was so badly shaken) tremors of all sorts had afflicted the earth, particularly around the "Ring of Fire." A major one devastated a city in Japan named Kobe, which meant "the door of God." On June 9, 1994, a tremor estimated to have been *four hundred miles* below the surface had been felt from Bolivia to Canada. Another shook the California town of Joshua Tree (as we recall Joshua blowing the shofar around Jericho before the walls fell).

In 2012 there were two massive quakes (8.6 and 8.2) in Indonesia, followed hours later by three more in Mexico.

There was perplexity: the Indonesian quakes were of the magnitude normally associated with major catastrophe, yet there had not been much surface damage.

What was happening at levels below those experts could study? Scientists speculated that a gigantic tectonic system known as the Indo-Australian plate was in the early stages of breaking up.

"The shocking number of earthquakes that have rattled the globe, especially along tectonic plate boundaries, since the double magnitude-eight earthquakes struck off the coast of Northern Sumatra on April 11, 2012, could be early indication the planet may be shifting towards a new catastrophic model," noted a blog, while Romania's top seismologist, Gheorghe Marmureanu, told the *Bucharest Herald*: "There is no doubt something is seriously wrong. There have been too many strong earthquakes. If you keep seismically shaking the earth, like a bottle of soda, its structural integrity eventually will become compromised and it will start to fracture like an egg. In this case, the fracturing will be thermal dissipation by hyper-volcanism, mega-thrust earthquakes, and greater tectonic boundary plate agitation around volcanic arcs and subduction zones . . . if this is what's indeed happening, the pressure will continue to build in the interior of the planet until it eventually destabilizes all tectonic plates in a spectral pattern of continuous seismic oscillation. Every earthquake generates and emits enough kinetic energy through the earth to potentially trigger more seismic disturbances. The quakes are a surprise that cannot be easily explained by current scientific knowledge. With the Indonesian quake for example, statistically, there should be one big earthquake in this part of Asia every five hundred years. However, since 2004 there were already three quakes with a magnitude over eight, which is not normal."

Would one trigger another? Would there be a quake "storm"?

On January 4, 2013, there was a magnitude-4.6 quake in Venezuela that was immediately followed by a magnitude-4.3 under the Ceram Sea in Indonesia and a magnitude-4.9 in the same region. The next day came a magnitude-5.1 in the Mid-Indian Ridge followed less than five hours later by a magnitude-7.5 along the Cascadian fault in southeastern Alaska. Another of magnitude-six hit Alaska later that same month. It was like the entire planet was resonating from the heightened seismicity (rumbling, humming like a bell).

Keep in mind how the 1990 prophecy said that *"chastisements will differ according to regions, and like the great evil, will not always or usually be immediately noticeable for what they are. In the period also will be a warning that involves not fire from the sky but fear of fire from the sky, and strange loud rumblings."*

As for those who felt the sounds they'd heard had come more from *above* than below, noted a blog: "This isn't the first time that such sounds have been heard. Particularly in the last three decades of the nineteenth century, strange sounds were reported in the heavens, ranging from explosions to metallic clanging and even 'harplike' sounds. Around the world, people have begun to hear strange sounds . . . bone-chilling, unexplainable, echoing, resonating, harmonic, crashing, metallic clamoring racket. It has forced many to think again about the coming apocalypse. In the current wave, some percipients have reported what sounds like the jumbled voices and music of a distant radio or television set. To date, scientists theorize about 'distant sounds' that might somehow be transported to faraway locations due to unusual meteorological conditions. But what about aerial harps . . . or the continuous droning of trumpets? That, of course, would require conditions not known to exist. Nor are there any substantiating seismic events, explosions, or head-on collisions. The sounds seem to come out of nowhere."

Some posited a tantalizing link to the aurora borealis. "In our opinion, the source of such powerful and immense manifestation of acoustic-gravity waves must be very large-scale energy processes," explained a team of researchers. "These processes include powerful solar flares and huge energy flows generated by them, rushing towards earth's surface and destabilizing the magnetosphere, ionosphere, and upper atmosphere. Thus, the effects of powerful solar flares: the impact of shock waves in the solar wind, streams of corpuscles and bursts of electromagnetic radiation are the main causes of generation of acoustic-gravitation waves following increased solar activity."

It was tantalizing because it had been an "unprece-dented" display of the northern lights on January 25, 1938 (from Europe to North America) that Lucia dos Santos of Fatima said was the great sign prophesied to her by the Blessed Mother in 1917 as the harbinger of a great coming war (which arrived soon after when Hitler swept into Austria). Now, nearly a century later, the auroras were making strong appearances. They were happening again, as activity on the sun grew strong—as solar storms and flares grew in size, sometimes threateningly. They were seen from the Arctic to Texas. Some looked like curtains of luminosity. Some looked like there were angels in them.

Many of the auroras looked like fire from the heavens and although the fear mentioned in the prophecy didn't seem connected to solar activity, there was concern—not yet fear—that an eruption on the sun could flare to such an extent as to take down our entire electrical grid, something that experts at the National Oceanic and Atmospheric Administration's space weather division told me, in an extreme case, was a distinct possibility.

"I read your article about strange lights in Jersey," wrote another correspondent. "I saw them too. The sky turned green for a few seconds about the same time as reported in the article. I live in Rutherford, about an hour Northeast of Bridgewater (New Jersey). My windows face west. I was up and happened to be looking out when the sky just turned a bright green for a few seconds then went away. Thought I was seeing things. Never happened again. Then I forgot about it until I read your article. Didn't last as long as people in the videos, but I definitely saw it."

There were fireballs. There were streaks of light. They had become commonplace. Sometimes they were associated with the sounds. There were striations in the sky and dark clouds putting one in mind of a vision that legend had it George Washington received in which he saw three major threats to the United States in the way of black vapors from overseas that were announced by a shadowy angel who placed a trumpet to his mouth and blew three distinct blasts (one that foretold the foundation of America, another the Civil War, and another an event in the future).

20

Regional chastisements, smaller chastisements—precursors—would precede an active stepped-up period during which still larger events would precipitate. There would be the stage of *precursors* and the stage of *precipitation*.

We were edging toward the precipitation.

Literally.

Events were expanding rapidly. When rain came, there was more of it. In Britain it had been "biblical." When snow came, there was more of it—snowiest Moscow in a century. Tornadoes? We hardly reported them any longer, unless they leveled a whole town. Droughts that had been confined to several counties or a part of a state or even an entire state were searing countrysides far beyond. In fact, there was the chance we were entering a stage of mega-droughts in many areas. They were multi-state. In 2012, *eighty* percent of the U.S. was deemed "unusually dry" or "drought" and a sixth or more was splashed red on maps indicating "severe"—including the critical Corn Belt. When rain did come, it was severe; storms were unprecedented. *Precipitation.* "From highways in Texas to nuclear power plants in Illinois, the concrete, steel and sophisticated engineering that undergird the nation's infrastructure are being taxed to worrisome degrees by heat, drought, and vicious storms," reported *The New York Times* on July 26, 2012. "The frequency of extreme weather is up over the past few years, and people who deal with infrastructure expect that to continue. Leading climate models suggest that weather-sensitive parts of the infrastructure will be seeing many more extreme episodes, along with shifts in weather patterns and rising maximum (and minimum) temperatures. 'We've got the "storm of the century" every year now,' said Bill Gausman, a senior vice president and a 38-year veteran at the Potomac Electric Power Company, which took eight days to recover from the June 29 'derecho' storm that raced from the Midwest to the Eastern Seaboard and knocked out power for 4.3 million people in ten states and the District of Columbia."

Added this newspaper six short months later:

"Britons may remember 2012 as the year the weather spun off its rails in a chaotic concoction of drought, deluge, and flooding, but the unpredictability of it all turns out to have been all too predictable: Around the world, extreme weather has become the new commonplace. China has endured its coldest winter in nearly thirty years. Brazil is in the grip of a dreadful heat spell. Eastern Russia is so freezing—minus fifty-degrees Fahrenheit, and counting— that the traffic lights recently stopped working in the city of Yakutsk. Bushfires are raging across Australia, fueled by a record-shattering heat wave. Pakistan was inundated by unexpected flooding in September. A vicious storm bringing rain, snow, and floods just struck the Middle East. And in the United States, scientists confirmed this week what people could have figured out simply by going outside: last year was the hottest since records began."

Some thought it was the shift in the earth's magnetic pole, which always fluctuated but now was moving by thirty miles a year—such that we would soon be searching for "north" over Siberia (actually, "true north" was where the axis of the earth hypothetically was).

There was no need to get too technical. The upshot was that when the earth's magnetism fluctuated so did its interaction with the sun's magnetic field, and this interaction could affect climate and provoke great instability. If there was enough of a flux (as another news service put it), "anything can happen.

"And what normally happens is that all hell breaks loose."

These media outlets did not realize how literally true this "hell" may have been.

Neither did they really have a handle on why the climate was doing what it was doing scientifically.

Many theories were tossed about but the truest: it was a planet spinning out of control in concert with its spirituality; God was leaving it on its own. There was a superstorm cycle. The instability would be noticed in all else—from ground quakes and the rumblings to asteroids. It was *God* Who kept everything together—or let it go on its own and begin to fall apart (to a degree). Scientists called this "entropy." Polar shifts had occurred often in the history of the earth. It meant "north" was no longer quite where it had been. It caused alteration in aeronautical navigation equipment. Compass needles in Africa were already drifting off each decade by a degree. There was more to come.

Events that had started and then stepped up in the 1990s were precipitating weather extremes of greater frequency, intensity, and duration. The storms, the droughts, the wind, the solar flares would continue until a monumental event or series of events took us to the stage of Denouement—the upshot of what had been building since 1990, a parting of the curtain. One definition of "denouement" was "the final clarification or resolution of a plot in a play or other work" and this tied right in to the way the latest extension of the original prophecy said, *"Not until the initial event will the curtain be drawn that reveals the entirety of the plan, and even then, it will be parted only slowly, in the woes of purification."*

Curtain. Play. Stage. Interestingly, the word denouement came from the old French word *dénouer*, which meant to "untie" or "unknot," and could bring to mind the cord on a rope on a curtain on a stage. But really, it meant: an unfolding, a loosening of what had been tightly bound, what had been shielded from our view, what had been secret. Now we were getting somewhere. At least, we seemed able to create a delineation—perhaps sort of a schedule. *"The angels have their instruction from east to west, and now a timetable has been set in motion,"* said the revelation back in 2004; if a timetable had been pushed into action, this meant or seemed to mean that a new time or stage had begun around the time of the Asian tsunami—which had occurred four days after the 2004 addendum.

Events were precipitating, rolling. They were approaching the status of "mega." But had the curtain parted? Not yet. It would part upon precipitation of a certain occurrence. Both the 2004 and 2010 prophetic dictations made allusions to "event" in the singular. The latest one, the 2010 locution, said the curtain would be drawn with the *initial event*. These were very rich words. Something big— and singular—would bring us into the time of Denouement. The curtain would part. We would not see the stage. Right now, we were still staring at the curtain. We were watching it billow. We were hearing the noises behind stage. There was a shuffling. Once in a while, a loud accidental noise. Furniture was moving. Backdrops were being placed. Perhaps the orchestra was tuning instruments—drums that rumbled, boomed, horns that blared, high-pitched, resonating strings.

"Initial" also meant that there would be other events. So the Denouement would be a time of a number and perhaps many happenings in the same act.

But there would be that initial one and it would be distinct in some way as also foretold in 2004 when that message had said *"the event to come will surprise everyone who has offered a prognostication, and will show even recalcitrant scientists, though not all, that there is a fundamental alarm in Heaven over their arrogant and wayward course. Nothing that is artificial in a way that disrupts what God intended will be allowed to stand."*

They tied together perfectly. The subtlety seemed beyond what one might fabricate. All three major messages interwove. It would take a brilliant person, a clairvoyant, to forge such phraseology years apart so expertly, so exactingly, in the midst of world happenings that also dovetailed. It made one matter clear: those who, in this time of darkness— during the Precipitation—had expected enormous occurrences were not wrong; something enormous was in the wings. Their error was with pronouncing it too soon (or in too much detail). *"In this time, expect the error of premature expectation, but not [error in] the truth of the expectation itself,"* intoned the prophecy as if to underscore how around the world presumptuous revelations were calling for this and that to happen on such and such a date—usually in the very near future, next week, or next month, during Lent— even as the underlying impulse was legitimate. Something approached. The error was in premature expectation and the error was also in specificity: it was enthralling when a "prophet" spelled out all that would happen in terrific detail, a temptation to which many succumbed as such specificity was often of the devil. The devil was in the details! In other cases—when it came to expectations—we were simply forming our own interpretations and drawing our own conclusions with our own timetables—premature because we desired long-prophesied events (at least, long for us) to "finally" come.

We wanted things to be done and over with. We didn't want the evil to drag on. We were *excited* to have the curtain lift—to finally see how the drama was fashioned. What would the stage look like? Would it be a scene out in nature or inside a government office or on a battlefield? How many parts were in this drama? Who would be the star? Was the high point indeed Christ in a towering manifestation? How would special effects manage *that*? What would occur just before? And just after?

We knew one thing: the trials of our time (and disasters could be defined as trials) were "now" headed to a "crescendo." Was the crescendo the same as the "initial event," the surprising "event to come"? Were we talking synonyms here?

Another clue: the initial event, according to 2004, would in some way pertain to science. It would involve technology; at the least, it was something that involved scientists. If it was to be a sign indicating what the prophecy had called *"alarm"* at science's *"wayward,"* arrogant course, one could deduce that the events would include something that aimed at scientific creations. *"There is going to be a major disruption in a region of the world that will affect everyone,"* said the prophecy—again using the singular.

An event. A region. It would not affect just scientists; it was for everyone. There would be a precise circumstance—a punctuation. This caused me to think back to the reputed apparitions in Bosnia-Hercegovina, where a seer claimed her first secret pertained to a particular part of the world—something that would be confined but heard all over. The punctuation would be in the form of a "disruption." A disruption meant that what we have in place—perhaps what *scientists* had set into place—would be dismantled or halted, at least for a time. The original prophecy said that it was the end of the technological era. Many inventions would be broken down. Some aspect of our society if not the society as a whole would be thrown into a different state. Arguably, it did not have to be something that aimed directly at science. It brought to mind part of a vision from Saint John Bosco in which he saw that "the population had declined greatly in the cities and in the countryside; the land was mangled as if by a hurricane and hailstorm." It could be a social, economic, or military event. It would be a disruption that would get the attention of everyone. But if it was aimed in a special way at our technological "achievements"—as so clearly implied, when it said the event would *"show even recalcitrant scientists"* that there was *"a fundamental alarm in Heaven"*—this caused the mind to roam more toward events like a sun flare or electromagnetic pulse or other situations that took down the electronic grid. The original prophecy said, *"This will fall, and all of its creations with it"*—referring to *"the science which has denied God."* If not utter confusion, the event—in keeping to the definition of "disruption"—would interrupt or impede progress—break or burst, "rupture." And in fact the later definition seemed closest to both the 1990 and 2004 missives. A major event, aimed at science.

Or was it simply that such an enormous event would speak to scientists and everyone else (or almost everyone, "though not all") simply because it would be so *unexpected*—and perhaps inexplicable? In the annals of prophecy, in the apocrypha, perhaps in the mythology, was an Austrian monk named Johannes Friede who reportedly had lived between 1204 and 1257 and had said: "When the great time will come, in which mankind will face its last, hard trial, it will be foreshadowed by striking changes in nature. The alteration between cold and heat will become more intensive, storms will have more catastrophic effects, earthquakes will destroy great regions, and the seas will overflow many lowlands. Not all of it will be the result of natural causes, but mankind will penetrate into the bowels of the earth and will reach into the clouds, gambling with its own existence. Before the powers of destruction will succeed in their design, the universe will be thrown into disorder, and the age of iron will plunge into nothingness. When nights will be filled with more intensive cold and days with heat, a new life will begin in nature. The heat means radiation from the earth, the cold the waning light of the sun. Only a few years more and you will become aware that sunlight has grown perceptibly weaker. When even your artificial light will cease to give service, the great event in the heavens will be near."

One could guess it would be the great sign or miracle that would surprise scientists—"experts" (because they didn't believe in signs)—but there also was the phraseology in 2004 that said nothing artificial in a way that contravened the natural intention of the world and humanity would be allowed to stand, implying changes across the board. One could name a litany of creations that interfered with Creation. Cars. Roadways. Plastics. Thousands of chemicals. Contraception. Did this not interfere with creation? Oil. Nuclear reactors. We now had electricity everywhere (instead of the Holy Spirit).

But few creations were as stark and challenging to Heaven—to the Creator Himself—as what was transpiring in the world of genetics.

How we could sit around and watch what they were doing without jumping up in screaming protest was not answerable.

It was like we were being constrained. We were blinded. It was astounding. They were re-creating Creation. It was beyond Styrofoam. It was beyond DDT. Life was being synthesized. There were now spider genes in goats to create milk from which proteins for strong fibers could be extracted; cats and dogs that glowed under a black light (when their genetic material was changed with an enzyme known as *luciferase*); firefly genes in tobacco plants (to make plants visible at night); and all the genetic food. Peas. Potatoes. Canola. Corn had been engineered to create its own insecticide (170 million acres of this!), soy to resist herbicides, papaya to repel viruses, rice with genes that had been reconfigured to allow a high amount of vitamin A, tomatoes to have a longer shelf life, dairy products infused with genetically-modified growth hormones that had increased milk production in more than twenty-percent of the American herd but with unknown human consequences.

Note the common theme: beneficial effects. It was the word from the first sentence of the first paragraph of the first prophecy. Convenient. Beneficial. (*"In four years there will arise a new evil the likes of which mankind has never before encountered. It will arrive almost imperceptibly, with few people noticing the depth of its evil, for it will appear to have beneficial and convenient aspects."*)

If by their fruits we would know, then already we could deduce there was danger—reports of lab animals developing disease or giving birth to deformed young after being fed food that was changed from the way God made it. As if we knew more! When the prophecies referred to science as arrogant, it was an understatement. The lambs had been silenced—and altered. There was that cloned sheep, Dolly (which died ugly and young). There were frozen embryos— babies—millions of them. Those babies who were born, who got past contraception and abortion, were often laden with chemicals that had passed through mother's milk or umbilical cords, some of these deformed due to genetically-modified foods. Synthetics were everywhere and went to the tremendous statement in 2004 that referring to God had said, *"There are those who would reconfigure the very creatures He has formed, and who meddle with the texture of life.*

"For this reason, the Lord will allow a huge reorientation. If not for the action of Heaven, what God has created on earth will soon be damaged beyond recovery.

"A very dramatic effect already is in progress as regards the support structures of what man calls nature."

In Texas, a herd of cattle succumbed after feeding on biotech grass (unexpectedly, it emitted cyanide), and whether due to chemicals or electromagnetism or genetic meddling (if not regular parasites), many wondered about the collapse of bee colonies. They wondered if genetic corn had led to the disappearance of butterflies. It was like Satan was making his final stab. In 1991—just over a month after the original 1990 prophecy—a seer from Medjugorje had relayed a message from the Blessed Mother that said, *"Satan is strong and wishes not only to destroy human life but also nature and the planet on which you live."*

He had once attempted to ascend to the throne (cast down by Michael) but now before final defeat, the devil would try again. It was his version of Noah's Ark; there were cloned goats, carp, donkeys, dogs, ferrets, camels, fruit flies, frogs, horses, monkeys, buffalos, rabbits, rats, deer, cattle, and wolves. There were pigs with human blood and mice with human brain cells and a rabbit with human DNA. We could "harvest" spare parts. They hoped to grow human organs on pigs. Through a combination of altered genes, replacement organs, and computer parts, we could achieve immortality. "I and many scientists now believe that in around twenty years we will have the means to reprogram our bodies' stone-age software so we can halt, then reverse, aging," boasted a futurist named Ray Kurzweil. "Then nanotechnology will let us live forever. Ultimately, nanorobots will replace blood cells and do their work thousands of times more effectively."

Already, babies had been born with genetic material from three parents and thus already we had humans who were altered genetically.

Most outrageous were those who proposed combining the DNA of chimps and humans to create a "humanzee."

21

And, thus, things we created (without God) were going to fall.

Precipitously.

There would be a major event.

It would be followed by others.

Down the line, there would be at least a couple of massive ones.

Would they be related?

Would one disaster lead to another?

Might a quake—a quake of unprecedented size—cause a massive volcano?

Might flares from the sun disrupt our electrical grid and serve as a precursor for a new era in which the sun scorched us or changed its radiation in the opposite direction?

At Fatima, again, and at so many places, strange phenomena involved the sun.

I was sent a photograph of what one woman thought was a formation that looked like an angel with a flaming sword in the solar orb as it set over mountains; another sent me the photo of a cloud formation that looked (call it a "simulacrum") like a towering angel.

This was "pixelated" in a way that amplified the form (or perhaps meant it had been "photo-shopped" to start with; I believed it), but there were plenty of others convincing in their authenticity that indicated the enhanced presence of angels around us and huge in the sky or the aurora and threw the mind back to the lines of prophecy which said, *"The angels have their instruction from east to west, and now a timetable has been set in motion. When the huge light is seen, I will act in a way I have not acted before."*

The scenarios were endless. A super-volcano could spew ash shutting photosynthesis down for years or a flank of the Hawaiian island could tumble into the sea (causing a massive tidal wave) or the same could occur in the Canary Islands or an undersea quake could erupt near Vanuta or Spain or a hurricane could hit Miami or New York or a mega-quake could rip through California from north to south or along the Mississippi or an asteroid could hit the Atlantic or a comet could hit L.A. or a suitcase nuke could explode or the power grid could fail or a drought could end sources of food or a fantastic epidemic could break out or a nuclear plant could contaminate the Caribbean—or the Pacific, the North Atlantic—or an economic collapse could lead to uprisings or a war could erupt in the Middle East (this time with nuclear weapons) or India could fight Pakistan or the magnetic poles could move even more rapidly or the axis of the earth could flip or a force from space could knock us from orbit or the sun could scorch us or . . .

Scenario after scenario. Warnings? A dam could break, a tornado could destroy Dallas.

War. Always war. When one looked in the Bible, military action—invasions, prolonged conflicts, massacres—

were most often the chastisement. Almost always! Would it start with Israel or Russia or China or somewhere obscure?

Did it matter?

The important point: as the Blessed Mother once said, *"the West has made civilization progress, but without God, as if they were their own creators."*

That was in October of 1981.

"The first secret has to do with our church at Medjugorje," said seer Vicka Ivanković-Mijatovic, according to scholar Father René Laurentin. "It has to do with the sign, humanity in general, and each person. The secrets speak of the Church in general. Some concern us personally, others the Church and the world."

"Vicka, some of these messages at Medjugorje involve chastisements for the sins of the world, don't they?" asked a lawyer named Jan Connell of the seer in another interview.

"Yes. The Blessed Mother said there will be punishments for the sins of the world," replied Vicka, who by 2013 was forty-eight years old (an age we need to keep in mind).

"Do you know anything about the end times, the apocalypse?"

"No, nothing."

"Should people be afraid?"

"Not if they are prepared. If we are afraid of these kinds of things, we don't have confidence in God. Fear of this kind does not come from God. It can only come from Satan who wants to disturb us, so that we close ourselves to God and are not able to pray. With God, you can only have confidence and strength to go through any troubles."

"Will God's mercy stop at some point?"

"If we are open to the Lord's Mercy, it never stops. If you don't want God's Mercy, it stops for you."

"When the permanent sign comes in Medjugorje, will it be too late for many to convert?"

"Yes."

"Will the permanent sign happen in your lifetime?"

"Yes."

"What happens to those who don't really believe enough right now to convert and want to wait until the permanent sign comes?"

"For those people, it will be too late."

"How do we prepare?"

"The best preparation is to pray every day, go to Mass, and read the Bible. With prayer and penance the chastisements can be substantially lessened. I can only say: prepare. For all eternity, you will thank God if you do."

The Blessed Mother had also said, *"Monthly Confession will be a remedy for the Church in the West."*

What was the rate of Confession?

From what I could tell: three-quarters of Catholics never attended Confession or did so once or less a year.

"The Mass is the most important and the most holy moment in your lives," the dear mother had also intoned.

And so it was. Those who attended, who prayed, had little to fear. They would be warned. They would "feel" things. They would be led. They had repented. That was the key word: repent. They were in *union*.

Here we jumped right back to prophecy—the 2010 one: *"For these times, you have the Rosary, and even more so, the praise. In union with God comes all protection, as the dark spirits are now allowed to materialize in full due to the pretense and aspirations of man."*

"In union with God."

If you had that, it could only be the devil causing you fear. The Rosary was astonishingly potent. True safety came in fifteen decades a day.

A key word also, *the* key word: praise. There was something about praise and thanks that caused transcendence, that spurred great focus, that shook loose whole strongholds and principalities, that evoked an enormous spiritual shield. When faced with evil, praise worked wonders. *Praise God. Praise You, Jesus.* The devil was set back. This also happened with fasting; Satan hated it! Fasting is what had kept him at bay in the desert. It had kept him away from innumerable saints. It was a practice behind powerhouses like Saint Pio, Saint Francis. Did Catholics do enough? Did they pray with enough spontaneity? Praise was a sacrifice. It operated like fasting.

Fasting put the enemy—and untoward events—at a distance.

So did reading Scripture.

Yet, this had largely been lost, as had been the ancient practice—dating to the Pentecost—of speaking in tongues. The mantra was "Jesus."

Power here! Protection. We could form a "bubble." This was a real message. We could *disengage* disaster. It did not have to happen. We didn't have to have an outbreak of ebola. We didn't have to have a famine. We didn't have to wage war. We didn't have to incur epidemics. Few were those who knew how very many times the Blessed Mother had appeared throughout history at spots threatened or afflicted by plague—halting it (when her words were heeded, when there was repentance).

It was a big deal: calling people back to repentance. In 2012, the evangelist Billy Graham, had announced that despite his age, the circumstances were so desperate in America that he was setting upon a forty-day mission to call for n*ational repentance.*

He had been slowed by a hospitalization. Would others take up the cause? Our bishops had requested the same thing: an interior look, a self-illumination.

A purge.

But we would hear none of it. There was "pretense." A pretentious person was too blind to note interior darkness. At times, we were all guilty of this. The prophecy said that the blatant manifestations of evil were due to pretense and that made sense because pretense went to pride and pride was the power of the devil who was prince of pride and ruler of "this world" (*John* 12:31). Pretension came from worldliness and worldliness was the gleaming car, those large diamonds, an obsession with clothes, with stocks, with sports, with entertainment. Two streets said it all: Fifth Avenue and Bourbon Street. Or Manhattan, period. Or South Beach. Or Rodeo Drive. Or Anywhere, America. Satan flashed things at us because he was the shining darkness. When one wondered how a sinful person could seem so lucky, so "blessed" (with the material), one had to weigh the fact that Satan could and very frequently did bestow worldly comforts. God provided what we needed. The devil provided luxury. Extravagance. Excess. God was looking for simplicity. Wealth blocked that and worked against what was pure and here once more we saw the essence of fasting—deprivation, which was the opposite of gluttony. Ours was a society that gorged. Ours was a society that also *gouged*. One led to the other. "Good business" was now seeing how much you could squeeze out of a fellow human being, to cajole, to trick, to slick over, no matter what needs they had; it was good business. Just about impossible it was, in our time, to believe an advertisement. Everyone looked for an angle to do what served self when the call of Heaven was to serve others.

We were too pretentious for that. We needed the car, the house. We extolled—revered—those whose claim to fame was precisely their selfishness! When you went into a store, you weren't paying for what the raw material plus labor plus shipment cost (as Catholics taught); you were paying markups of a hundred or two hundred percent that was sent into the hands of too few for McMansions. The pretentious, the arrogant, were our role models while the humble were dismissed as losers. This went against what Jesus and every modern Pope, particularly John Paul II, so strongly admonished against.

The material had obscured the spiritual. That wasn't capitalism. That was greed. Capitalism held that you charged what it cost, plus labor, not what the market could "bear." It was all a front and the first stage in possession, some said, was the "pretense"—a mask the evil spirit placed over the face of a victim or a person put over his or her own face through ego which speaking of epidemics just simply *raged*. The power of pride brought evil to the fore and many gloried in it and now there was so much energy from that darkness that the devil—empowered, energized, emboldened,—wasn't even bothering to wear much of a mask. His visage popped out from everywhere. There were the glazed eyes of a shooter in Colorado and a massive summer ritual called the "burning man" out west (a Woodstock-like, occult event) and pagan revelry everywhere from the incredibly ribald Mardi Gras in Rio or New Orleans (where there was also the Southern Decadence Festival) to Olympic ceremonies where semi-nude dancers danced and nuns were props and musicians struck poses that were sexually charged and there was makeup to bring out the demonic and the closing song imagined one world and "no religion too" and like burning man or the "cremation of cares" at Bohemian Grove the sacred phoenix bird rose in great illuminative fireworks and a massive cauldron (yes, a cauldron) flamed. Many good people were being held under the deception and tyranny of a culture that promoted occultism in the guise of pageantry. I was constantly sent church bulletins in which parishes advertised questionable meditative practices as the occult had radically and almost pervasively infiltrated centers operated by nuns (at one annual Catholic conference, the main speaker was a New Ager; at another, a witch). The motif—the taint—was everywhere. Thank God, there was Heaven. Thank God, there were those who got a glimpse of it. Thank God for afterlife visions. The depictions of it could cause light to overcome the greatest dark. There were the living waters that were so consistently described by those who had near-death episodes and the incredible gigantic trees and flowers like but totally unlike anything on earth and the odor of sanctity and the luscious nature of fruit that was both real and ethereal and like everything in Heaven, too good and brilliant and magnificent (and different) for depiction. Only through praise and prayer and the Eucharist were we illuminated. With the Eucharist, we were elevated above worldliness; we could see behind the forest, the brush; we rose above the terrain. Things just beyond and often way beyond were now visible—while the worldly had a view that was like someone driving on a highway and seeing only the most proximate trees and asphalt lanes. With prayer and love (the single most important standard of judgment), we began not only to glimpse and feel and even taste Heaven, but to see life on earth with Heaven's perspective. In the context of eternity, earthly matters collapsed to the wayside; "big deals" were not big deals; they were naught but simple stuff; one day they would be eclipsed by glory. At Kibeho the seers said heaven was a place of ultimate bliss where colors were like music and music like colors, where you could breathe water and drink light, where everything was alive (with praise).

But there was also hell, and lust—along with greed, hate, and non-belief—bought a ticket there. Anger and lust empowered the devil. He fed off it. His demons fed off it. They had *precipitated*—as events also would soon precipitate. There was a riot of sex. You could turn nowhere without seeing something salacious. "If God doesn't punish America," Graham's wife told him, "he'll have to apologize for Sodom and Gomorrah."

And Babylon. And Nineveh.

We were blind. There was darkness—except for those who prayed. With the Rosary came enlightenment and with the Rosary came that buffer. For mysterious reasons, Christ had given His mother a special role—*the* role, next to His—in staving off evil. And how it flourished—spread! How evil spirits were showing themselves! The Virgin had called it the devil's "shameful face" and to perceive it one had only to buy a movie ticket and look at the face of the Joker in *Batman* or all the zombies, all the vampires. Where *wasn't* that shameful face these days?

Depictions of him were now vivid. There was no more hiding. The dark knight was rising. It was the Joker now. It had been Darth Vader. He was coming out. New Orleans? It had dodged a bullet. It wouldn't dodge them all. God was sending pre-chastisements. In *Numbers* (11:1) was shown how the Lord sent disaster nearby as warning—to the "outskirts of the camp" ("Now the people complained about their hardships in the hearing of the Lord, and when He heard them His anger aroused. Then fire from the Lord burned among them and consumed some of the outskirts of the camp")—as we now saw massive wildfires that approached cities like Colorado Springs or Denver or Malibu or San Diego or Los Alamos or San Francisco or right up to the suburbs of Sydney in Australia and the same with storms—disasters that could have—*should* have—been greater, even far greater, that came within a hairsbreadth, as with tornadoes in Oklahoma or near Dallas or on the East Coast or hurricanes like "Andrew" which in essence was a ten-mile-wide tornado that in a direct hit would have devastated Miami, as other storms even larger had also threatened so many densely populated places but veered at the last moment to the "outskirts."

Hurricane Fran. Hurricane Charley (once projected to hit Tampa, but ending up at Punta Gorda). Hurricane Hugo. Even "Sandy" did not directly target New York.

The list was a long one. In many cases, it was the ritzy side of town that came under most severe threat. Spectacular was how *few* were dying as yet in American disasters—too many, if it was a person in your family; too many, if even one—but greatly less than how many died in floods and monsoons and typhoons and quakes in India, Asian nations, and places like Haiti (where the voodoo had practically begged for it).

You knew God's mercy was still functioning in many parts of the world and that there was still time—waning, but time—before a great and sudden step-up in events by the limited damage. Had anyone envisioned what it would have been like had "Katrina" swept slightly west and filled downtown New Orleans with twenty feet of water or a storm like it smashed through downtown Houston or Tampa?

The storms, the fires, the terrorism were still glancing blows. In India, they were used to monsoons that displaced millions.

One day, they would not be so glancing.

One day, death tolls would come more in line with what occurred in Haiti or the Philippines or China. Did we really reckon just how *many* massive cities were along vulnerable coasts or the "Ring of Fire" (which was showing signs of coming to life)? What would happen if New York or Miami or Philadelphia or Washington, D.C. were covered with water, or all of the above, all at once?

About three billion people—nearly half of the world's population—lived within a hundred and twenty miles of an ocean.

By 2025, that figure was likely to double.

One day, some region in America or Europe would find itself under water as Manila did in 2012, when eighty percent of this massive city was inundated.

In the Philippines, that wasn't an apocalypse: it meant folks wading through water that was ankle-deep. Once more, God's mercy had shown itself. There were sixty-six dead. (The puzzle was why a country like the Philippines— one of the most actively Catholic nations on earth—was so continually pounded.)

The Spirit moved where the Spirit willed. We could never know God's calculus. Only He could calculate the secret thoughts and morality of every single person in an area. These matters were too great for us. Only on the other side would we know for sure. In Denver, lightning hit a shrine dedicated to Mother Cabrini. (God and the devil threw thunderbolts.) We were tested—witness a cathedral in Christchurch, New Zealand, ruined by a quake, or churches destroyed by tornadoes in the Midwest or a shrine in south- east Arizona—Our Lady of the Sierras—that was all but wiped from the map during raging wildfires.

In Jasper, Indiana, fire erupted at a Catholic nursing home named Providence Home Health Care Center and also burned a statue of Jesus, Whose right Hand—the hand of blessing—seemed like a ball of fire to onlookers who were in the Adoration chapel.

Ten days prior, the roof of the high school gym had collapsed due to heavy rain.

One had to remember: there were such things as curses. There was such a thing as spiritual warfare. More numerous were the cases, however, whereby sacred places miracu- lously escaped mayhem as we saw once more at that shrine dedicated to an apparition in Wisconsin and it was hard to count how many photographs were taken of statues from around North America that survived hurricanes, floods, and fires—that still stood in the midst of huge fallen branches. On the Niagara River, a little chapel dedicated to the Archangel Michael once survived a flow of ice that scoured everything else along the shore during an historically cold winter in which the river moved like a glacier—all but this chapel!

At times God chastised; at times He protected, miraculously; at times He did not. We were left to our devices. We neglected to see grinding, long-term chastisements. At times, things happened in His (seeming) absence. At other times, He struck fast and pointedly at immorality, causing a storm, for example, to shut down "decadence weekend" in the French Quarter or a rare tornado to rip a steeple off the flagship Lutheran cathedral in Minneapolis while national leaders of that congregation were there across the street at that very moment, preparing to vote on whether to have a more accepting policy toward homosexuality.

The tornado was just a hundred yards wide and moved over a distance of half a mile—just enough to knock off the steeple, disrupt the meeting, and also destroy the roof and windows of a famous local music store called the "Electric Fetus."

At the same time, tornado warnings swept through Toronto, Canada and a vicious storm felled a hundred trees in New York's Central Park.

Blessings and curses, curses and blessings.

The same week, too, lightning destroyed a Presbyterian church in DeBary, Florida (for no obvious reason).

Meanwhile, during Hurricane Charley, a Catholic church in Punta Gorda was completely ruined but for the tabernacle next to which a candle somehow some way still flickered.

"The church split apart and imploded," said the pastor. "Pews riveted into the ground were ripped and tossed around like twigs." (But not the light for the Blessed Sacrament.)

"I just wanted to comment about the catastrophic storm we experienced here in Southern Ontario on Thursday August 20, 2009," a woman named Corinne Aird of Hagersville, Ontario, wrote to me. "Environment Canada confirmed that seven tornadoes touched down in Durham, Vaughan, Collingwood, Milton, Newmarket, Markdale and Gravenhurst. In Vaughan alone, there were over six hundred homes damaged or destroyed. Last year I started praying daily for the Precious Blood of Our Lord's shoulder wound to protect our home and those of family and friends and our roads as we travel to and from our destinations. This is of particular concern to me, because I live in Hagersville and drive fifty-seven miles to my office in Mississauga. That Thursday I left Mississauga at 5:00 p.m. under a frightening black sky and prayed that I would get home safely an hour and a half later. I felt such calm in knowing that God would look after me and my son, who was driving home from Hamilton. Five minutes after I got in the door, the black sky that spread all across southern Ontario opened up, but we were spared from the high winds, lightning strikes, and tornadoes. The magnitude and severity of this storm left no doubt in my mind that this was a sign from God. The following morning as I passed by Hamilton airport on my way to work, I saw a gray sky with a black cloud in the shape of a dragon. It was shocking and reminded me of the Book of Revelation. Please remind people how important it is to pray for protection for their loved ones in these storms."

Said *Psalm* 91: "He that dwelleth in the secret place of the most High shall abide under the shadow of the Almighty. I will say of the Lord, He is my refuge and my fortress: my God; in Him will I trust. Surely He shall deliver thee from the snare of the fowler, and from the noisome pestilence. He shall cover thee with his feathers, and under His wings shalt thou trust: His truth shall be thy shield and buckler. Thou shalt not be afraid for the terror by night; nor for the arrow that flieth by day; nor for the pestilence that walketh in darkness; nor for the destruction that wasteth at noonday. A thousand shall fall at thy side, and ten thousand at thy right hand; but it shall not come nigh thee."

I remember an incredible photo taken of lightning striking the world's tallest statue of Jesus, "Christ the Redeemer," causing an eerie luminosity to surround the seven-hundred-ton monument in Brazil and turning it into towering light. Noted a newspaper: "According to reports, a strange aura appeared around the 130-foot figure's head and chest before disappearing in a flash. Shocked locals believe that Christ the Redeemer looked as if it had been illuminated by God's Hand. It has also been reported that the 130-foot figure, on the summit of Rio de Janeiro's Corcovado Mountain, was left unscathed even after the uncanny event."

22

The event in South America was interesting for reasons beyond its escape from damage.

In the original 1990 prophecy, towards the end, were the words, *"As for the antichrist, remember Europe, and especially Central Europe.*

"Yet know too that God's Hand will be evident in South America."

What did it mean by *"too"*?

What *was* it that might happen in *South America*?

Obviously, looming was some development or event. If it had to do with Jesus, it would come after chastisements . . . after the breakdown, if we accepted it . . . because that's when the earlier part of the prophecy said Christ would manifest *"in a series of supernatural events similar to the apparitions but much more powerful."* It also seemed to be in the period of an antichrist.

The exact scenario was impossible to figure. Nothing stood out as likely. But there were a number of matters to consider. One was that South America still maintained a massive Catholic population. There were one hundred and seventy-five million Christians in Brazil alone and a hundred and twenty million of them were Catholic (two and a half times the number in the U.S.). That made it the single largest population of Catholics anywhere.

In Argentina, the figure was thirty-three million . . . or nearly ninety percent of the population.

While Catholicism was diminishing as Pentecostals made inroads, along with secularism, the Church was similarly robust in other parts, notably countries such as Venezuela, which had boasted the great mystic, Maria Esperanza. I had been to an apparition site there and encountered the greatest sun miracle I had ever witnessed: Mary, in the pose of the Miraculous Medal, formed by rays of the sun.

I also had visited a reputed site of apparition in Ecuador where pilgrims had seen a giant silhouette of Mary in the sky over the highlands and thousands of flashes of light (like a laser show).

These were nations, along with ones like Colombia and Bolivia and Chile, that were ninety percent or more Catholic. Thus there was fertile soil. Was it poised for some sort of spectacular, unprecedented, future manifestation?

The continent had a long history of Marian apparitions. Many of them were unknown to the rest of the West. Much of it had begun in the sixteenth century. I spelled them out in a book called *The Last Secret*. On January 21, 1577, a group of Immaculate Conception nuns in Quito were gathered in the choir for vespers when extraordinary rays of light pierced the dark and shone on images that decorated the altar, particularly a statue of Mary holding Jesus and a scepter. There wasn't even a lamp for the tabernacle and yet the illumination had been so bright that passersby noticed it. The light focused on Mary and seemed to increase in brightness until the statue appeared to move and take on the appearance of a living person.

The figure of the Infant she had been holding in her left arm vanished and the statue transformed itself into a representation of the Immaculate Conception with numerous angels around her.

Villagers stopped in to see what was going on, knowing the chapel should have been dark, and they too witnessed the phenomena.

These events had been recorded by Church officials and so were others witnessed by crowds in Chile and Paraguay, signs in the sky or deliverance from plague, as in 1604, when an image of the Madonna was credited in Arequipa, Peru, with stopping an outbreak of the "black vomit."

Did these past apparitions hint at plagues in the future? Did they hint at further signs in the sky?

Might Christ tower as an apparition in South America as He towered for the time being in the way of the lightning-struck statue of Christ the Redeemer in Rio?

Meanwhile, in Central America, in Panama, the president had announced plans for a statue of the Blessed Mother . . . as "Santa Maria la Antigua" . . . that, standing taller than the Statue of Liberty (at more than three hundred feet, and taller than the current tallest one of Mary, in Bolivia, which was one hundred and fifty feet), would be the tallest statue of *any* kind in the world. Devotion such as that caused fertile soil.

Of course, Latin America was also the region of origin for the miraculous image of Guadalupe, arguably the most famous such image of Mary in history, at least in the Americas . . . and one that was constantly showing up in all those silhouettes and reflections and other reputedly miraculous manifestations across the continent.

Every time there was a claim that Mary had appeared on some object, or nearly each time, it seemed to be shaped like Guadalupe, whether on an overpass in Chicago or a garage in Texas or that glass building in Clearwater, Florida (where the massive silhouette of her, since smashed by a vandal, darkened on September 11, 2001).

Something was generating in Latin America, and while history could be tedious, not so in the case of the Blessed Mother, for there could be signs in those past events.

Other epidemics had been halted in Venezuela and there were instances of radiating images or more apparitions as in the Peruvian city of Orcotuna, where the seer, a humble Indian woman named Rosa Achicahuala, had testified that one night while mending by candlelight she'd heard a dog bark and peering outside saw a beautiful girl bathed in moonlight.

The girl's face was framed by golden hair and her dainty feet rested on a flat rock in the middle of a flowing stream.

She was washing a baby's tiny shirt and when she finished she squeezed the last of the water and shook the garment, then spread it over the twigs of a bush to dry.

Rosa had tried to approach but when she did the apparition disappeared. This happened night after night with the addition of angels and melodious singing.

Finally, one night, Rosa was able to draw near enough to ask, "Why do you wash at hours so late? What is your name? Who are you?"

Softly the lovely young woman had replied, *"Listen, Rosa. I have chosen you as my faithful servant. Do not be afraid. I am Queen of the Heavens. I will take care of your every need."*

Immediately Rosa had fallen to her knees and kissed the hem of the Lady's robe. "My little mother, what do you want me to do?"

"I wish only to entrust you with the building of a little chapel close by this spring where I will be venerated under the name of 'Virgen de Cocharcas,'" said Mary.

Why South America was chosen as such a center of activity remained a mystery but a center it was . . . with Saint Rose of Lima experiencing daily visions of Mary and missionaries encountering her in prayer or in dreams or through statue miracles. "Have confidence, my son, your fatigue will take the place of purgatory for you," she'd told a missionary named Father Michael De La Fontaine who was prostrate. "Bear your sufferings patiently and on leaving this life your soul will be received into the abode of the blessed." The spiritual war had been apparent on February 2, 1605, in the frontier region near Ëquira, Colombia when hermits and priests holding a festival in honor of the Most Holy Lady of Purification heard a frightful clap of thunder that resounded through the valley as Mass began. One author recounted that "the sky obscured by dark clouds (was) ripped repeatedly by lightning flashes. Then winds of hurricane force blew up, cataracts of water coursed down the hillsides, and soon the Gachaneca River overflowed with a roar like that of wild beasts.

"All this happened in a very few minutes and was accompanied by voices of the devil that threatened death to all. The crowd attending the Mass began to cry out in terror and many fled up into the hills. Those who remained quiet although not without fear were those within the chapel and they had faith in the power of the Virgin. The voices of the demons could more and more horribly be heard and at times the frame of the chapel creaked and shook on its foundations."

The Mass had proceeded and as a priest prayed for deliverance the rain suddenly stopped and a fire ignited by lightning was likewise extinguished.

That was the war (the war we now saw picking up such steam in modern times) and Mary was going right into the heart of the enemy.

She was converting Coromoto Indians in places like Guanare, Venezuela, where a chief was on his way to a place he was cultivating in the mountains sometime toward the end of 1651 when near a shallow ravine with a smooth-flowing stream he and his wife saw a beautiful woman gliding over the water. *This* time the mysterious female spoke to the chief in his own language and told him to go see the missionaries and have them pour water over his head so that he could go to Heaven.

Were these types of phenomena about to culminate in something far larger, far more extraordinary . . . somewhere in South America?

There was more in the past. There had been the appearance on February 2, 1634, of Mary in Quito to another Immaculate Conception nun named Marianna Torres of Jesus.

She had been praying before the Blessed Sacrament when the perpetual lamp suddenly went out. As in the previous event, the chapel was totally dark and like the earlier episode at the very same place there was a soft heavenly light.

This time Mary appeared in the light and allegedly spoke a long prophecy, one that if authentic was one of the most impressive in Church records.

"My heart-loved daughter, I am Maria del Buen Suceso, your mother and protector," Mary reportedly had said. *"The sanctuary lamp burning in front of the Prisoner of Love, which you saw go out, has many meanings. The first meaning is that at the end of the 19th century and for a large part of the twentieth century, various heresies will flourish on this earth, which will become a free republic. The precious light of the faith will go out in souls because of the almost total moral corruption. In those times there will be great physical and moral calamities, in private and in*

public. The small number of souls keeping the faith and practicing the virtues will undergo cruel and unspeakable suffering. The second meaning is that my communities will be abandoned. They will be swamped in a sea of bitterness, and will seem drowned in tribulations. How many true vocations will be lost for lack of skillful and prudent direction to form them! Each mistress of novices will need to be a soul of prayer, knowing how to discern spirits. The third meaning is that in those times the air will be filled with the spirit of impurity which like a deluge of filth will flood the streets, squares, and public places. The licentiousness will be such that there will be no more virgin souls in the world. The fourth meaning is that by gaining control of all the social classes, the sects will tend to penetrate with great skill into the hearts of families and destroy even the children. The devil will take glory in perfidiously feeding on the hearts of children. The innocence of childhood will almost disappear. Thus priestly vocations will be lost. It will be a real disaster; priests will abandon their sacred duties and will depart from the path marked for them by God. Then the Church will go through a dark night for lack of a prelate and father to watch over it with love, gentleness, strength, and prudence, and numbers of priests will lose the Spirit of God, thus placing their souls in great danger.

"Satan will take control of this earth through the fault of faithless men who, like a black cloud, will darken the clear sky of the republic consecrated to the Most Sacred Heart of my Divine Son. This republic, having allowed entry to all the vices, will have to undergo all sorts of chastisements: plagues, famine, war, apostasy, and the loss of souls without number. And to scatter these black clouds blocking the brilliant dawning of the Church, there will be a terrible war in which the blood of priests and of religious will flow.

"That night will be so horrible that wickedness will seem triumphant. Then will come my time: in astounding

fashion I shall destroy Satan's pride, casting him beneath my feet, chaining him up in the depth of hell, leaving Church and country freed at last from his cruel tyranny. The fifth meaning is that men possessing great wealth will look on with indifference while the Church is oppressed, virtue is persecuted, and evil triumphs. They will not use their wealth to fight evil and to reconstruct faith. The people will come to care nothing for the things of God, will absorb the spirit of evil, and will let themselves be swept away by all vices and passions."

It was difficult to discern the authenticity.

Had Mary really said these things so long ago, or had someone later put words in her mouth in recounting the apparition?

If someone had, it had been impressive. It was prescient. It bore similarities to what had been said at LaSalette . . . great similarities. (Too great?) At LaSalette, Melanie had quoted Mary as mentioning that a *"deluge of filth"* would flood *"the streets, squares, and public places,"* and LaSalette also had said men would *"become more and more perverted"* and *"evil books"* would be *"abundant"* and the *"spirits of darkness will spread everywhere a universal slackening in all that concerns the service of God."* Like LaSalette, it saw desecration. It saw an emptying of the convents. Like LaSalette: plague and a "dark night" and disasters of all sorts, particularly war, flowing with the blood of religious. There would be a persecution that included a period with no *"prelate."* There was the reference to "sects," which was interesting in light of Masonry, international corporations, and Bohemian Grove as well as the global network of bankers.

Whatever the case with that old Quito "prediction," there was electricity in South America and particularly Brazil where besides that lightning at Christ the Redeemer, you had a priest who was drawing tens of thousands . . . sometimes hundreds of thousands . . . for Mass and visions with prophecies pronounced in several places like Ecuador (in the Andes, where the antichrist was foreseen as already alive, if "very young," in 1991) as well as apparitions, starting in 1983, at San Nicolás de los Arroyos, Argentina, where the messages (if not the apparitions themselves) had earned the imprimatur of the local bishop, Mario Luis Bautista Maulion, who told me the words from San Nicolás were "very spiritual" and "approved" . . . messages that in several ways tied directly into the 1990 prophecies.

These were recorded by a devout middle-aged housewife named Gladys Quiroga de Motta who said she saw Mary on the twenty-fifth of each month during which throngs (including bishops) would gather. Her messages saw massive spiritual contamination over much of the world (she had a vision of a great battle between good and evil, two-thirds of men in darkness) and . . . like 1990, like LaSalette, and Quito . . . persecution of Catholicism: an oppression that Gladys said was already in progress.

This was important . . . for the 1990 prophecy had clearly stated that the manifestation of Jesus would follow persecution.

What was currently transpiring in the world, whether in sterile Europe, or the antagonistic humanistic corners of America, or countries where Muslims were murdering Christians, did not yet seem like The Persecution. But it was a forerunner. Like so many other events that were occurring, it was precursory.

The 1990 missive had said that the big persecution, the real trampling of the Church, would follow the *"breakdown of false society."* That had not yet transpired. At Medjugorje, one reputed seer, Ivan Dragičević, asked if when the Blessed Mother's secrets unfold there will be a great trial for the Church, said yes . . . "absolutely so." We already were encountering a foretaste, he said, in tests of faith.

But attack by the devil was in full swing in the invisible world and this too was persecution: assaults by demons, especially on families. Gladys had a vision of enormous monsters that came in her direction or of human beings with huge heads and ears, but a bright wall that suddenly fell between her and the assailants. *"The enemy is mercilessly challenging me; he is tempting my children openly,"* the Blessed Mother was quoted as telling Gladys. *"It is a struggle between the light and darkness, a constant persecution of my beloved Church. My daughter, there is darkness and loss everywhere! Evil continues to spread; it is the evil one in his apparent victory! [But] the work of God will finish with Him; God's Justice will save the just."*

Many were blind, said the messages, *"to the Lord's warning."*

Blessed, said Mary, were those who feared the Lord's judgment.

It was not mankind that was abandoned by God but God Who was abandoned by mankind.

As for the Blessed Mother, her great enemies were materialism and pride. Pride was what we all had to work at ridding. It was crucial to do this. Pride was a *"very serious sin,"* said Mary. We all needed to purge any vestiges of it!

Did we pray to do so? Did we realize how cleverly pride could hide?

She spoke, did the Virgin, about the atheism and *"total indifference of God"* in the large cities of the world.

She said the state of the world was why she appeared so frequently. Not everything in the world was corrupt, said the Blessed Mother, but a great part was . . . the taint was touching everywhere . . . and the corrupt parts, the really corrupt parts, had to be *"completely renewed"* because there were so many who were enemies of the Lord . . . those who despised Him.

"I again visit here on earth," said Mary, explaining that her visits to Argentina, to South America, were *"more frequent and more lengthy, since humanity is living very dramatic moments."*

Souls, she said, were *"drowning in vanities."* They were *"succumbing in the most complete materialism."*

"You must be warned, children, because the plague is big," she said. Humanity was "hanging by a thread." The devil wanted *"full domination."* He wanted to destroy.

"All humanity is contaminated," said Mary, *"it does not know what it wants, and it is the evil one's chance, but he will not be the winner. Christ Jesus will win the great battle, my daughter. You must not let yourselves be surprised; you must be alert."*

Many times we would be threatened, the Blessed Mother was saying, but if evil was rejected, it would self-implode; it would be destroyed; it would evaporate. She described this evil as consuming the world like a *"fire."* Here we had this theme again of sulfur, of brimstone. Because his end was approaching, the devil was pouring out everything he had . . . *"astute and calculating,"* wanting to destroy but in the end the one who would self-destruct. She had already begun a key fight with him. She would win with the help of *"humble sons."* Believers were to have peace. The devil was taking his *"last chance by availing himself of human weakness . . . pride."* However dark it seemed, *"a new time has begun"* . . . this also is similar to what the 1990 prophecies said. In a way that seemed directly tied with the original 1990 prediction of the Second Coming, Mary was quoted by Gladys as saying not only that God would quash the devil *"with Him"* (which obviously implied His Son) but that *"the very intense light of Christ is going to be reborn, for just as on Calvary, after Crucifixion and death, the Resurrection took place, the Church too will be born again through the strength of love."* As we have seen, the locution of 1990 had described Christ as manifesting after the chastisements and new world order and persecution *"in towering light."*

The messages were weaving in and out of each other.

At San Nicolás, the Blessed Mother allegedly said too that *"the coming of the Lord is imminent."* and that *"Christians should be prepared."*

These were messages that bore an imprimatur!

Were there issues in translation?

One wondered. The Blessed Mother at first had been quoted as saying that most but not all the world was corrupt, then also as warning that *"all"* humanity was contaminated.

Was there a misunderstanding there, or was it a matter of different expressions to convey the same idea: that the world was operating in a terrific shadow (with evil certainly touching everyone, in some fashion)? In South America, in 2013, a horrible fire would kill . . . at a nightclub in Santa Maria, Brazil . . . at the same time as was surfacing information on another Church-approved apparition on the continent, this time at the edge of the Amazon in a river city called Itapiranga, in the territory of jaguars and monkeys, of anaconda, where a young man named Edson Glauber and his mother Maria do Carmo had been reporting supernatural visitation from the Blessed Mother since 1994. Noted the local bishop, Carillo Gritti, who issued a *nihil obstat* and *quominus imprimatur*, "The signs of our times are dramatic. It is my sincere belief that devotion to Our Lady of the Holy Rosary, and Queen of Peace, can help us, in the drama of our time, to find the right path, the path towards a new and unique coming of the Holy Spirit, He Who alone can heal the great plagues of our time." The first apparition had been on May 2, 1994, when Mary came as a girl of about seventeen, subsequently appearing with both Saint Joseph and the Christ Child. The apparitions were most prevalent on Saturdays and during one, the Blessed Mother had foreseen the great Asian tsunami that would occur years later. The visits were said to be in preparation of some kind and to help men avoid "great evils that were coming to the world." That was language that arced straight back to the 1990 prediction and its warning that a "new and great evil" would arrive in "four years."

Noted a website dedicated to the alleged apparitions (which were formally approved only through the first four years):

"On December 26, 2004, occurred the great earthquake and tsunami in Asia that killed more than 200,000 people: the fact is that it was prophesied many years before and revealed to Edson in Itapiranga in 1996 and then on February 11, 1997, in Arari, when he met with his family at the site of some friends. At that time, before people present, the Virgin showed Edson various scenes and asked him to draw what he was shown. One of these visions was the earthquake and tsunami that would kill thousands of people in Asia. This drawing the Virgin asked Edson to put on the wall of his home in Itapiranga so people could see it, meditate, and pray that it not happen in the world, but many did not take seriously this request for intercessory prayer for the conversion of world and saw these drawings and prophecies as nonsense and lies. Many over time came to say: time has passed and nothing has happened. But people do not know God's timing. The Madonna began to reappear for longer times in 2004 to Edson again wanting to gather children in prayer, calling them to intercede for the world, but unfortunately once again this was not heard and catastrophe arrived, killing many. In 2005 the Virgin often prayed with Edson for the carrying out of [heavenly] plans and asked him to sacrifice more for this work. On another occasion, in an appearance, Jesus asked him if he wanted to help save more souls to Heaven (July 29, 2007). Edson accepted and Jesus placed the crown of thorns on the head of Edson and told him: *'Learn to offer your sacrifices and penances united with the merits of My Passion, so they become very precious in the sight of my Eternal Father.'* Soon after this appearance Edson offered this sacrifice to the Eternal Father together with merits of the Passion of Christ for the salvation of all souls and then Bishop Carillo Gritti came to Itapiranga (May 8, 2005) to publicly celebrate Holy Mass for the first time for the pilgrims."

Said the seer himself: "The Virgin is sealing us for God with her motherly blessing, preparing the small remnant of the Lord. This is achieved through the action of the Holy Spirit, when we lead with their blessing and their thanks at the table of the Eucharist, to receive the body and Precious Blood of His Son Jesus, for it is through Him that we are sealed, as Scripture says (*Ephesians* 1.13): 'In whom ye also trusted, after that ye heard the word of truth, the gospel of your salvation, and having believed, ye were sealed with that Holy Spirit of promise.'"

"Peace my dear children!" she allegedly said. *"I come from Heaven with my Son Jesus and St. Joseph to bless the families. My children, today, on this special night, where you celebrate the birth of my Son Jesus, I tell them that it is peace in their lives that is the light that illuminates your path in this world. Be of Jesus now, delivering all your hearts, and my Divine Son will relieve them and comfort them when they feel slaughtered and without faith. Pray, pray with love, pray to always feel the Presence of my Divine Son so that it will be present in a special way. I love them and tell them that if they want to have the peace and love of*

my Son in their families they should open their hearts to Him, give Him everything with faith and trust and never doubt. Thank you for your presence here tonight. Take the blessing of my Divine Son to their families. Take our love: the love of our most holy hearts to their brothers. Do not worry and do not despair. God is on your side dropping all barriers and opening the way before you, so that your work will spread and shine strongly, destroying the darkness of Satan. Satan will be destroyed by the obedience and humility of those who wish to live my appeals to the heart and love. I bless you all: in the Name of the Father, the Son and the Holy Spirit. Amen!"

In another message on Christmas Day in 2012, the Blessed Mother was quoted as saying, *"My children, this is the hour of his return to God. After this probation major changes occur in the world. Do not let the grace of God be wasted in vain. Welcome to my messages in their lives and they perform great miracles of conversion, peace and love. I bless you all: in the name of the Father, the Son and the Holy Spirit. Amen!"*

There was the idea of a manifestation, a "second coming," or something of that nature . . . certainly events that would be "major." In Venezuela, Maria Esperanza had spoken of Christ coming in such a way as to knock on everyone's door and it seemed as if she had been depicting a time when His Presence would manifest in various ways. His Spirit would become increasingly intense. If nothing else, it was a "coming" spiritually. But that could presage a physical one . . . or at least one that might be seen with the physical eyes. The mind roamed to conceptions of how it might be . . . perhaps reports and testimonies of Him in a place where His mother had been appearing or in a *number* of places where she had appeared. Can we imagine seers at apparition sites suddenly reporting the Lord Himself in a corporeal apparition like Lourdes, like Fatima . . . but of course (as 1990 intoned) *"more powerful"*?

"My second coming will be different than My first, and like My first, it will be spectacular to many but also unknown initially to many, or disbelieved. Yet truly I tell you, the arrogance of the world will have been broken, and so many more than normal will believe."

The word "spectacular" stood out. So did the concept that this coming would be much different than Bethlehem.

It would not be as subtle; it would not be in a manger. It reminded one more of what was said in *Matthew* 24. He would come on a cloud . . . as Mary now came on a cloud. He would not be seen by everyone. Or at least it seemed not everyone would see the series of manifestations because many . . . it said . . . would still disbelieve.

What would they disbelieve? Reports from afar? Reports from remote areas like 12,000 feet up the Andes, or even in Bosnia-Hercegovina or a place such as Kibeho?

In deep Africa, a statue of Mary recently bled in Ivory Coast (in August of 2012). Also, in India. In Indonesia. Stuff was crystallizing. There was a concatenation. A manifestation loomed after major events had broken down our infrastructure . . . the infrastructure that so violated nature and in its arrogance removed us from God; distanced Him.

This would be *"broken"* as the prophecy had said the pride in New York would be *"broken"* (eleven years before September 11 . . . as the pride indeed was broken, at least temporarily, before it was so arrogantly restored).

"I will come not as a man of flesh, but like My mother, who already nurses Me and holds Me in her arms, as a light and power."

"I will come in towering light."

Oh the times! Was the idea of Christ appearing in or with light related to that 2004 addition which had said,

"When the huge light is seen, I will act in a way I have not acted before"?

That seemed more like something such as the northern lights or a comet or some kind of astronomical marvel (or fright).

A *"huge light."* Again the mind soared. Might it be a sudden brilliance of the sun . . . something over the horizon? It seemed less related to the manifestation than to events that would precede that manifestation . . . to the breakdown, to the unprecedented chastisements. For it followed that sentence which said, *"The angels have their instruction from east to west, and now a timetable has been set in motion."*

Was it linked to something else as well?

While the prophecies thus far had come in three main parts . . . the first main one in 1990, then shorter additions in 2004 and 2010 . . . the receiver had reported a "word of knowledge" in between that had said (again esoterically):

"When you see the great smoke rise, Satan will have touched the earth. His manifestation will be near. He will seek to destroy what Christ has built, as Jesus came to destroy the work of the devil. In the end, the Cross will predominate, but not before the end of an era that has strayed."

23

If a light was coming, if there were going to be—and perhaps had been—great loud rumblings; if the pride in New York was going to be busted further; if there were going to be regional chastisements as forerunners—as there had been now so many—there was going to be smoke also and a manifestation of the devil.

Drama indeed.

Chilling.

Reminiscent of Pope VI who after Vatican Two had used the metaphor of precisely this, "smoke," to describe infiltration by evil.

Great smoke would rise from the bowels of the earth. Again, did that mean something volcanic? Or might there be a *"huge light"* as in "comet" that then would send up a *"great smoke"* as it hit land or vaporized in a gyre of ocean? Comets were winging around. The most visible in memory was expected in 2014. However that played out, others had been noted in 2013 and that year the dramatic, shocking retirement of Pope Benedict XVI—the first papal abdication in six centuries—had been followed not only by lightning that twice struck St. Peter's Basilica hours after the announcement but four days later by meteorites that caused such a sound—booms, rumbles—in Siberia where more than a thousand were injured by shattered glass. Fireballs also were reported over Florida, Cuba, and California, heightening trepidation. It was the greatest such strike in more than a hundred years and was not only the same week as the Pope's announcement but the same *day* as an asteroid made the closest pass to earth of any its size in recorded history (closer than some communications satellites). And soon after this, small quakes shook the Vatican and Castel Gandolfo, where Benedict, as Pope Emeritus, had just arrived for his retirement, while cardinals mulled his replacement. Comets. Plenty of comets. In 2036, there was going to be—was expected to be, anyway—another close pass, this time by a much larger asteroid called Apophis.

A smash? A flash? Smoke? The prophecy, like the other words, was chock-full of implications. There were fresh clues. It was also, of course, an additional mystery but one laid out for us if we accepted this mini-locution (from February of 2008) as to how the cosmic battle was viewed in the larger picture.

Jesus had come (as He Himself said, in *1 John* 3:8) to destroy the works of the devil.

Now Satan was going to answer in kind or attempt that.

He would destroy, try to annihilate, what Jesus had built.

As much as anything—as quickly as anything—that brought to mind the Church.

Might the "smoke" be the smoke announcing a new pontiff—but actually an antichrist?

That was a dangerous concept, perhaps an evil one; a good man, a holy man, could thusly be slandered. I trusted no prophecies claiming this.

It didn't seem like this would qualify as the *"great smoke"* (however important the announcement of a new papacy was) because the other addendum had spoken in very similar language of a *"great light"* with the initial sense of something to do with coming natural events or supernatural phenomena—the earth or sky.

Yet vigilance was not a bad thing.

Who knew?

A *"great smoke"* might also describe massive mushroom clouds from a nuclear exchange—which also, initially, would cause a *"huge light"* (known as the "event horizon").

Certainly, Satan wanted to see this, urgently. He would revel in war. He wanted to *damage*. He lived in smoke. He formed in vapor. During 9/11, incredible demonic images were formed in the smoke and dust and flames, pouring forth from the Trade Center. The prophecy implied that Satan would not just be influencing nor sending his minions but would manifest himself, somehow, somewhere, perhaps everywhere.

As a miracle-worker? As an antichrist? Did it confirm the time-honored conception about the dragon, the beast, 666, the Son of Perdition?

This could not be discerned but the small prophecy about smoke certainly confirmed the idea, first mentioned in 1990 (three times), that an era, a major period in human history, was drawing to a close.

"The change of era."

"Your era is ending."

"The end of your technological era."

And now: *"the end of an era that has strayed."*

An entire era!

Interestingly, there was the mention, however, of how the Cross would predominate which could be viewed either as a metaphor—a manner of speech—or related to the prophecy from Saint Faustina that one day there would be a great Cross of light in the sky announcing Jesus' return.

"Souls perish in spite of My bitter Passion," she said Jesus warned in the 1930s *"I am giving them the last hope of salvation; that is, the Feast of My Mercy . . . If they will not adore My mercy, they will perish for all eternity. Speak to the world about My mercy. After it will come the Day of Justice. You will prepare the world for My Final Coming. Tell souls about this great mercy, because the awful day, the day of My justice, is near . . . While there is still time, let them have recourse to the fountain of My mercy."*

The current period of mercy, Faustina said she was told, had been *"prolonged"* and as we have seen with all the storms, quakes, and fires that had greatly threatened (but so far consumed little, in the way of human life) what the Polish saint had been told, by Jesus, was a sign of the *"end times."*

It was remarkable how many mainstream Catholics followed Faustina and yet ignored her utterly apocalyptic pronouncements—even followers of this devotion!

"You will prepare the world for My final coming," she claimed Jesus said.

Woe to them who did not recognize this time, He had added—a reminder of San Nicolás, where Mary had called those who ignored the special nature of our era *"senseless."* At Medjugorje, she had told seer Mirjana Dragicević Soldo in March of 2013, *"I am calling you not to be hard of heart. Do not shut your eyes to the warnings which the Heavenly Father sends you out of love."* The Virgin had also said to Faustina: *"You have to speak to the world about His great mercy and prepare the world for the Second Coming of Him Who will come, not as a merciful Savior, but as a just Judge. Oh how terrible is that day! Determined is the day of justice, the day of Divine wrath. The angels tremble before it. Speak to souls about this great mercy while it is still the time for granting mercy."*

How—one might wonder—could a canonized saint revered by none other than John Paul II (who initiated the Divine Mercy feast day and died during its vigil) be ignored *(tanquam is absentis)* by so many in the pulpit?

"Speak to the world about My mercy . . . It is a sign for the end times. After it will come the Day of Justice" (Faustina Diary, 848).

It was something that was virtually never mentioned in homilies due to skepticism over private revelations (which was the priest's right) or for fear of offending secular types (not just in the media and pews but in Catholic bureaucracies).

The "justice" referred to in certain of Faustina's revelations may have pertained to World War Two—which was just around the corner in the mid-1930s, when Faustina, a resident of Poland, was receiving her messages—but the references to Christ's return seemed to spell a larger and longer scenario that was in keeping with the 1990 prophecies.

Like 1990, Faustina saw a sign coming.

Her prediction: "before the day of justice arrives, there will be given to people a sign in the heavens of this sort: All light in the heavens will be extinguished, and there will be great darkness over the whole earth. Then the sign of the cross will be seen in the sky, and from the openings where the hands and the feet of the Savior were nailed will come forth great lights which will light the earth for a period of time."

Was this the *"huge light"*?

Back in the days of Constantine the Great was the account of a cross-like symbol in the sky. Before a great battle, he and his soldiers had witnessed it above the setting sun.

That same century a doctor of the Church, Saint Cyril of Jerusalem, had encountered something similar in the Holy

Land. Perhaps this we most directly relate to Lent. Wrote St. Cyril: "On the nones of May, about the third hour, a great luminous Cross appeared in the heavens, just over Golgotha, reaching as far as the holy mount of Olivet, seen, not by one or two persons, but clearly and evidently by the whole city. This was not, as might be thought, a fancy-bred and transient appearance: but it continued several hours together, visible to our eyes and brighter than the sun. The whole city, penetrated alike with awe and with joy at this portent, ran immediately to the church, all with one voice giving praise to our Lord Jesus Christ, the only Son of God." In the famed *Imitation of Christ*, Thomas á Kempis, an ascetic who lived in the fifteenth century (and also claimed to converse with Jesus), wrote that "the sign of the Cross shall appear in Heaven when Our Lord shall come to judge the world."

There was going to be a Cross—of some sort. 1990 didn't say this. But neither did it rule such out. What the 1990 prophecies indicated was the Lord coming in some kind of glory, and I note that the word glory in the Old Testament was used to describe the luminous cloud around God and also that the dictionary defined it as something of resplendent beauty.

Its synonyms were words like "brilliance" and "effulgence."

Towering light.

Was the luminosity itself—of Jesus, in manifestation— what was foreseen as the huge light? *"When the huge light is seen, I will act in a way I have not acted before."*

That didn't preclude the towering light of the manifestation, but it seemed to indicate something else, something before the largest events, and thus before His appearance— if appearance there was to be. In 2004 it had been preceded by the sentence, *"The angels have their instruction from east to west, and now a timetable has been set in motion."* That too was resonant with Saint Faustina—who had seen an angel as "executor of Divine wrath" in a way that strikingly reminded one of the image of the angel in the third secret of Fatima, *"clothed in a dazzling robe, his face gloriously bright, a cloud beneath his feet,"* as we now saw in 2004 that the angels were at the ready at all corners and were granted insight into the very workings of Heaven.

"From the cloud, bolts of thunder and flashes of lightning were springing forth, and only then were they striking the earth," said Faustina of a chastisement that would have occurred (but for her prayers) in the 1930s (in a major Polish city). "When I saw this sign of Divine Wrath which was about to strike the earth, and in particular a certain place, which for good reasons I cannot name, I began to implore the angel to hold off for a few moments, and the world would do penance."

Note the remarkable similarity to the *"penance, penance, penance"* that ended up being part of the Fatima secret (which at the time was still secret and had been granted to Sister Lucia two decades before). Note also the similarities when it came to luminosity. In the third secret, the flaming sword in the left hand of the angel was described as "flashing" and giving out "flames that looked as though they would set the world on fire." *Fear of fire.* *"And we saw in an immense light that is God,"* said Sister Lucia. *Huge light.*

Both the third secret of Fatima and the 2004 missive used the expression of a large, extraordinary luminosity, in just slightly different ways: Sister Lucia as part of a vision and the 2004 prophecy as part of what seemed like a more physical event.

Precursors? There were those who saw strange squiggly lights, formations in clouds, and even the letters "CHRIST" in a photograph of the sky above Medjugorje—a sky that, in the photograph, was suddenly and inexplicably dark, as in Faustina's vision (despite the fact that it had been, at Medjugorje, midday). Others photographed a "cross" above Ground Zero. Or reflecting in water. Or on fences. Some of the "crosses" were remarkable. I received hundreds of accounts. I received photographs. Something was coming. But what? We had to be cautious not to jump the gun, nor to be deceived. Yet, it was certainly a constant in the world of prophecy—not just a manifestation, but a "coming."

1990 itself had used that term (albeit in *lower case*).

Angels?

A man from Iowa who had "died" and was unconscious for eight hours after a brutal car accident in 1974 and afterward was known for alleged healings said he was shown the world of angels, "what I call the Armies of God.

"I was taken to a very large area. I don't know where it was and I don't know what part of Heaven it was in, but I was taken there in an instant. I was in the air and looked down on possibly thousands of angels lined up in ranks and units. They looked just like soldiers getting ready to go on parade. I knew—I understood—that they were standing where they were standing when God created them for the purpose He created them. They were God's warring angels and they would come down and fight battles for us. Some of them had swords that were fifteen-feet long and on fire.

"They had supernatural weapons that I do not know how to explain.

"I knew that some of them could speak words and cause whole nations to just crumble and fall into the sea. They were armed, some with words, some with swords, some with spears that had special purposes, and all with the power of God. Some of them were clothed with the power to move the earth. Others were clothed with the power to bring judgment, but they all had the power to defend and to keep God's children. Oh, the power of God that is there and available to us. There are literally legions of angels that are at the disposal of the Holy Spirit on our behalf. I saw angels that were in charge of the weather and I saw angels that were in charge of protection."

It seemed, didn't it, that something was disturbing the earth's crust. When I was in Louisiana, they spoke to me about a sinkhole that was eight acres across, probably caused by the brine industry. There was the poor man in Florida who disappeared into another sinkhole that swallowed his bedroom, with no warning (this too in 2013). Elsewhere were road collapses and landslips. In California, a strange pervasive odor of what was attributed to methane escaping from crevices on the floor of the Pacific Ocean, perhaps due to a profound shift of tectonic plates. There were scientists who believed South America was slowly being yanked away from Central America and that the Andes would one day fall upon what was called the Nazca Plate. Nearly two thousand miles below the Pacific were what geologists believed to be continent-size pools of molten material called thermo-chemical blobs that might be aiming to converge (one day, at any rate), causing a great unleashing of fire or molten material on the surface. They figured that was a hundred million years away. Yet, our lack of knowledge—in every field—was unnerving. Right after the asteroid buzzed earth in February of 2013, another twice its size, also ready to buzz by (if twice as far out) was discovered.

Many anticipated the occurrence of that "something."

"In March this year, 2012, I attended a retreat day near to where I live in the UK and during praise and worship time I received the words repeatedly, *'I call the nations to peace,'*" said Rose, another viewer of our website. "Someone asked if anyone had received any 'words' from the Lord during prayer but I felt too shy to speak. That same night I had a dream where a lady came up to me and, in a serious yet loving tone, said: *'It is just beginning.'* At those words I was propelled backwards and started sliding down a tunnel of light at some speed. On either side of me were what looked like television screens. I was travelling horizontally and not going downhill so I didn't feel like I was falling. I could see each screen clearly as I passed. The screens were in color and I 'saw' many things I would rather not have seen. It was like watching the worst bits of a violent movie and yet I felt it was all real either happening or about to happen. There were people fighting, soldiers at war, civilians stabbing each other. There seemed to be every color and race in the world in the pictures I saw on the screens. There were Europeans, Asians, Americans, Africans, all fighting either against each other or with each other according to the screen. I thought to myself to call on the Lord's Name in case the dream was not from God and so I called out: 'In the Name of Jesus I command this to stop.' I called that out three times. I have never had a dream that didn't disappear after calling on Jesus' Name three times if it was from the devil. The power of Jesus' Name is tremendous against hell.

"But I still continued on down the tunnel and I tried to grab onto a screen to stop myself but couldn't and then suddenly I found myself awake on the bed with such a feeling that it was awful but with a strong surge in my heart to pray for peace in the world. Really, I had witnessed many horrible things; it was like watching news reports when Rwanda was undergoing the genocide a few years back."

In Kibeho, had not the Blessed Mother said that without change, what had occurred in that nation would occur worldwide?

Conflict. Weather. Judgment.

That angels had a role in judgment—purification, chastisement, denouement—was made clear in *Revelation* where angels were seen standing on the four corners of the earth and sounding out *fire* and *hail* and a mountain *ablaze* (thrown into the sea) and the water and blood, pouring out God's judgments: festering wounds, a dying river, the sun scorching with fire, a time of darkness—after spiritual warfare and the fall of Babylon.

Now, in the recent prophecies, we were being told something similar—strikingly. Again, the words rushed back: *"The angels have their instruction from east to west, and now a timetable has been set in motion."* The angels (plural) had their orders from east to west (implying their positions or stations). When Dr. Howard Storm had his near-death episode, it was angels who also indicated to him—*allegedly*—God's timetable. And it was intense. For according to Storm, Our Lord plans to completely transform the earth into a natural, far more mystical place, and to do this within two hundred years.

In the process, claimed Storm, the United States, if it did not radically stop its disengagement from God, would be reduced to a third-world nation, a simpler state, on the way to a transformed planet.

This was an experience that had occurred in 1985.

It took us back to Paul VI and his "smoke." For decades it had been said that when he made his famous statement (on June 29, 1972), that the "smoke of Satan" had entered through a crack in the Church, he was alluding to distortions of Vatican II, especially in the way of modernizing devotions and Mass, or perhaps the pervasiveness of liberalism. Some had even taken it to mean actual Satanists were operating at the Vatican. It may well be that a modernistic religious course after Vatican II was part of his comment on smoke, and perhaps he also had the whiff of coming scandal. But a detailed translation of what he'd said on that fateful day (the ninth anniversary of his coronation, during a Mass for the solemnity of Peter and Paul) provided the almost startling realization that Paul VI was speaking *in much broader terms* than simple concern over how Vatican II might be interpreted or how Mass would be celebrated and was instead *alluding to the infiltration of modern psychology, sociology, and scientism* into the ranks of his clergy and the hierarchy who served as shepherds. In short, it appeared, in the wake of a new summary devised by translator Father Stephanos Pedrano (and presented by *The American Catholic*), that the Pope, in June of 1972—thirteen years before Storm—and then at a follow-up at a general audience on November 15 of the same year, was warning of a scientific mindset pervading Catholicism and the world, especially the West: that the Church was succumbing to modern notions of "research" and "objectivity," which, instead of accenting the genius of God, sought to cast doubt at every turn and served to negate the very roots of Christian mysticism and supernaturality.

Indeed, the Pope, as it turned out, had both implied and directly stated that it was the adoption of modern psychological notions to replace spiritual theories that had bred a new attitude of skepticism toward miracles and had begun to count Satan (and the smoke) as naught but "superstition."

"There is doubt, incertitude, problematic disquiet, dissatisfaction, confrontation," said Paul VI—immediately after saying that "from some fissure the smoke has entered the Temple of God" in his famous homily, which was often excerpted out of context.

"There is no longer trust in the Church. They trust the first profane prophet who speaks in some journal or some social movement, and they run after him and ask him if he has a formula for true life.

"Doubt has entered our consciences, and it entered by a window that should have been open to light. Science exists to give us truths that do not separate us from God, but make us seek Him all the more and celebrate Him with greater intensity. Instead, science gives us criticism and doubt.

Scientists are those who more thoughtfully and painfully exert their minds. But they end up teaching us: 'I don't know; we don't know; we cannot know.' The school becomes the gymnasium of confusion and sometimes absurd contradictions."

This denial of the supernatural, this "state of uncertainty," was now holding sway in the Church. "There was the belief that after the Council there would be a day of sunshine for the history of the Church," he had intoned. "Instead, it is the arrival of a day of clouds, of tempest, of darkness, of research, of uncertainty."

Here we had a Pope in effect foretelling what would be said in the 1990 prophecy.

Instead of faith, there was now skepticism. Instead of exorcism, there was psychology. Instead of the miraculous there was technology. Nothing was accepted unless it could meet the narrow protocols of a laboratory.

When Vatican II opened the windows of the Church, it had been looking to the sunshine of deep past Christian faith—but instead science and its philosophy of doubt was allowed like dark smoke to waft in and contaminate.

"How has this come about?" asked the summary translation. "The Pope entrusts one of his thoughts to those who are present: that there has been an intervention of an adverse power. Its name is the devil, this mysterious being that the Letter of St. Paul refers to." Observed the Holy Father further: "We believe that something preternatural has come into the world precisely to disturb, to suffocate the fruits of the Ecumenical Council, and to impede the Church from breaking into the hymn of joy at having renewed in fullness its awareness of itself."

One might add that while in olden times bishops had led processions to sites of reputed miracles and had done so immediately, in our hyper-academic climate they ignored such reports altogether. The Pope mentioned the loss of the religious habit and exterior manifestations of the religious life. And this was important.

But it was the idea that Paul VI was referring, beyond simple liturgical matters, to a larger infiltration (one that eventually would empty the pews) that caused surprise.

And it took us to the words in the 1990 prophecy, which had said: *"My greatest nemesis is science, even more so than the media. The science that alters life, the science which creates a counterfeit heaven, the science that toils with the womb and genes, the science that has filled the air with the power of the enemy, the science which creates chemical witchcraft and fouls the earth, the science which seeks to create life but cannot in actuality even sustain it, the science which has denied God. This will fall, and all of its creations with it."*

24

When it did, claimed Storm, it would leave us with that more natural world, even a radically natural one—if "radical" was a word that should be used in simply turning the planet back to what God had created.

Were we really going to see the dismantling of inventions? Could so *much* of it be wrong?

One had to discern. One had to be skeptical. One also had to remain open. It took prayer: no one knew but through the Holy Spirit what would transpire; no one knew but through the Will of God. I didn't want to live without a car or air conditioning!

But this is what the prophecy had claimed: that we were unaware totally in our lust for convenience of how far we'd strayed from God's Plan. Not everyone was surprised by this radicalism. I remember receiving an e-mail from a Catholic woman in Colorado who felt she experienced visions and said, "Man was not made to fly around earth. The speed of cars is in total disharmony with the natural speed of the organic body. Zipping about? Where is there an example of that in the Holy Scripture? All the good these technologies have done? Instead of pleasant, peaceful, clean souls in clean bodies, we are like little flames roaring about. Walking is the proper harmony for a soul in a body. We now have massages, therapies, whirlpools, saunas, gymnasiums, and medications galore because our disharmonic body-soul union demands some harmony. True followers of Jesus should actually be praying for the dismantling of all our technologies because we live in an extremely unreal world and we could be spiritually enjoying the goods Heaven gives us daily. God has allowed all this evil to grow very rapidly without chastisements because at this point, all these things that come from the evil one must become full so that when God chastises, these same evils will be banished and never returned."

I also recalled an article about a group of Catholics on a 350-mile pilgrimage from Denver to Chimaýo, New Mexico. Said one, "Going by foot is so important because it is a natural pace. It was what we were built to do. When you walk, it is with all senses. When you are in a car, you turn off senses. There the sense of smell has no meaning. You hear music or conversation. When you walk alone in the wilderness, you smell the variations of the vegetation. You even taste the herbs as you crush them underfoot."

This, of course, was at odds with the modern way and it was incredible how we had been duped into believing that any convenience—because it was "convenient" or "progress"—was automatically good. Could anyone really believe we were meant to cause splendid creatures—birds, sea life, mammals—to go extinct? Did we realize that when America was first discovered birds were so numerous that they darkened the sky? How many knew that when settlers first arrived squirrels came right up to them, unafraid of humans? And how many noted the disappearance of butter-flies due to chemicals and electromagnetism as well as collisions with the grills and headlights of cars—gorgeous monarchs and other types that like so very, very many animals had been sculpted in a way that was exquisite beyond anything we could imitate, vastly more intricate than could be produced through the randomness proposed by evolutionists?

It was this Godlessness, and greed, that excused the ravaging of nature. During an annual slaughter of dolphins in Japan, seawater turned almost Biblical red. Sad it was: how those who had the sense to oppose abortion failed to support life in other forms (*"the smallest of what lives is precious in my sight"*)—and how, conversely, those who supported the environment often also supported abortion. We were in a time of confusion. We were in that period of *"disorientation."* It was irrational. We poisoned the water we drank! The Lord in *Genesis* had said to "subdue" the earth—not necessarily to reinvent it, to transform it, and certainly not to destroy it.

As a statement by the Franciscans, reflecting on its founder, said:

"The thirteenth-century society in which Francis lived was characterized by a nascent market economy. It was a time of obsessive pursuit of profit and privilege, and appropriation of land and power by the wealthy few at the exclusion of the destitute many, accompanied by pervasive violence. Unfettered greed, the loosening of the fraternal bonds of communion with society, and a sense of entitlement on the part of the wealthy few became a dominant path toward advancement, security, and freedom. Within this context, Francis and his followers set out to call individual people and their contemporary society to conversion. They did so by seeking security, freedom, and fulfillment in solidarity with the poor and marginalized, and in communion with God and God's Creation. Francis' insistence on strict poverty was not ascetical in a narrow sense, but expressive of a fundamental trust in the God of abundance and a manifestation of his radical commitment to live his life in gratitude and in solidarity with the marginalized, and in kinship with all God's creatures."

Added the statement (after pointing out that the oil industry deployed 2,870 lobbyists and had spent hundreds of millions fighting pollution regulations, something it could well afford (considering its $137 *billion* in 2011 profits), "As we reflect on the signs of the times, we may realize that the edifice of the dominant worldview is beginning to crumble. It is a worldview in which human beings have seen themselves as separated from the rest of God's Creation and free to pursue the dream of unlimited material growth and consumption. In its place, the edifice of a new, alternative vision is beginning to emerge."

"The very artifice of your societies is false and against the accordance of God's Will," said the 1990 prophecy. *"This artifice shall not last."*

As the *Catholic World Report*, in summarizing the Pope's views, noted (in 2012), "The created order is not an evil from which we flee—it is part of who we are. This implies that our planet is not a trough from which we gorge our appetites or a limitless dump into which we cast our refuse. Rather, from Genesis and throughout the Old and New Testaments, Creation is meant to be humanity's common home—the place in which the one, holy, Catholic, and apostolic Church must go and make disciples by preaching the Gospel of life."

The Holy Father had said too that those alarmed by what was being done to nature "had come to realize that something is wrong in our relationship with nature, that matter is not just raw material for us to shape at will, but that the earth has a dignity of its own and that we must follow its directive. The importance of ecology is no longer disputed. We must listen to the language of nature and we must answer accordingly."

The language of nature? How about dead fish! Tens of thousands on the coast of Peru, on the shores of Lake Erie, in Louisiana. Across southern California, a stench hovered from fish that had died in the shrinking Salton Sea, just like the Sea of Galilee and Dead Sea—Galilee!—had also dwindled in Israel.

At the River Jordan, I watched river rats as they navigated the waterway just upriver from where the garbage got really bad and downriver a ways from where the Lord had been baptized. In many cities, birds (three thousand in one Arkansas area) had fallen from the sky, *just fallen*. In many regions, honeybees were gone. Bats in the Northeast were dying.

Animal kills from Texas to Sweden.

Tons of sardines had washed up in Japan.

In the province of Assam, India, sparrows had all but disappeared.

That was not to impute every such death to contamination. There were fish kills and bat kills that occurred naturally. Life on earth was meant to be passing. But across the landscape, nearly *every* landscape, were ribbons of asphalt and electrical lines, like scars on the planet. We had cut ourselves off from Creation, and when we were cut off from Creation, we were cut off from the Creator Himself.

Did it strike anyone as interesting that the Blessed Mother had specifically mentioned "materialism" at three major apparition sites—San Nicolás, Kibeho, and Medjugorje—two of them approved by the Church?

There were two main definitions of materialism: first the philosophy that everything in the universe, including the mind, was due to physical agency and only the physical (the foundation of atheism) and second the preoccupation with material objects, which went to the age-old, biblical sin of idolatry. In fact, as one expert on demonism, Father Yozefu-B. Ssemakula, of Uganda, wrote, "It is because the sin of idolatry plays us so efficiently into Satan's plan of destroying us, and what belongs to us, that I believe the enemy tries to make it so available. He will consequently set all sorts of traps on our way to sweep us into it. And when he fails to get us into the crude superstitious worship of him through other creatures of God, he reverts to making us worship him through creatures of man (man-made objects), such as money and all its derivatives. He seems to get to the same result, only in the second case, instead of being clothed with Santeria, or messy African religious rituals, for example, it is clothed with sleek cars and luxury homes."

Yet, we were in such a confused time that our moral heroes were now materialists or political commentators who were courted by the oil industry.

One thing was for sure: Christ had been a *non*-materialist and so one had to at least consider visions of people like Dr. Storm, who during that near-death brush, upon rescue by Jesus, and then angels, was shown a future that involved "a beautiful natural wooded setting."

"There was no evidence of human intrusion or man-made devices," he wrote. "They told me this was the future and we were in a garden that people tended. People came by and talked with each other. I inquired about what they did. They raised children mostly. Everyone spent the majority of their time with the children teaching them about love and the wonders of the natural world. They all participated in child-rearing and teaching as the most important activity in their lives. They ate what they grew immediately without cooking. The clothing was all finely woven fibers. There was little metal except in ornaments. Everybody was a student of nature, which they knew intimately and with which they could communicate. People valued the life experience they had been given in this world because they knew it was a precious gift from God. I was amazed because I thought the future world would look like the science fiction I had been raised on," added the former atheistic college professor. "The future I was shown was completely different than what I expected. People lived in extreme simplicity and harmony. There was no want. Everyone was happy. There was no conflict. 'How will it happen?' I asked. They answered, 'God is changing the world now. God wants worldwide conversion. God is going to awaken every person to be the person he or she was created to be. Those who accept God's Will shall flourish and those who deny God's Love shall perish.' 'Will the United States,' I asked, 'be the leader of the world in this change?' [They answered:] 'The United States has been given the opportunity to be the teacher for the world, but much is expected of those to whom much has been given. The United States has been given more of everything than any country in the history of the world and it has failed to be generous with the gifts. If the United States continues to exploit the rest of the world by greedily consuming the world's resources, the United States will have God's blessing withdrawn. Your country will collapse economically which will result in civil chaos. Because of the greedy nature of people, you will have people killing people for a cup of gasoline. The world will watch in horror as your country is obliterated by strife. The rest of the world will not intervene because they have been victims of your exploitation. They will welcome the annihilation of such selfish people. The United States must change immediately and become teachers of goodness and generosity to the rest of the world. Today the United States is the primary merchant of war and the culture of violence that you export to the world. This will come to an end because you have the seeds of your own destruction within you. Either you will destroy yourselves or God will bring it to an end if there isn't a change. God sees the people of the United States becoming increasingly greedy, self-centered, and uncaring. There must be a turning to God or the reign of the United States will end.'"

It was tough talk. It hurt our patriotic pride. But had we already seen glimmerings?

There was the collapse of the World Trade Center, which had all but brought our system of transportation crashing down. There was "Katrina," after which mayhem broke out at gas stations (including fatal violence) as customers vied for dwindling supplies or tried to drive off without paying. This also occurred with other storms: looting or violence over a "cup" of gasoline. In New Orleans (where the annual Southern Decadence Weekend had been ruined by "Katrina" and where it was delayed again in 2012 due to Hurricane Isaac), police had to fire on those who sought to ransack evacuated stores. There was chaos at the Superdome. There was financial distress. The "seeds" of our own destruction were in fake mortgages, false profits, bloated financial paper, greedy bankers, hyped-up stocks, and lustful developers, all part of the 2008 denouement during which (but for artificial propping) Fannie Mae and Freddie Mac would have collapsed and Lehman Brothers did fall.

Others too should have fallen, most of Wall Street.

For now, we could still play a game of shells. We could still shuffle. We could still prop. But a crash seemed in the cards—a crash because our nation had become an economy without a product and was now being recognized as having lived a charade as had also Greece and Ireland and Spain and—in South America—Argentina and really the majority of nations that had modern "economies."

We were living beyond our means, on borrowed time. Everyone seemed to be on a bloated pension. But who would pay the pensions, as retirees began to outnumber wage earners? We were in an era of "flash mobs." This was a nation where ghetto kids had sneakers that cost up to $300 and where the greatest problem was not starvation but obesity and waste: we tossed away forty percent of our food, a plastic bottle after a couple of sips. Disarray. Flash riots. A breaking down. We were seeing the glimmering. There was a coming upheaval. That was the key word: upheaval.

It also came from blatant immorality, such as abortion.

There was not just abortion and late-term abortion but trafficking in fetal parts. In fact, some of the most popular vaccines for polio, hepatitis, measles, mumps, chicken pox, rabies, and other afflictions came from stem-cell lines that had been derived from abortions. Moreover, companies were using vaccine enhancers ("adjuvants") derived from products such as peanuts, pumping these concoctions into the bloodstreams of our young. *Was this why there were so many peanut allergies?* Some went so far as to claim that deadly vaccines harboring new viruses were released or one day would be released intentionally (either to boost vaccine sales by causing viral symptoms or to cull the population).

These were, as yet, "far-out" claims. There was no proof. There was no firm evidence. There were only suspicions—perhaps, paranoia.

But we knew one thing: there was that population philosophy espoused by the Georgia monuments, and materialism was out of control. Almost anything that benefitted big corporations, including pharmaceutical ones, was allowed. If one wanted to look for the formation of one-world structures, one was wise to start with international cartels. According to WHO there were cases where pharmaceutical companies had inserted *live* viruses in vaccines to facilitate approval of vaccinations for the viruses they released in clandestine fashion. This was discovered only when a researcher in Czechoslovakia decided to test the vaccine on ferrets and all the lab animals died.

It was a stretch to as yet call this a "plot." But were we meddling with nature! There were genetically-modified adjuvants, as there were now also genetically-modified corn, tomatoes, potatoes, cottonseed, canola, papaya, rice, peas, dairy products, and soy.

Was it a conspiracy or did it get back to simple greed?

Another factor was our simple reverence for science: the belief that anything "new" was "progress" and progress was always good; as we will see, that was a tragic assumption.

There were always benefits: cows engineered to produce more meat (with less fat) and plants to grow with less water and mosquitoes that passed a lethal gene to their offspring. That reduced the number of insects but raised the specter of transmitting a bio-engineered protein to humans (and other animals).

It was like DDT when it first came out and there had been ads with a happy housewife declaring with a big smile, alongside farm animals, "DDT is good for me!"

Soon, it was found that DDT was devastating the environment.

Now, it was genetically-modified plants. Downsides? When the French tried to modify the genes in trees, no wildlife (not even fungi and birds) would have anything to do with the small patch of forest (which by the by could send its pollen for a distance of up to four hundred miles).

We were dabbling with life at its most basic and infinitesimal level. With nano-engineering, we were going as small as science could see. Amazingly, in some cases they were not only altering and mixing plant genes, but mixing plant genes with those of animals. They were inserting human and animal genes, in some cases, into the DNA of crops. We were going to levels we didn't even know existed a few short decades before. It was in the years leading up to the 1990 locution that development of sophisticated DNA techniques allowing for the genetic transformation of plants and animals took place—along with U.S. government approval for use of genetically-altered growth hormones in dairy cows. Might we one day find ourselves with not a single authentic, unmodified stalk of corn? One academic paper, written by a noted biologist, cited this crucial period precisely as 1983 to 1989. "In the 1990s, Pfizer Corporation's genetically-engineered form of rennet used in making cheese was approved, but it received little attention," she said. "The American Medical Association and the National Institutes of Health independently concluded that meat and milk from cows treated with [the growth hormone] rBST were as safe as untreated ones. A year later, the American Pediatric Association approved rBST. In 1993, the FDA gave approval for rBST in dairy cows. Researchers at Cornell University have also produced rPST used in pigs to produce lean pork. In 1994, FDA finally gave approval for Calgene Corporation's Flavr Savr Tomato, the first genetically-engineered whole food approved for the market."

1994.

This occurred despite indications that modified food might be causing an outbreak of allergies as well as other forms of toxicity that could be carcinogenic. Foreign genes, it was noted, might also activate nearby genes not meant to be activated, or change and suppress others—causing unexpected mutations. "Plants engineered to contain virus particles as part of a strategy to enhance resistance could facilitate the creation of new viruses in the environment," warned the researcher. "Religious concerns are also voiced as some of the reasons for opposing genetic engineering of foods. For example, Jews and Muslims may be aversive to grains that contain pig genes and vegetarians may similarly object to vegetables and fruits that contain any animal genes."

Bio-engineered foods now comprised most of our soy and corn—the majority—as well as large percentages of the potatoes, tomatoes, canola, rice, peppers, papaya, and other products I mentioned. Incredibly, companies were not required to directly inform us of such modification on labels. In certain cases, human genes had been inserted into plant chromosomes to yield large experimental quantities of human serum and insulin. Goats had been engineered to produce human-like milk. Cassavas had been engineered to have a higher nutrient level. There was talk of fashioning bananas or potatoes to carry vaccines. What would happen, however, if it all fell into the wrong hands? Was there not a huge danger in that the gene-altered-seed-and-crop market was dominated by a handful of multi-national corporations, who now could have a stranglehold on the food industry— corporations that in some cases had decades-long relation- ships with global financiers. Astonishing it was that one of the greatest dangers known to mankind has been over- looked as the world debates issues that paled by compar- ison.

Not war, not health care, not the economy were anywhere nearly as acute a concern as the simple, startling fact that a handful of major global corporations had all but taken control of the world's food supply and were doing so not only through massive "factory farming" and an outra- geous overuse of chemicals but by genetically engineering seeds to produce altered crops with unknown health hazards.

This was a huge issue that could largely be tracked to quiet organizations such as the Rockefeller Foundation—

which has funded much of the research sparking global agricultural trends. Some saw it as a push for a single global superstructure. By 2002, Monsanto and Pioneer-HiBred of Dupont had controlled sixty percent of the U.S. corn and soybean seed markets—which consisted almost entirely of seeds that had been genetically modified, reported F. William Engdahl in *Seeds of Destruction*. The implications of new technologies allowed "three or four private multinational seed companies to dictate terms to world farmers for their seed," said the author—pointing out that gene-altered seeds were often fashioned so they produced plants that were sterile, forcing farmers to buy new seed every year. The plants were also engineered to withstand increased use of herbicides sold by the same companies.

Some geneticists were meddling with peas, tomatoes, peppers, wheat, rice, or corn to alter them such that "in one broad, brazen stroke of his hand, man will have irretrievably broken the plant-to-seed-to-plant-to-seed cycle, the cycle that supports most life on the planet," as one critic put it.

"Corn and soybeans constituted the most important animal feed in U.S. agricultural, which meant that nearly the entire meat production of the nation as well as its meat exports had been fed on genetically modified animal feed," Engdahl wrote (and this was all very germane to the prophecies). "Few Americans had a clue as to what they were eating. No one bothered to tell them, least of all the government agencies entrusted with a mandate to protect citizens' health and welfare."

Studies showing adverse effects had been quashed despite signs of trouble. Toxins used in 25 percent of modified crops were found to be harmful to mice, butterflies, beetles, weevils, and lacewings—perhaps too accounting for the disappearance of bees and other animals—while a study in Russia indicated that half the offspring of rats fed on genetically-modified soybean diets died in the first three weeks of their lives. Mutated ingredients were now in most processed and fast foods, along with everyday items such as milk and popcorn. The proliferation had continued under U.S. presidents from both major political parties and gained special momentum under President George H. W. Bush. Some traced the trend not only to genetic engineering pioneered by Rockefeller-funded laboratories, but also to a memorandum penned by Rockefeller-protégé and former Secretary of State Henry Kissinger, who in April of 1974 wrote that national security memorandum known as "NSSM 200," which had been kept secret for fifteen years.

"By the early years of the new century, it was clear that no more than four giant chemical multinational companies had emerged as global players in the game to control patents on the very basic food products that most people in the world depend for their daily nutrition—corn, soybeans, rice, wheat, even vegetables and fruits and cotton—as well as new strains of disease-resistant poultry genetically-modified to allegedly resist the deadly H5N1 bird flu virus, or even genetically altered pigs and cattle," wrote Engdahl. "Three of the four private companies had decades-long ties to Pentagon chemical warfare research."

One might point out that Monsanto also had produced saccharin, DDT, PCBs, and dioxin.

Certainly, no one accused any company or person of intentionally harming the public. The worry: that the race for profits had run roughshod over concerns for health and was set to destroy small farms (so important to American spirituality at its founding) while the incredible concentration of agribusiness in the hands of a dozen or fewer corporations might allow future takeover by a global entity bent on using crop production as a "weapon" or means of control. Engdahl argued that the policy of the Rockefeller elite consisted of adopting a "world population plan of action" for drastic global population reduction policies in order to preserve resources and maintain order.

Was the goal for those with great wealth to be genetically nurtured while poor less "desirable" elements were reduced in number, an idea known as "eugenics" (and popular in Nazi Germany)? In fact, the greatest force behind the memorandum, as well as many projects connected to its goals—the Rockefeller Foundation—also had funded notorious German eugenics programs until 1939, charged Engdahl.

"John D. Rockefeller III was appointed by President Nixon in July 1969 to head the Commission on Population Control," he wrote. "Among his recommendations were the establishment of sex education programs in all schools, population education so that the public appreciated the supposed crisis, and the repeal of all laws that hindered contraceptive means to minors and adults. It proposed making voluntary sterilization easier and liberalizing state laws against abortion. Abortion had been regarded as a major vehicle for fertility control by the Rockefeller circles for decades, hindered by strong opposition from church and other groups. A fierce resistance from the Catholic Church, from every Communist country except Romania, as well as from Latin American and Asian nations, convinced leading U.S. policy circles that covert means were needed to implement their project."

Why the scope and implications of this memo as well as Rockefeller involvement in eugenics had never created an international sensation was mysterious, for their studies and policies had a profound influence on every president since that time and in many ways could be interpreted as the fountainhead for catchphrases such as "freedom of choice," "sex education," and "sustainable development"—listing as it did the "right of the individual couple to determine freely and responsibly their number and spacing of children and to have information, education, and means to do so."

Meanwhile, the implementation of the memorandum was connected to organizations like the Council on Foreign Relations, the Trilateral Commission, and, yes, the Bilderberg Group—all linked to Kissinger and founded at least in part by the Rockefellers, whose interest in limiting world population reportedly dated back to its patriarchs in the late 1800s.

Or at least, these were the charges. "The secret Kissinger plan was implemented immediately," stated Engdahl in his book, which focused on the global purveyance of genetically-modified food. "The thirteen priority countries for population reduction were to undergo drastic changes in their affairs over the following thirty years. Most would not even be aware of what was happening. The Brazilian government [for example] was shocked to find that an estimated forty-four percent of all Brazilian women aged between fourteen and fifty-five had been permanently sterilized. Most of the older women had been sterilized when the program began in the mid-1970s." Those sterilizations—carried out by organizations such as the International Planned Parenthood Federation and Family Health International—were all under the direction of the U.S. Agency for International Development.

From their inception, argued some, elite foundations were intent on reducing "inferior" breeds and as far back as the 1920s funded the American Eugenics Society and Margaret Sanger's Planned Parenthood Federation of America, which had become the country's largest abortion-provider.

Could men have really plotted something so nefarious? One had to be very careful not to accuse "elitest" or corporations simply because they had a global reach. Would they actually seek to actively cause human deaths—or at least prevent births? And if so, was it farfetched to worry about something like a flu bug or bio-warfare agent being unleashed one day on the unknowing masses—fears stoked when the swine-flu was found to have strange DNA components?

Perhaps. Perhaps it was paranoid. Perhaps it went too far. For the main part, it was a matter of corporations seeking simply to corner a market. There were always flu bugs. Their DNA shifted naturally. And many argued convincingly that genetic food was good for humanity at large. It certainly increased production. And there was no doubt that the environment was overburdened and that sustainable development—as the Vatican even argued—was crucial. But the history of powerful men thinking along the lines of "culling the herd" and the Rockefellers' profound interest in genetic and viral research made one wonder if such past policies may be what was behind an undercurrent of subconscious fear that seemed to have intuitively spread among those who were afraid of everything from forced euthanasia in health-care policies to man-made viruses (or fear the vaccinations used to treat viruses) to HAARP to aerosols from planes ("chem-trails").

Fears were running rampant—perhaps, out of control. And a sin it was, to impute anyone as wanting to "cull" a population, including the Rockefellers. Gates had bought Monsanto stock, but to think he had done so for a nefarious reason seemed at best unfair; he was also seeking to improve sanitary conditions (by increasing third-world access to toilets). If he wanted people to die, why was he trying to save them? Why was he seeking to improve education? Whatever their birth-control policies, there was absolutely no reason to believe that any group had engineered swine flu as part of a memorandum or policy.

One had to be cautious not to fall into the "everything-is-a-conspiracy" mindset.

But the fear was more understandable in light of certain researchers (some with alleged links to the Rockefellers). "One of the more prominent members of the American Eugenics Society in the early 1920s was Dr. Paul Bowman Popenoe, a U.S. Army venereal disease specialist from World War One, who wrote a textbook entitled *Applied Eugenics,*" charged Engdahl. "In sum, Popenoe said, 'The first method which presents itself is execution . . . Its value in keeping up the standard of the race should not be underestimated.' He went on to eloquently advocate the 'destruction of the individual by some adverse feature of the environment, such as excessive cold, or by bacteria or by bodily deficiency.'"

These were the types of things of which we needed to be aware, without casting aspersions. For the most part, it was a matter of hyper-capitalism or philanthropy that had become pretentious. Did Bill Gates really know what the world needed and what it should be like because he had so successfully fashioned computer operating systems? Did oil and banking money give the Rockefellers or anyone else the cachet to design a new world order (without references to God)?

More than anything, it was an indictment of science.

This was permanent stuff. No one knew the risk of cancer and other disease. These genes could transfer through the soil. They could ride the wind. There was no telling what new viruses and bacteria could be generated. So worried were Mexicans that they had stockpiled seeds from ancestral corn—afraid it was doomed to genetic contamination. In India, they were trying to ban our products. The same was true in much of Europe—though the United States had sued the European Union in an effort to force them to open up for our genetic markets. If there was spiritual contamination, this also showed itself at the physical level. The war with the demonic was fought all over; there was a new arena every week. Remarkably, far under public radar, dabbling scientists had gone so far as to use *agrobacterium*—a soil bacterium that causes crown gall disease in plants (including tumors)—to transfer genes from one plant to another. What would happen if humans were exposed to too much of this bacteria, and altered ones? Might it be responsible for other medical effects—including bizarre ones? Across America were those claiming to be afflicted by Morgellons disease, whereby strange multicolored and thus far unidentified fibers were sprouting from their skin—causing a tormenting itch and emotional trauma. One team that scanned the fibers with an electron microscope confirmed that the Morgellons fibers were unlike any natural or synthetic threads. When they took skin biopsies, they found "all Morgellons patients screened to date" to have "tested positive for the presence of *agrobacterium*, whereas this micro-organism has not been detected in any samples derived from the control, healthy individuals." Their conclusion was that the bacterium may have been involved with these little threads that were erupting from people. Such playing with nature at such infinitesimal levels brought to mind that incredible line from the 2004 message: *"A very dramatic effect already is in progress as regards the support structures of what man calls nature."*

Didn't everyone see how many odd ailments had sprouted up—not just the deluge of cancers, not just AIDS, not just asthma, but the Lyme disease, the nervous disorders, the awkwardly huge size of many youngsters (growth hormones), the allergies, the symptoms in young or old of what may have been overexposure to electromagnetism as well as chemicals and genetically-modified substances in this brave new world where we were now all constantly barraged with radio waves, Wi-Fi, the magnetic fields around electrical wires, TV and computer radiation, cell phones, cordless phones, and many other emanations (from electric blankets to digital clocks) that we never really calculated?

God did not intend this.

And it wasn't a "culling" of the populace.

It was simple blindness—spiritual, as well as scientific.

No one was controlling this; the conspiracy was too vast for humans; it was a conspiracy at a supernatural level.

Strange stuff. Certainly, Satan had fallen as a bolt of electricity. Meanwhile, the 1990 prophecy had used the term *"chemical witchcraft"*—and in fact not only were the fruits of chemistry frequently awful, as they replaced natural means (and did this so expediently), but it also took one back to alchemy and before that *pharmakeia* and the dabbling of ancient wizards.

Might God have been behind many modern inventions? He might. Who could discern, from this earth? Who would like to live without modern surgery, without penicillin?

But—spurred by globalists—we had gone to an astonishing extreme; when someone contracted cancer, we tried to cure the person with even stronger toxic agents (chemotherapy). This was extremely profitable for international pharmaceutical conglomerates as well as doctors, who would have little to do with the natural (or the supernatural).

Yet more often than we realized, the supernatural intersected with the natural. Thomas Edison was so sure that inspiration came through the supernatural that he spent much of his time trying to invent a device to contact the spirit world. One of history's great chemists, Friedrich

August Kekulé, described in his *Textbook of Organic Chemistry* (1861) how he had a dream from which he developed his formula for multivalent atoms and discovered the famed chemical benzene (a widely used human carcinogen):

"I was returning [to my lodgings] by the last omnibus, 'outside' as usual, through the deserted streets of the metropolis, which are at other times so full of life. I fell into a reverie and lo! the atoms were gamboling before my eyes. Whenever, hitherto, these diminutive beings had appeared to me, they had always been in motion; but up to that time I had never been able to discern the nature of their motion. Now, however, I saw how, frequently, two smaller atoms united to form a pair; how a larger one embraced two smaller ones; how still larger ones kept hold of three or even four of the smaller; whilst the whole kept whirling a giddy dance. I saw how the larger ones formed a chain . . . I spent part of the night putting on paper at least sketches of these dream forms."

Kekulé also saw a snake in one of his visions.

What was good? What was of Satan? What about oil?

One could look back on the vaunted, revered formulations of mass production and the industrial revolution and particularly the invention of electricity and automobiles and wonder: how in the world could we think this was remotely in keeping with nature, yet how many of us would want to live without them? Was oil—from which so much of our electricity, asphalt, pharmaceuticals, and chemicals came—in God's designs? Were we tapping into a combustible residue from prehistoric vegetation, or was petroleum a misunderstood component of geological strata, a sort of lubricant between crustal layers, not meant for combustion in the atmosphere? Those kind of radical questions were arresting in light of the 1990 prophecy whereby Jesus had said we didn't realize *"the fundamental mistakes of mankind"* and another by Serbian mystic Mitar

Tarabich, who died in 1899 and as recorded by a priest had said, "People will drill wells deep in the ground and dig out gold, which will give them light, speed, and power, and the earth will shed tears of sorrow, because there will be much more gold and light on its surface than in its interior. The earth will suffer because of these open wounds. Instead of working in the fields, people will dig everywhere, in right and wrong places, but the real power will be all around them, not being able to tell them, 'Come on, take me, don't you see that I am here, all around you.' Only after many a summer, people will remember this real power, and then they will realize how unintelligent it was to dig all those holes. This power will also be present in people but it will take a long time before they discover it and use it. Thus man will live for a long, long time, not being able to know himself. There will be many learned men who will think through their books that they know and can do everything. They will be the great obstacle for this realization, but once men obtain this knowledge, they will see what kind of delusion it was when they listened to their learned men."

Lost in all the links between storms and warnings from Heaven was that besides voodoo and the ribaldry of the French Quarter, Louisiana was one of the nation's hotspots for drilling oil and manufacturing synthetics (*"chemical witchcraft"*).

There was that sinkhole near Bayou Corne. There were the cancer clusters elsewhere. In New Orleans, coeds at a college near some of the pollution had once reported that on bad days their nylons would begin to disintegrate. It was a "black" region on cancer mortality maps.

Lost too was the fact that when hurricanes "Rita" and "Katrina" swept through, they had destroyed more than a hundred platforms and drilling wells.

Esperanza had speculated that one day we'd come up with inventions that would take care of energy needs without violating nature, tapping into what she called the "stellar curvature." With the Holy Spirit, said Esperanza (whose own family was in the oil industry), humans could find the inspiration for vastly more natural means of working with nature. She prophesied such a change in course as following a "great struggle among nations that will take place, brother against brother." The new inventions, said the mystic (who had foreseen the internet), would be "more revolutionary than computers." She described such inventions as coming from "secret forces" hidden in rhythms of nature and what she called the "sacred canticles." She had synopsized an alleged message from the Lord on March 18, 1981, that speaking of leaps in technology had said (in her words): "This will come about with the sun and with the drive of magnetic forces of earthly energies: volcanic forces, wind, water, certain kinds of seaweed because phosphorus will be better assimilated. In short, no element will be wasted, everything will be used."

The point, as Dr. Storm and the 1990 prediction indicated, was that our artificiality would be dismantled. That theme ran through all three major "1990" messages: that our modern way of living was going to be brought down, and not just for blatant sins like abortion.

There was going to be a breakdown into more of a peasant way of life and then would come Jesus in a way different from His First Coming. He would not be in regular physical form. There would be no manger. Scripture too said this: He was coming in light, in supernatural light, in glory. *"Know this about the world,"* He had allegedly said in 1990, *"I would not appear on television, nor ride a car, nor travel in an airplane.*

"Would I come in such a manner?

"Would I live in such a world?

"You think of the changes in very simple ways, without realizing the fundamental mistakes of mankind.

"The very artifice of your societies is false and against the accordance of God's Will.

"This artifice shall not last.

"Your very conceptions of happiness and comforts are a great evil and falsity.

"They will not stand."

A breakdown would come.

Then would be some sort of a "coming."

None was directly quoted in a way that was definitive as foreseeing the same, but there were indications that the three Church-sanctioned visionaries at Kibeho saw such an arrival. According to Father Gabriel Maindron, a priest who had been close to Kibeho, the seer Alphonsine "tells us that Our Lady came to Kibeho in order to prepare us for the coming of her Son"—that it was "close at hand"—but those words had not been confirmed with the seer herself (now cloistered in Italy) as was also the case with Marie-Claire. The predictions of the approved seers, however, were serious nonetheless. She had been quoted as saying that "humans' time on earth is nearing the end." *"Repent, repent, repent,"* Marie-Claire said the Virgin had warned. *"When I tell you this, I am not addressing myself strictly to you, child, but I am making this appeal to all the world. Today, man empties all things of their true value. Those who are continually committing sins are doing so without any acceptance that what they are doing is wrong."*

"We will know (the secrets) when we are being instructed to reveal them," added a Medjugorje visionary.

It was claimed that a German monk named Ludwig Heinrich who lived in the seventeenth century had said, "In the last years of the twentieth century, one will see the disappearing of countless animal species, killed by man. But at the end, it will be mankind who will condemn man to death, because everything that grows on the earth will contain the essence of the death. The air will be the blow of the death, and as soon as the man breathes it, he will breathe the death."

25

There would be a breakdown and the question was whether this breakdown would be gradual or sudden—from a series of trends and events or a singular one.

It would be a combination. There would be many events and trends punctuated by ones that were massive.

Already, society was melting down and would continue to do so with indeterminate periods (and false recoveries) while events rapidly followed each other; an event one day, and then also the next, and not always related. A priest once saw it as like snow in the spring but one was also tempted to again look at 9/11: If there had been omens, if there were harbingers, in the way of a sycamore that had fallen, perhaps there were also hints in the very way the two towers collapsed. First one floor, then the next, then a cascade. It had been completely unexpected. The planes seemed to just be there in the sky, as coming events might suddenly just be there. There might be little time in between certain secret events. The World Trade towers did not collapse instantly. It took an hour and a half for the first tower to fall, and it was interesting how it did. First, there had been the surprise in the sky. Then there was the fire. There was the great smoke.

The fire spread. The top started to crumble, almost as in slow-motion but then with increased speed as one floor buckled after another. Each was like an event—to those on those floors. One floor fell on top of the one below in a "pancake" effect like a chain reaction that built up speed and then crushed all below until it exploded on the ground in an incredible ball of debris, smoke, and chemicals that would afflict those near it for the rest of their lives and cause another building at Seven World Trade Center (where the city's emergency management office was ironically head-quartered) to likewise implode.

I recalled visiting that building to interview officials on what they thought was the greatest future cataclysmic threat to New York. They had spoken about hurricanes. They had spoken about plagues. They had addressed an earthquake, and terrorism with poisons.

No one had mentioned the possibility of what was to occur a year later across the street.

Nor did they suspect that their own building would be turned to rubble.

The Trade Center horror had been at once unexpected and sudden, then gradual but powerful, then totally devastating. No one had anticipated planes flying into the two buildings (and the Pentagon). No one expected the towers to collapse. And if *Isaiah* had spoken during September 11, 2001, so too did it speak in 2012—this time with storms in a stormy political era, in a divisive time, in a raucous, name-calling time when first a hurricane ("Isaac") interrupted the start of the Republican convention in the U.S. and then its remnants circled back a few days later to cause the Democrats to relocate an outdoor event and then came Hurricane Sandy to disrupt the most populated region in the entire nation as well as throw a dynamic into the presidential race.

It was something that went beyond politics. Politics was only important to a point. There was far more at work. In the case of "Sandy," it had belted the most materialistic corridors in the Northeast—among the most extravagant on earth—taking aim at New Jersey (per capita the wealthiest state) and also washing away oceanfront homes on Long Island, pummeling tony Connecticut (and rich little communities like Westport), throwing furniture on the streets of Brooklyn, badly damaging a town called Babylon, swamping the gay weekend hotspot of Fire Island, closing subways (thought to be so invincible), putting three of the world's busiest airports out of service, shutting down Wall Street (where the golden bull remained), and—most pointedly—causing floodwaters to cascade onto the site of the new Freedom Tower, this skyscraper that was built in defiance of the 9/11 event, causing little waterfalls, right there at Ground Zero (and causing politicians to once *more* vow to rebuild). Noted one report: "Perhaps as startling as the sheer toll was the devastation to some of the state's well-known locales. Boardwalks along the beach in Seaside Heights, Belmar and other towns on the Jersey Shore were blown away. Amusement parks, arcades and restaurants all but vanished. Bridges to barrier islands buckled, preventing residents from even inspecting the damage to their property."

One small attack on the Trade Center in 1993 had preceded the huge one in 2001 (also foreseen by Esperanza) and then there was the collapse of financial markets and now a hurricane battering New Jersey and Long Island and the Battery—and still most remained oblivious or simply refused prophecy. "Sandy" could be considered a derivative of "Cassandra" which etymologists said came from a term for the "unheeded prophetess" who had attempted to warn Troy. As I said it meant unheeded warning!

Somewhere in the collapse of biblical "towers" or the aftermath of storms or the tsunamis or societal upsets was the clue or were the clues to an event or events in the "secrets."

There was *Judges* 9, where "all the men of the tower of Shechem also died, about a thousand men and women."

There was *Isaiah* 30: "On every lofty mountain and on every high hill there will be streams running with water on the day of the great slaughter, when the towers fall" (mentioning, two verses later, "a consuming fire" and also punishment for not hearing the prophetic voices of warning—but instead heeding "oppression and guile," seeking protection of the pharaoh).

On the day of the great slaughter, said the Bible, collapse would come in "an instant" (back to the notion of suddenness) and "when the towers fall" (it added), the light of the moon "will be as the light of the sun, and the light of the sun will be seven times brighter" *(Isaiah* 30:26).

Was *this* what the 2004 addendum spoke of as a *"huge light"*?

"Therefore, her young men will fall in her streets, and all the men of war will be silenced in that day," declared the Lord of Hosts in *Jeremiah* 49. "I will set fire to the wall of Damascus, and it will devour the fortified towers."

"He destroyed their fortified towers and laid waste their cities," added *Ezekiel* 19—mentioning a "young lion" and the "sound of his roaring." (This was interesting, in etymology, as "Osama" meant "lion.") "I will bring up many nations against you," said that same part of the Old Testament.

26

Meltdown, sudden disasters, invasion, upheaval, more events. It fell into what was indicated as our own future. One mathematician created a model showing that each fifty years the United States experienced upheaval starting in 1870 with the Civil War and then 1920 with workers plus racial unrest and 1970 with the Vietnam War and more societal disorder and the next coming, according to his theory, around 2020 (this time, he said, with conditions that would be "much worse" than 1970).

There would be a period of Intensification followed by a period of Precipitation followed by the Denouement.

We were crossing from "Intensification" to "Precipitation."

The "Denouement" would be sudden. In the view of some mystics events would pick up from 2015 to 2020, progress with special vigor until just before or around 2020 and then in a major way by 2025 on through the mid-2030s. This was guesswork. A mystic named Venerable Magdalene Porzat, who died in 1850, supposedly had said, "When the feast of Saint Mark shall fall on Easter, the feast of Saint Anthony on Pentecost, and that of Saint John on Corpus

Christi, the whole world shall cry, 'Woe!'" That intersection of feasts (Saint Mark's May 25, Saint Anthony's June 13, and Saint John's June 24) would occur in 2038. Dr. Storm had given that much larger frame of time (by the end of this century or the next). Like Ground Zero, there would be fire; there would be mayhem; the smoke would clear and the evil would be gone, banished, with a planet now to use in a way that brought men closer to God (and not mammon). We had failed the test of 9/11. We had failed "Sandy." We still had time. The events were to sanctify us. We did not have to see a meltdown, at least not one with massive disasters (much greater than "Katrina").

But a meltdown was already well underway.

Little economic markers went lockstep with "little" weather events and "little" societal breakdowns and many tremors. April 2011 was a record month for tornadoes, with 758. It nearly tripled the old record. Small quakes were constant and not so small ones more frequent. A powerful underwater jolt shook Sumatra in 2012, a quake larger (magnitude-8.6) than thought possible for its type that ruptured along multiple fault lines at nearly right angles, as if through a maze. ("The shocking number of earthquakes that have rattled the globe, especially along tectonic plate boundaries, since the double 8.0-plus magnitude earthquakes struck off the coast of Northern Sumatra on April 11, 2012, could be early indication the planet may be shifting towards a new catastrophic model," noted one website that logged natural disasters.)

How many didn't see the connection! The quakes were not yet catastrophic. They were small for now. But there were those rumblings. Or a "hum." It was as if tectonic plates were resonating, as a musical instrument resonates, perhaps due to water or oil or molten rock sloshing deep below. Now, in California. Now, in Seattle (there more of a strange hum). In Costa Rica, there was a television report of a strange mechanical pounding, rhythmic and marching, machine-like, from what seemed like the depths; several days later, there was a magnitude-7.6 quake. In India, also rumblings. Supernatural? Perhaps. I read the near-death account of a neurosurgeon who during his episode found himself in a dark, "primordial," earthen underworld where he heard "a deep, rhythmic pounding, distant yet strong, so that each pulse of it goes right through you . . . mechanical, like the sound of metal against metal, as if a giant, subterranean blacksmith is pounding an anvil somewhere off in the distance: pounding it so hard that the sound vibrates through the earth, or the mud, or wherever it is you are."

There was that aspect: like a resonation from a dark spiritual dimension. But also: something was wrong deep in the earth. Something was out of balance. Something would occur that geophysicists would not anticipate. It would be as unexpected as the Trade Center. "I could see traffic moving through the downtown area," said one who "saw" a coming quake. "However, my attention was focused on the base of a huge building. Again came the prelude and the earthquake. Autos were literally flung off the streets into buildings by the violent movements of the earth. A horrible chorus of creaking, scraping, and grating sounds filled the air, not unlike masts of great sailing ships in a storm, as the skyscrapers swayed to and fro. The giant building began to shear off from its base about twenty feet from the sidewalk but surprised me by not falling. Brick, stone, glass, debris of every sort fell into the streets below like hail driven by a storm wind."

That was a vision of a quake in the Midwest.

Such intriguing notes I received, from those who perceived "visions."

There was this sense of something impending—something upsetting, but in the end great.

Good was going to occur. The world was going to transform.

Before it did?

One had also to consider "plagues."

As I said, it was an epidemic that wiped out up to a hundred million after Fatima. Flu. At Kibeho, the Blessed Mother had shown the seers villages that would be abandoned and soon after, AIDS destroyed whole settlements.

Rwanda bordered the Congo which bordered Cameroon where some believe the first HIV virus crossed from a chimpanzee that had been slain for bush meat.

Deep in Africa a bug lurked that caused viral hemorrhagic fever. It reared its head on occasion, frightening even seasoned epidemiologists. For they knew if this fever, causing blood to pour out of the mouth, nose, eyes, and other orifices, borne by ticks, turning organs to something like coffee grounds, ever mutated to where it allowed the host to live long enough to spread it around and could be transmitted by casual contact (a simple sneeze), it would be globally catastrophic. There were any number of high-order threats. Every year seemed to bring consternation. There was SARS. There was swine flu. There was bird flu. There were the strange, terrifying viruses from Asia and the Middle East. Hospitals had become zones of contamination. Bacteria were defying antibiotics. In 1996 a bacterial strain (*Klebsiella pneumoniae*) was found with coding for an enzyme that conferred resistance in other bacteria to every known treatment. This bacteria was dangerously similar to those that commonly pervade our bodies, opening the chance it might bequeath its resistance to them. As a newspaper in the United Kingdom, *The Mail,* reported during October in 2012, "Last month, a forty-nine-year-old man entered London's Saint Thomas Hospital with a raging fever, severe cough, and desperate difficulty in breathing. He bore all the hallmarks of the deadly SARS virus that killed nearly one thousand people in 2003—but blood tests quickly showed that this terrifyingly virulent infection was not SARS. Nor was it any other virus yet known to medical science. Worse still, the gasping, sweating patient was rapidly succumbing to kidney failure, a potentially lethal complication that had never before been seen in such a case. Using the latest high-tech gene-scanning technique, scientists at the Health Protection Agency started to piece together clues from tissue samples taken from the Qatari patient, who was now hooked up to a life-support machine. The results were extraordinary. Yes, the virus was from the same family as SARS. But its make-up was completely new. It had come not from humans, but from bats."

Some of these diseases—virulent, fatal diseases—were in the same family as the common cold.

One leading virologist, John Oxford at Queen Mary Hospital, University of London, a world authority on epidemics, warned we must expect "an animal-originated pandemic to hit the world within the next five years, with potentially cataclysmic effects on the human race. I think it is inevitable that we will have another big global outbreak of flu. We should plan for one emerging in 2017-2018."

Did that mean stockpiling food and medical essentials in a world where everyone had to disconnect or even flee from each other?

The answers would come only through prayer. There was also the prospect of food shortages. Here we were back to Asia.

In China, where, tempting God, authorities forced women to abort babies if they already had a child—and where moneychangers black-marketed elephant tusks (and made ashtrays from severed gorilla hands), and where pollution was far worse than most countries, where, in 2012, the Yangtze, as if as another sign, turned red—Christians in Shandong were said to have recorded a mysterious prophecy in 1995 at a clandestine prayer meeting where "everyone was singing 'in the Spirit' together (*1 Corinthians* 14:15), not in their own language, but 'as the Spirit gave them utterance,' all in harmony but all singing different words. Someone audio-taped the meeting. Later, when they played back the cassette, they were shocked!" reported one evangelical. "What they heard was not what had happened there at all but the sound of angels singing in Mandarin a song they had never heard before, and with a musical accompaniment that had not been there. When my friend first heard the tape, before anyone told him what it was, he exclaimed, 'Those are angels!' Actually, there was no other explanation. A Chinese Christian co-worker translated the tape." The actual words (for discernment):

"The end is near. Rescue souls.

"The famine is becoming more and more critical.

"There are more and more earthquakes.

"The situation is becoming more and more sinister.

"People are fighting against each other, nation against nation.

"Disasters are more and more severe.

"The whole environment is deteriorating.

"People's hearts are wicked, and they do not worship the true God.

"Disasters are more and more severe.

"Floods and droughts are more and more frequent.

"There is more and more homosexuality and incurable diseases.

"Disasters are more and more severe.

"The climates are becoming more and more abnormal.

"The earth is more and more restless.

"The skies have broken.

"The atmosphere is distorted.

"Disasters are more and more severe."

Then a chorus:

"The end is near. The revelation of love has been mani-fested.

"Rise up, rise up, rescue souls.

"The end is near.

"Rise up, rise up, rescue souls."

As for the West, Dr. Storm—Reverend Storm (for he became a minister)—recounted of his encounter with angels:

They showed me that what would happen is that people would begin robbing the grocery stores, hoarding goods, and killing one another for gasoline and tires, and as a consequence everything would break down and would end up in chaos."

We had scares every year—false alarms. We saw this with the bogus Mayan 2012 prophecy. We saw this with Y2K. Moreover, humans often rose to the challenge (with help from the Holy Spirit). Even now, at a quickening hour, there was time. Terror was only for those who lacked faith.

But Storm insisted we were not out of the woods, that there would be a purge as God ushers in a new Kingdom during the next two hundred years.

How close was that? How close was purification?

"Too close," Storm told me. "Way too close. And God doesn't want this to happen. God doesn't want to do it. What God wants is love, hope, faith, and goodness."

The planet would be swiftly altered. Right now, left and right, society was beating nature down, and at such a pace that when a northern Michigan man named David Milarch who had been a weight-lifter and arm-wrestling competitor had *his* alleged near-death revelation, it included instructions by an angel to stockpile the DNA of large, old-growth trees so they could be propagated to help replenish earth in the future. Milarch began an organization called Archangel Ancient Tree Archive and set about taking the DNA from the most magnificent trees on the planet, trees that would absorb carbon, that would purify water, that in some cases emitted anti-bacterial, anti-viral, and even anti-cancer agents, such as redwoods and sequoias and bristlecone pine thousands of years old, trees that were dying or had been unceremoniously chopped down for money's sake. Willow and yew. Thousands of trees. It was remarkable. For this experience was almost precisely the way the 1990 prophecy had taken place, it too occurring in the middle of the night, involving an angel, and recorded on a legal pad, words that, like 1990, astonished the recipient, but occurring in 1992 (a time during which the prophecy of two years before still had not been brought into the public realm). This occurred weeks after his clinical "death" when one winter night, claimed Milarch, "I awoke just after one a.m., surprised to find the bedroom lit by the warm glow that had given me such comfort. The light grew brighter and brighter until it was blinding. I covered my eyes with my hands, but it barely made a difference. 'Okay, I'm listening,' I said. 'Just tell me what I need to do.' A soft, warm female voice said, 'Get a pad and pen and go to the living room.' I rose out of bed, found a legal pad and a pen and sat nervously on the edge of my leather chair. But the voice was gone. My eyes grew heavy. I awoke with a start and looked at the clock, 5:55 a.m. But what about . . . I looked down at the pad in my lap, page after page, filled with a detailed, formal outline. I stared in wonder at the words: Dying trees. Champion species. Cloning. Reforesting. It was my handwriting, but nothing I'd ever even thought about. I had no memory of taking any of it down. My heart raced as I read through what I'd written. The earth's trees and forests getting sicker, weakened by pollution, drought, disease, and bugs able to survive the warmer winters. I was to clone the biggest, strongest, hardiest trees—trees that had lived hundreds, even thousands of years—so the world could one day be restored to its natural order by the giants of the forest. I felt like Noah, a simple man told to become a ship-builder and a zookeeper."

The earth was like a dull negative of Heaven.

But it was supposed to remain in line with the picture, with what was more gloriously manifested in eternity, and earth had not. As the new Pope said, in explaining why he took the name of Saint Francis, "For me, he is the man of poverty, the man of peace, the man who loves and protects creation. These days we don't have a very good relationship with creation, do we?"

Every baby dead from abortion was an insult to God's Plan. That was true of all sin, all lack of charity, all degra-dation of Creation. We would pay a price. It was way back in 1946, claimed a man named James Wilburn Chauncey, of Georgia, that he "died" of bacterial spinal meningitis, his vital signs disappearing to such an extent that a doctor told the nurses to prepare his body for the morgue and cremation to prevent spread of the highly contagious (and, back then, almost always deadly bacteria). Chauncey claimed that during a period of two hours he was taken by Jesus and angels to various parts of eternity.

"There were all these trees with fruit on them and beau-tiful vegetation and the sky was just so blue," said this man, who was a Baptist. "I don't remember any clouds. I saw the 'river of life' and on one side were people who had lived after the Crucifixion and on the other side people who had lived before, biblical-like people, people like out of the Old Testament, and they looked to be in their twenties or thirties and were dressed in the attire that they had worn on earth. Jesus came out of a large building and I heard lots of singing praise music. The atmosphere was sweet like honeysuckle. The building Jesus had been in was made of something like stones or blocks and cut with three levels of stairs. No one went beyond the first layer. There were columns and it was like all white, sort of like Roman buildings, but really not like that, not like anything. I call it stone but it could have been something else. I wasn't allowed to go to that section, just to this gate. People kept coming out. I was told it was all my bloodline.

"Then they showed me what would happen to me and the earth and this consumed a lot of the time. We went to the edge of paradise, like a cliff, and you could see the blue earth hanging there and when you wanted you could just zoom in on various places on earth. I could smell smoke and heard booming noises and it was like I was seeing over the northeast toward Europe these armies moving from the north over Syria (it could have been Iran, or Russia) and continuing southwest and southeast, bypassing Israel. They conquered all of Africa and Asia except for China, then they started across the rest of Europe and across to England.

"The English fought very hard. Wars, fires, earthquakes, conflicts, and death were occurring all around the world, and then it was upon the shores of America. After England I saw missiles lobbed from boats at New York, Washington, Philadelphia, Cincinnati, Jacksonville, and Atlanta and some other place but at this point they weren't nuclear. That was followed by a landing of troops and I looked toward the other side of America when I heard some huge blasts and I looked toward Mexico and New Mexico. There were troops coming from Mexico and South America and they were Islamic. I kept getting that Russia has a pact with the Islamic countries. After this, there were nuclear blasts. Atomic bombs started falling."

Looking closer, Chauncey claimed to have focused on the western coast of America, where he saw "great earthquakes and tremendous explosions intermixed with the invasions. Mountains rose, land disappeared, and crevices opened up across the land." He recalled seeing a massive, pear-shaped "lake" stretching from around lakes Superior and Michigan across Nebraska, Iowa, the Dakotas, Kansas, and parts of Wisconsin and Minnesota, on down through the Mississippi River, which he saw as vastly wider.

"Mountains had fallen; canyons disappeared; the courses of rivers were changed, and much land disappeared," he wrote. "Portions of Texas and Arizona were now lakes. What had been deserts of the west were now green and lush with trees and vegetation. Asia, Africa, Europe, and the world over became lush with vegetation, clear water, lakes, and rivers, and an abundance of fish, fowl, and animal life." Afterward he was shown "animals and people began to appear from places where they hid during the terrible time of destruction. As the rain fell [after phenomenal drought], and the animals began to emerge from their hiding places, I looked toward what was left of the North and South American continents. One thing has been made perfectly clear to me. Humanity can cause a delay or shifts within periods of time, but humanity cannot prevent them unless all humanity totally rejects evil."

And so we discern. Was it a revelation from Heaven or a deception to dilute legitimate prophecy? Real? Or symbolism? Chauncey said he had been shown weapons that made no sense at the time but that he now sees in modern combat, including the stealth jet, which he said he used to draw as a child, to the consternation of teachers. "Seeing these weapons now convinces me that we are on the threshold of disaster," he asserted, adding that the events would occur during the presidency of a young man.

It was frustrating, trying to wade through it all; it was difficult. Maybe it was impossible. All prophecy (*1 Corinthians* 13:19) was "imperfect." Did it all go to *2 Timothy* 4:3 (wanting to have "ears tickled")?

Ignored often was how a chastisement could come in the form of what already had occurred, by way of HIV, abortion, homosexuality, pornography, selfishness, addiction, rancor, divorce, and terrorism, or start as a little drought that went on for a year and then another year and spread over regions.

At LaSalette the Blessed Mother allegedly had said that there would be disease, there would be crop failure, there would be a famine; that later, in the end times, *"water and fire will give the earth's globe convulsions . . . and terrible earthquakes will swallow up mountains and cities . . . earthquakes will swallow whole countries . . . The fire of Heaven will fall . . . the earth will be struck by calamities of all kinds (in addition to plague and famine which will be widespread). There will be a series of wars until the last war . . . At the first blow of His thundering sword, the mountains and all nature will tremble in terror, for the disorders and crimes of men have pierced the vault of the heavens . . ."*

At Kibeho fire was at center stage, fire was the theme. Here too, an abyss had opened.

In the vision before the genocide, trees were seen to be aflame.

That may have occurred during the onslaught. It may have happened as troops battled.

But fire, it seemed, was in a larger picture. Remember what Nathalie Mukamazimpaka had said: "I saw mountains crashing into each other. Stones coming out of the earth, nearly as if they were angry. I saw storms crashing against each other and fire coming from them. I don't know what this means. I was told that people are causing this and that it is coming." And Segatashya: "After all souls chosen by God have been led into Heaven, a great fire will erupt from deep within the earth and the world will be consumed in flames, and all those who rejected God and refused to believe will burn in the fire."

The "time of visitation," said the seers, was nearing an end.

"If you don't take refuge in God," Mary had asked there, *"where will you go to hide when the fire will spread every-where?"*

And so it seemed like nearly a consensus: great social and military upset and natural disasters that would involve fire. The 1990 prophecy didn't say that. It said *"fear of fire."* But interpretation remained open. *Something in a region of the world would affect everyone,* said the addendum in 2004. That could be a volcano and volcanic activity appeared to be riding a surge. *From deep within the earth.* There certainly had been volcanic activity around the world and the magma, the spewing smoke, in some cases, the lava seemed to closely follow the rumbles of quakes: little and sometimes larger volcanic eruptions in Indonesia and Guatemala and Japan. One could view a map of current eruptions and count more than twenty on a particular day, and scientists most recently had detected a huge expansion of the magma bubble beneath one of history's most notorious volcanic sites, that of an island near Greece called Thera or Santorini, which 1,600 years before Christ erupted with such power that it destroyed the ancient Minoans; villages had been steeped with up to one hundred and fifty feet of ash and there had been a darkness so total "that not even lamplight could penetrate it," said an historical account— a darkness that affected land within a hundred miles and lasted up to three days.

There was a great tidal wave.

It was one of the most famous eruptions in all of recorded history.

Rock vaporized.

There were severe food shortages after, as sunlight was blocked.

Another had been Krakatau in Indonesia which now was also showing signs of returning to life and in 1883 had erupted so violently it was heard nearly three thousand miles away, caused a tidal wave that killed at least thirty-six thousand, emitted a glow (*"huge light"*) that was noticed as far away as Connecticut, and affected global weather.

Now, there were signs of volcanic activity in Nicaragua, Columbia, Costa Rica, New Zealand, Japan, Chile, the Canary Islands, Hawaii, the Aleutians, and in the Pacific—underwater, where there were more mountains and volcanoes than on the surface and where an eruption could not only surprise but devastate fantastically (generating walls of water and gigantic plumes of ash skyward).

Near Vesuvius was a massive, recently discovered volcano that was calculated to pose a threat to the three million people in an area just a couple miles from the famous volcano that had destroyed Pompeii—a Sodom-like city—not long after the death of Jesus.

Fire! There was a "supervolcano" under Yellowstone National Park. There was one in Siberia. There were a number under the ice.

When the strange odor was detected across southern California in 2012, some wondered if it was from a hidden volcano near the Salton Sea (not so far from L.A. and San Diego).

There had been activity at Etna.

There were volcanoes rumbling under Antarctica.

In 2012, a ship in the Pacific happened upon a stretch of pumice that covered 4,660 square miles of water east of

New Zealand and had been triggered by more than a thousand small quakes over a period of just two days along the "ring of fire."

I remember visiting the volcano on the Big Island of Hawaii and the alien feeling in a helicopter watching the fiery lava that cascaded toward a cliff into the Pacific: steam at what seemed (when I later drove up to it) like the edge of the world.

There were 1,500 active volcanoes—forty in the lower 48, sixty in Alaska—and as many as ten thousand under ocean waves.

It would take just one "supervolcano" to have global repercussions, shutting down photosynthesis.

It is what we faced if we kept up the transgressions, if we kept abusing the earth, if we didn't do something drastic to change the way modern life had evolved—so out of control that those toxics were now in every human newborn; animals were abused everywhere; roads dissected everything God had put there; herbicides were sprayed right onto freshwater lakes (to kill certain plants, and make way for fishermen to take more fish); insecticides were blasted alongside and into our homes, or hosed onto our lawns, our shrubs, seeping into groundwater, killing streams and springs, wafting miles through the air; plastics now truly omnipresent and reconfiguring nature; trees were felled at the merest whim, genetic crops sending pollen to who knew where, artificial radiation nearly as pervasive as gravity, abrasive synthetics a staple in household cleaners, and artificial light fading out the stars, cars burning up not only lubricant but now corn (ethanol), and oxygen in grand megalopolises that created their own localized clouds (called the "heat-island" effect). Did not everyone flying out of Mexico City—after a visit to see, for example, the Virgin of Guadalupe—not notice the plume of hydrocarbons that stretched from that city for hundreds of miles—or that the aerosols from Los Angeles, its particulates, were clouding up vistas at the Grand Canyon and toxics from China were landing in the U.S. (alongside non-biodegradable debris from the Japanese tsunami)? Pope Francis emphasized this in his very inaugural homily: that we needed to safeguard the weakest, the poorest, as well as the ecology. "Today amid so much darkness we need to see the light of hope and to be men and women who bring hope to others," he said, reminding us that "to protect creation, to protect every man and every woman, to look upon them with tenderness and love, is to open up a horizon of hope, it is to let a shaft of light break through the heavy clouds. Let us protect Christ in our lives, so that we can protect others, so that we can protect Creation!

"The vocation of being a 'protector,' however, is not just something involving us Christians alone; it also has a prior dimension which is simply human, involving everyone. It means protecting all Creation, the beauty of the created world, as the Book of Genesis tells us and as Saint Francis of Assisi showed us. It means respecting each of God's creatures and respecting the environment in which we live. It means protecting people, showing loving concern for each and every person, especially children, the elderly, those in need, who are often the last we think about. It means caring for one another in our families: husbands and wives first protect one another, and then, as parents, they care for their children, and children themselves, in time, protect their parents. It means building sincere friendships in which we protect one another in trust, respect, and goodness. In the end, everything has been entrusted to our protection, and all of us are responsible for it. Be protectors of God's gifts! Whenever human beings fail to live up to this responsibility, whenever we fail to care for Creation and for our brothers and sisters, the way is opened to destruction and hearts are hardened. Tragically, in every period of history there are 'Herods' who plot death, wreak havoc, and mar the countenance of men and women. Please, I would like to ask all those who have positions of responsibility in economic, political, and social life, and all men and women of goodwill: let us be 'protectors' of Creation, protectors of God's Plan inscribed in nature, protectors of one another and of the environment. Let us not allow omens of destruction and death to accompany the advance of this world!"

It was nearly as if Francis had read the 1990 prophecy. This was the Pope!

The same spirit was moving. It was incredible and caused one to wonder: did Francis fulfill another part of the prophecy, toward the end, mentioning that as regards an antichrist we should be vigilant when it came to Central Europe, *"Yet know too that God's Hand will be evident in South America"*?

Was Pope Francis that sign or part of it? And if so, were we indeed in a period prefiguring a manifestation of Jesus— along with manifestations of evil, warnings, and chastisements?

Many looked to a prophecy alleged to be from Saint Malachy that seemed to see the Pope after Benedict as *Petrus Romanus*, as the last, the "Peter of Rome" who would nourish the flock in trying times, and while his name— Jorge, Mario, Francis—didn't seem to fit, the essence of nurturing a harried flock might, for trying times seemed in the cards, perhaps during his pontificate, and if not, shortly thereafter.

If we kept up our sin—not just the sins we all knew about, not just homosexuality, not just abortion, not just theft, not just murder, not just fornication, but also the gluttony, the materialism, the abuse of nature, nature was going to spit us out. LaSalette said this! *"Nature is asking for vengeance, because of man, and she trembles with dread at what must happen to the earth stained with crime."*

27

Would the fire come from below, above, from a comet? Was there "dark matter" up there? What about past weather mysteries? Two thousands years before Christ, a drastic unexplained flux in climate had destroyed societies in the Akkadian Empire of Mesopotamia, the Old Kingdom of Egypt, and the settlements of Greece, Turkey, and Israel; the Old World had collapsed; that was two thousand years before Jesus; we were now two thousand after. Wrote Dr. Harvey Weiss of Yale, "Seasonal rains became scarce, and withering storms replaced them. The winds cut through northern wheat fields and blanketed them in dust. They emptied out towns and villages, sending people stumbling south with pastoral nomads, to seek forage along rivers and streams. For more than a hundred years the desertification continued, disrupting societies from southwestern Europe to central Asia."

I had communicated with scientists who believed that at points in history—and not so long ago—asteroids had smashed in the Atlantic near Europe; we knew this: there were times of drought at one place, tidal surges, storms, and floods at others—mega events not so far back but greater than any we've witnessed.

The magnetic poles were moving at forty miles a year, indicating a complete reversal of polarity (as periodically has occurred through history) might occur.

That might affect the way earth was shielded from solar radiation, which would affect the climate.

Most did not believe it would be cataclysmic. (They speculated that such a reversal was gradual and would take ten thousand years.) Others were more fearful, wondering if the axis itself could suddenly tilt or "flip." A sudden, staggered realignment of the planet (not just its magnetism, but the earth itself) would be unimaginable. That could only occur, astronomers reassured us, if an object larger than or equal in size to earth suddenly affected our gravity. "Such an encounter would last a week in a deep encounter and the tectonic upheavals would be tremendous, horrible, ecetera," said one alarmist. "The surface of the earth would become molten as the tremendous tidal energies are dissipated. No one would possibly survive it, and the atmosphere would be transfigured. Currently, the earth is spinning about a thousand miles per hour at the equator, a lot less towards the poles. An appreciable change in rotation direction would produce winds with speeds of thousands of miles per hour everywhere. Anything not anchored to bedrock would be torn out of the soil and mixed with a world-enveloping hurricane of activity. The earth would remain engulfed in thick clouds of dirt, dust and debris for decades. I cannot imagine anything surviving such a catastrophe, because the solid earth would be wracked by earthquakes the likes of which have never been experienced by living organisms in over three billion years or more. There would be no spot on the earth not affected by one-hundred-to-five-hundred-mile-per-hour winds and earthquakes of magnitude-seven and much higher."

That was not to inspire fear but to give an example of endless scenarios—most of them unlikely and avoidable through prayer. The 1990 prophecy said there would be a cleansed world but not one that was *depopulated*. At Kibeho, none of the approved seers were quoted in a documented way as seeing the end of the world. Anathalie said nothing about a final apocalypse. While, as I said, a priest named Father Gabriel Maindron wrote, in reference to Alphonsine, that she "tells us Our Lady came to Kibeho in order to prepare us for the coming of her Son" (and that it was "close at hand"), his words were not direct quotes, as was also the case with Marie-Claire, who was likewise said to have stated that "humans' time on earth is nearing the end."

"Repent, repent, repent," she said the Virgin had told her. *"When I tell you this, I am not addressing myself strictly to you, child, but I am making this appeal to all the world. Today, man empties all things of their true value. Those who are continually committing sins are doing so without any acceptance that what they are doing is wrong."*

Anathalie's message: "Pray with the right heart. Include a bit of mortification. Make it an effort by the mind and body."

Don't look for suffering, she said, but neither rebel against it. Suffering brought back purity. It opened our hearts. In our lives, advised Anathalie, we will suffer, but this helped us gain entrance into Heaven. Our Lady wanted us to be happy yet also fearless. There was God's mercy, and that was infinite (if not always endless).

But the indications coming out of Africa—not just Kibeho, but with statues of Mary in places like the Ivory Coast and strange solar phenomena reported in that same part of the continent—were of major coming change. In the 1990s, phenomena involving bleeding images had been reported along Africa's west coast in Benin. On April 1, 1997, a statue in the community of the Franciscan Sisters in Gebegamey wept tears of blood, causing Vincent Metonnou, a journalist for the weekly *Le Forum*, to wonder why there were now so many similar "signs of sorrow" appearing all over the world: "Has the world lost the way?" he asked, concluding that the Son of Man was probably saddened by mankind's "villainy" (in the words of the newspaper). In August of 2010, a church dedicated to St. Paul in Nigeria "turned into a mecca of sorts as people from all walks of life thronged the church to catch a glimpse of what has been literally described as an apparition of Jesus Christ," reported *The Nigerian Observer*. "The uncommon but holy phenomenon according to Catholic faithful and enthusiasts present at the church premises, came up early Wednesday morning immediately after the offering of Adoration at the church. It has however generated so much frenzy amongst Catholic faithful and non-Catholics who jostled through the ever-busy Airport Road in the state capital to witness the rare spiritual occurrence. Similarly, the spiritual significance of the 'apparition of Christ' at the St. Paul's Catholic Church was further described to connote the signs of the end of time by Prince Ken Ebosele, a committed Catholic faithful who was present at the church to catch a glimpse of the 'apparition.' Prince Ebosele revealed that it was a reassurance of the fact that the salvation in Christ which Christians profess was not in vain, adding that the appearance of Christ was a manifestation of the presence of Christ in our lives. Others who pleaded anonymity disclosed that the 'apparition of Christ' at this critical period of human's sinful existence was clear indication that no matter how neck-deep we are involved in sin, the Almighty God has special interest in the salvation of human beings." On April 20, 2011, the bizarre video of an alleged miracle showed what looked like the Virgin of the Miraculous Medal in sunlight that blasted over the trees (causing loud cries from onlookers, who videoed it with cell cameras).

That was in Abidjan in Africa's Ivory Coast. Many claimed it was a hoax. Others were not quite sure. Did one have to be careful? In the early 1990s a nun in Kenya claimed phenomena that included eerie photographs of Jesus at three a.m. with glowing red eyes.

But there were also legitimate phenomena and Africa was special, producing amazing vocations, and a message from Benin, in 1995, where it was said a replica of the Holy Face began to shed blood later analyzed as type AB, RH positive and where—allegedly, powerfully—it was claimed that the Most Sacred Heart of Jesus said in locution: *"Always offer up My Most Holy Face to the Heavenly Father so that He will have mercy on you. I ask all of you that you honor My Divine Countenance and that you will give it a place of honor in your homes, so that the Heavenly Father will grace you abundantly and forgive you your sins. My dear children make sure to say every day in your homes a short prayer to the countenance of Jesus. Don't forget to greet it when you get up in the morning and ask His blessings when you lay down to sleep, so you will be arriving happily in the heavenly homeland. I assure you that all who have a special love for the Holy Face will be warned of dangers and catastrophes. I solemnly promise whoever distributes the devotion of My Holy Countenance will be spared of the punishments that will come over the human race. In addition, they will receive light for the days of horrible confusion that are coming towards the holy Church. Should they suffer death during the punishments, they will die as martyrs and receive holiness. Truly, truly, I say to you, those who spread the devotion to My Holy Face will receive the grace that no family member will be condemned and that those who are in purgatory will soon be released. But all have come to Me through the intercession of My Most Holy Mother, all the worshippers of the Divine Countenance, will receive a great light to understand the mysteries of the end times and they will be very close to the Savior. All these graces they will receive as worshippers of the Holy Face. Don't lose these blessings! For it is also easy to lose them."* The Eternal Father was likewise quoted: *"My children! In the horrible time that will come over the human race, the Holy Face will be very helpful (a real cloth to dry the tears); because My real children will hide behind It. The Holy Face will be a real blessing, so that the punishment that I will send over the human race will be lessened. In the home where it is exhibited will be light in order to be freed from the power of darkness. In the homes where the Holy Face of My Son is located, I will order My angels to mark them, and My children will be spared from the evils that will come over ungrateful humanity. My children become real apostles of the Holy Face and spread it all over. The more it is spread the less will be the catastrophe."*

It was like "pass over." Everyone needed to have an image of Him in their homes—His face—or even on one's person.

Most often the future was unexpected. So were timetables. The angels had a timetable, but that didn't mean anyone knew it. It did say in *1 Thessalonians*: "Now as to the times and the epochs, brethren, you have no need of anything to be written to you. For you yourselves know full well that the day of the Lord will come just like a thief in the night. While they are saying, 'Peace and safety!' then destruction will come upon them suddenly like labor pains upon a woman with child." Events would be unexpected.

As stated in 2004, and let us repeat, *"The event to come will surprise everyone who has offered a prognostication."*

That same message had pointed out that what was to occur—at least one of the huge events—would transmit to scientists the alarm in Heaven over what they were doing.

So at least *this* happening—the event or series of events alluded to in 2004—would somehow be linked to what science was doing or what it believed or didn't believe. What a shame! Science did so much good and yet now was casting itself as a nemesis. We could know this: prophecies in "secrets" at major apparition sites seemed to be very dramatic. At Fatima, they included the rise of Communism, massive persecution (that killed millions), a world war, and an angel about to torch the world (all in three secrets). What to believe? The Bible said not to despise prophecy, but to weigh it, take what is good, and leave the rest, avoiding evil (*1 Thessalonians* 5:20-22). Some locutions were evil. Some came from familiar spirits. Some came from the demonic— which sought to dilute and confuse and thereby discredit legitimate "words" (while causing terror). In many cases, the locution was in the imagination.

How far was too far? Was it not most prudent to simply take the essence of the prophetic "pulse"? For all prophecy, said the Bible (*1 Corinthians* 13:19), was "imperfect."

Often, it seemed to hinge on what would *occur if the world stayed as it was at the moment of the prophecy.*

At Kibeho, it had gone a good deal past that with seers such as Segatashya who like Agnes had not met with Church approbation but quoted the Lord as saying: *"Do not be afraid but have faith! For the one who does good will come with Me to Heaven. It is the one who does evil who will be met by fire. Today this world is full of hatred, and you will know that the time of My return is near, that I am on My way, when you hear of and see the wars of religion. Know then that I come, for nothing will be able to stop these wars. Know, too, that it will not be easy to recognize Me.. You will know that My return is near when you see wars erupt between the different religions of the world. When you witness wars of religion, you will know that I am on the way. Once the wars of religion begin, nothing will stop the fighting. Tell all men that there is not much time left. I will return soon. Hurry to do good, for Satan will one day disappear from this world, and then you will never be tempted again. But hurry, for there is little time left."*

That had been in 1982. (Segatashya died in 1994.)

"The Lord says in the end He will show many signs and He is showing many signs already," said Agnes—in 2010, on that roadside where we met her. "The time will come when the message will be listened to. Most of the secrets are from Jesus. He shares them as a friend would share secrets. He shows things to me when He wants prayer and fasting. They unite me with Him. Most of the secrets involve everyone in the world. Kibeho is something God is happy about because it is growing. He wants us to believe so much and have trust. Love is huge. It is above everything. He wants us to pray from our hearts. There are secrets that will be revealed to certain people prior to them happening. We need to wake up to God's Love. He has spoken about the end of the world but more than that about the end of each person's world."

As a teen, Segatashya—who later was killed by a Hutu death squad—said Jesus appeared to him in a sky that seemed like fabric which had been parted in two and was filled with "a million shining white flowers, which were more beautiful than you can imagine. A moment later Jesus appeared in the heavens, standing in the midst of the white flowers. He was bathed in a luminous light that both surrounded Him and shone out from within His Body. He was floating high above me, supported by the beauty of the great white light and the glorious flowers that were now sparkling like stars. He was the most handsome Man I'd ever seen. He looked as though He was in His early thirties, had a dark-skinned complexion, but His skin was not nearly as dark as a Rwandan's skin. He was dressed in the traditional tunic of a Rwandan man, and the material was glowing as though it had been sewn with threads of silver and gold. All the while I was looking up, I felt as though arms of love were wrapped around me. My soul was at peace, and my heart was happier than it had ever been."

There was great danger—eternal danger, said Jesus, according to this boy—for all who sought *"earthly pleasures above the truth of My words."*

This was all coming from a pagan boy who had never been inside a church and had never heard of the Bible!

"Everything on earth belongs to Heaven; nothing belongs to Satan," Jesus supposedly intoned to him. *"When God created man, Satan, in his jealousy and loneliness, set out to destroy mankind's relationship with God. Ever since mankind's creation, Satan has been trying to trick humanity with his lies and temptation, hoping that man will love the sin of the devil more than the goodness of God. Remember this, My child, God's Love and Light are the only safeguard against evil and eternal darkness . . . tell all those who will listen to prepare their hearts for the Day of Judgment, for the last days of earth draw near. Satan is the author of all lies and is not to be trusted; he has been trying to separate mankind from God's Love since Adam and Eve."*

"In the last days the sun will become very hot, and countless people will die from famine and the other calamities that will follow this famine," Segatashya quoted the Lord as foretelling. *"There will be many temptations from the devil in those times because there will be greater suffering on earth than the world has ever known before."*

As quoted by the pagan boy—who astonished priests and bishops with his sudden theological knowledge—the Lord said, *"There will be many earthquakes in all the corners of the globe. In some places the sun will beat down so relentlessly that the earth will dry up and crops will fail year after year. Winds will carry away all the soil, and never-ending rains will bring great flooding. Hunger will grip many nations. Many will fight each other for food, and scores will starve to death.*"

Segatashya had said of Jesus that "He is a much better being than any human I have ever known. His power is wonderful and terrifying, but so is the power of His love. He loves every person in the world with a force greater than the heat of the sun or strength of a thousand waterfalls. He created this world and everything that is in it, including all people everywhere. He told me that the world will end in fire and that He will come back to the world and carry everyone who lives with a pure heart and who loves Him up to paradise to be with Him forever. But our hearts must be pure when He returns; we must live like He lived when He was on earth long ago. He is the most honorable Man and purest spirit in the universe.

"On the very last day, the planet will tremble and the joy of the righteous will be overwhelming. After all souls chosen by God have been led into Heaven, a great fire will erupt from deep within the earth and the world will be consumed in flames, and all those who rejected God and refused to believe will burn in the fire."

The world was created by God, *"knowing that it will end one day,"* said Segatashya.

And so one day it would.

But to see the "end" as imminent—contrary to indications from Medjugorje, the 1990 prophecy, and other predictions, particularly those of Maria Esperanza—was a matter that gave pause. The end of the world did not seem nigh. The end of an era—a great, tumultuous, radical change—did. "I'm not going to tell you that we are all going to kill each other, that the world is going to end, that we are going to destroy each other—no, no, no," Esperanza, whose very name meant "hope," had remarked in 1992. "They said at the end of [the twentieth] century, everything is going to end. That's impossible. I don't believe it. It will continue throughout generations, and this world will continue progressing and becoming conscious and perfecting itself in order to live a life which is really happy, because individuals will find themselves, because they will feel God and know and learn how to respect Him and to love Him and to love their brothers and sisters."

On the way to "progression," however—on the way to a more natural way of living, in harmony with Creation—she, like Storm, saw a breaking down. "People of light must be conscious of their duties," said Maria. "We cannot be concerned about money or houses or big cars. No, the moment is arriving when we must leave all those things. The moment is coming. At this moment, right now, man is punishing himself through his egoism, through his lack of charity, through his lack of conscientiousness. As a result, we're about to be in a big war, but I have more fears for natural disasters because there are so many injustices in the world and the Lord is making Himself felt by His justice."

In Argentina, at San Nicolás, it was a bit more stark. *"The coming of the Savior is imminent,"* Gladys quoted Mary as saying in the 1980s. *"As the Gospel says, no one knows the date nor the hour, but the hour will come, and it is certain that the soul of the Christian must be prepared for that hour. Even the stones will be witnesses to it. The great strength of God breaks every plan which the enemy wants to prepare. If the devil acts ferociously, do not be scared. He attacks without compassion, involving whatever he can touch. Pray, because prayer strengthens. You are called by Jesus Christ to pray. The prince of evil knows that his sad kingdom is coming to an end. In this way, he shed his poison with all his strength. There is only a little left. His end is approaching. The evil one is astute and calculating. He wants to destroy, but here he will not be able to do it. Here, it is he who will self-destruct. A new time has begun. A new hope has been born; attach yourselves to this hope. The very intense light of Christ is going to be reborn, for just as on Calvary, after Crucifixion and death, the Resurrection took place. The Church, too, will be born again through the strength of love. My daughter, as previously in Fatima, today my visits are renewed on earth. They are more frequent and more prolonged, because humanity is passing through very dramatic times."*

It was to be recalled that appearances in places often preceded major events in those specific regions. That was true not only of Kibeho and Bosnia, but also alleged events in Syria and Iraq, where predictions of the end in Damascus and Mosul (the site of ancient Nineveh) were followed by devastating persecution and war. As in Rwanda, the apparitions seemed a prelude to domestic violence: a regional apocalypse. There at ancient Nineveh, churches were soon torched and thousands of Syrian Christians (perhaps including the seer, Dina Basher) injured, scattered, or killed. Dina had seen Jesus with a golden crown and like Segatashya had prophesied in 1991 that the Second Coming was near. As for Syria, that nation threatened to plunge the world into what Esperanza warned could turn into "the brouhaha of an atomic awakening" in which mankind would "succumb under fire: war and death," without conversion.

There was "fire" again. On the surface, there would be flames. In a spiritual or physical or in both ways, it would be an incendiary time, whether from the earth or sky or again both. Earth, sky, fire. This continued to be indicated and one could go back to mystics like the great Padre Pio who capsulated the societal breakdown as well as coming disturbances when in a passage about him and his concern for society author Bernard Ruffin (in *Padre Pio: The True Story*) noted that "by the mid-1960s, Capuchins [in his monastery] were permitted to watch television, which did not please Padre Pio, who felt that the programs did not lead to virtues desirable in Christian living. He also feared that excessive television viewing was a factor in the destruction of family life: instead of talking to each other, family members tended to spend evenings staring gape-mouthed, like zombies, at the set. He strongly advised anyone who asked his opinion not to buy a television set. Although he had once cautiously approved of his nephew's running a movie theater and had authorized a cinema in the *Casa*, Padre Pio grew increasingly negative about motion pictures. When the subject was broached, he was known to say, 'The devil is in it!' On at least one occasion he told a penitent that the reason his car had broken down the night before was that he was en route to the movies! Padre Pio was exceedingly pessimistic about the world situation and the future. He seemed to see the future, and it filled him with horror."

A Capuchin named Father Joseph Pius recalled specific prophecies from Padre Pio about coming events but said it was "best that they not be disclosed lest they prove too unsettling." When Pio was questioned as to what the coming years would bring, Father Pius reports that he often said, "Can't you see that the world is catching on fire?"

At Kibeho, Alphonsine had been quoted as saying that not just Rwanda but the world faced an "abyss."

"As one vision began to fade, Mary asked the stricken Alphonsine to sing another song, this time repeating two lines of verse seven times each," wrote a chronicler of the apparition. *"First: There will be fire that will come from beneath the earth and consume everything on earth . . . And then: The day will come to take those who have served You, God, we beg you to have mercy on us. . . ."*

28

The notion of fire, of something unexpected, of sudden acceleration—of something that "consumed"—brought to mind two simultaneous disasters that had started inexplicably on the same day (and some said the same hour) during October of 1871 in the Midwest, disasters that were connected to America's first approved apparition near Green Bay.

These were the historic fires in Chicago and Wisconsin (in the region of a town called Peshtigo, and also in parts of Michigan). When the Virgin Mary appeared clothed in white to the Belgian girl Adele Brisé on October 9, 1859, she had called for the *"conversion of sinners"* and warned that *"if they do not convert and do penance, my Son will be obliged to punish them."*

It had been a rowdy time: logging camps and rail construction and drinking and houses of ill repute and violence and exploitation of nature, not to mention religious indifference across Wisconsin, along with the more sophisticated evil in places like Chicago, Illinois. As recalled in *Firestorm At Peshtigo*, a classic book about the fire, "Peshtigo [not far from the apparition site, and especially

traumatized] was a town split between devotion and indul-
gence. On Sundays the people filled the Congregational,
Lutheran, Presbyterian, and Catholic churches. But on
Sunday nights, the streets belonged to Miss Delia and Hatty
Baker and to the men who frequented the saloons. When
someone was out of favor, loggers stomped on them with
their caulked boots. Half wild, half civilized, Peshtigo was
synonymous with progress." Wandering preachers stalked
the countryside, waving bibles and warning, as in our own
time, of judgment as small wildfires flamed at the outskirts
through the fall of 1871. Noted the book: "The commonly
held belief among the preachers was that after thirty years of
clearing, burning, and building, a moral drama had been
staged: man was the architect, not only of cities, farms, and
mills, but of destruction, and wounded Nature would fight
back." A newspaper editor named Benjamin Franklin Tilton
said that whether "doomed to chastisement for our sins or
for a solemn warning to the world, we leave for others to
decide. Certain it is, that the scourge of fire increased."

There were signs. Birds plummeted from the sky and by
September 21, 1871, a glare was noted as blazes erupted
from a drought that had left trees so dry and the ground so
parched that some of the small blazes spread several feet
below the soil or peat, occasionally visible like fiery
serpents that wiggled across the terrain.

It had been eerie stuff. Every day, here and there, more
blazes; several weeks of this. Cinders wafted in the air.
There were constant whiffs of distant smoke. Then—
between October 8 and 10—a low-pressure system formed
the pattern of a cyclone and the fires detonated across
parched countryside like something nuclear. Peshtigo.
Champion. Marinette.

And down in Chicago.

"Within the space of two hours on October 8, 1871, the
cyclonic storm front served to make the main fire a veritable

monster," said the authors. "The persistent surging and whirring rendered each obstacle in its path yet another opportunity to create more violent wind, which in turn created another vortex, which in turn strengthened the wind, which in turn fed the atmospheric turbulence—until the sky and the ground and everything in between was ablaze. Chicago was in flames, and Oconto County, Wisconsin, situated at eighty-eight degrees west longitude and forty-five degrees north latitude, had become a roaring ocean of fire."

What the passage did not say was that the flames near Peshtigo were unconnected to those in Chicago and that there had been other fires cropping up miles away in Wisconsin and Michigan—with no single point of discernible origin. In Chicago, where it was supposed to have started in a barn (until this legend, of a cow kicking over a lantern, was later discredited), a watchman at the courthouse was confused because, through his spyglass, the fire seemed to be coming from two different directions. Before it was over it would destroy more than seventy miles of road and 17,500 buildings, leaving a third of the city's residents homeless (but sparing a church, Holy Family, right near the famous barn, when the wind shifted). Was it simply an extraordinary meteorological result? Something more? A combination? The supernatural inflecting itself through various means on the natural?

What we know is that the greatest urban fire in U.S. history occurred at the exact same time as the greatest wild-fire, though they were separated by more than two hundred and sixty miles and by a lake from the eruptions in Michigan.

We also know they had come after the warning from Mary on October 9, 1859.

Now—twelve years later, to the day—here were explosive, fantastic, and parallel conflagrations. The wildfires extended from October eighth to the tenth, putting the ninth precisely in the middle.

The apparition occurred right where the flames would sweep through, incinerating 1.2 million acres.

A coincidence?

How? Why?

Brimstone?

There was a great harbinger—and mystery—here.

In Wisconsin, small fires that seemed like warnings suddenly seemed to join. "Heat radiation from these separate fires may have ignited nearby underbrush, logging debris, and other combustible material, creating even larger fires as the individual blazes merged together," noted a website devoted to the fire. "[Perhaps] above the heavier, smoke-laden air of northeastern Wisconsin was a layer of colder air. This cold air mass initially suppressed the convection whirls that these original smaller fires generated, causing them to burn sluggishly. When the swirling, over-heated air of the combined convection whirls finally broke through the blanket of cooler air above it, it was as if a giant furnace damper had been opened. The hot air rushed skyward and the colder air swept in from all sides towards the column of rising air. This updraft created a firestorm that ravaged approximately one thousand square miles. It incinerated the village of Peshtigo and other settlements and farms in both Wisconsin and Michigan."

As a scholar at Michigan State University recounted, "the great fire in 1871, damaged the entire Lake Michigan shoreline, destroyed the cities of Holland and Manistee, and spread across to Port Huron."

Blamed, in Wisconsin, on campfires used by loggers, rail workers, and hunters (as well as on farmers who slashed and burned vegetation to clear land), so powerful and extraordinary was the disaster some theorized that a meteor shower added to the woes or even sparked it. Experts scoffed at that. But there certainly were unusual characterizations: "black balls" that hurtled down in both Wisconsin and Chicago as if from a cannon.

The shapes had changed from minute to terrifying minute.

Was this what Lot would have seen, had he glanced back (as had his wife) at Gomorrah?

"Now waves of gas mixed into the smoke to cast an eerie glow over the roads," said the book, written by Denise Gee and William Lutz. "These round spheres suggested the presence of crispy, ominous, and darkly colored protruding mammatus clouds, which form just before a tornado makes contact with the ground. From minute to minute the shapes change; sometimes they even begin to blur, taking on the appearance of streaming virga. The survivors would never forget the sound. 'The sound of judgment,' some said. The sound of an angel heralding the end of the world, blasting gusts of fire from his horn. 'Like a thousand locomotives rushing at full speed,' some wrote. Like the devil had opened his mouth with a 'deafening, persistent roar that never stopped but kept growing louder,' or 'a pounding waterfall,' or a 'hurricane.' Survivors described 'streaks of bloody mist like meteors falling.' Dry lightning strikes were making a spectacular showing." One man depicted a fireball that "flung itself into a tree with the speed of a meteor and had sent a flurry of fire to the surrounding houses."

It was like a cloud of gas had descended and ignited. In Peshtigo, a holy priest named Father Peter Pernin rushed back to the rectory of one of two churches he served to retrieve a chalice and the tabernacle. Through the building, sparks blazed, flying from one room to the next and making a "sharp detonating sound" that convinced him the air was saturated with gas. "Many circumstances tended to prove that the intensity of the heat produced by the fire was in some places extreme, nay unheard of," wrote the priest later.

"The flames pursued the roots of the trees to the very depths of the earth, consuming them to the last inch. Immense numbers of fish of all sizes died, and the morning after the storm the river was covered with them." The speed of fires was virtually instant. "Faster than it takes to write these words is the phrase every survivor used," noted Gess and Lutz. "They used it to describe the speed of a fireball hitting a house and setting it into instant flames; they used it to describe the speed with which one house was lifted from its foundation, then thrown through the air 'a hundred feet' before it detonated midflight and sent strips of flaming wood flying like shrapnel."

Father Pernin rescued the wood tabernacle from the flames and fled to the river. The tabernacle, though wood, would miraculously remain intact, amid everything in ruins. Most people did not have such luck. Many burned to death as they bobbed in the water, the flames at one point hovering remarkably—eerily—over the waterway for a full horrifying hour. Babies died when their skulls were scorched. Floating logs burned on the water. Cyclones powered what seemed like huge blowtorches. Something was raining down. Was it all just downdrafts after convection? Massive trees were uprooted. There were chunks of burning coal. Homes were lifted uncannily from their foundations and thrown a hundred feet, exploding in mid-flight. There were tornadoes of fire. One had seemed to split in half and create flaring microbursts as it approached towns called Menominee and Marinette. In the New Franken-Champion vicinity, the seer Adele and a small group had taken refuge at a small shrine that had been cut from the woods to commemorate her apparition. They processed an image of Mary and recited a Rosary in a small chapel where against all odds they survived. Flames lapped right up to the fence of the five-acre shrine but then halted, scorching the palings but touching nothing on the grounds themselves (which were described as an "island of emerald" in a sea of ash). The book on Peshtigo meanwhile claimed at one point and perhaps with exaggeration that there was "a five-mile-high wall of flame and a vortex of wind." Bodies combusted (fueled by "fat drippings"). From 1,200 to 2,200 died (a number that is likely to be far below the actual count, for it left out many outlying rural areas). Even those who sought shelter in ponds and wells or in wet blankets on meadowland had been incinerated. "People simply became piles of ashes or calcinated bones, identifiable only if a buckle, a ring, a shawl pin, or some other familiar object survived the incredible heat," recalled Father Pernin in his own booklet (calcinated like a "pillar of salt"?). Bizarre black clouds spat lightning, he recounted. Perhaps this was marsh gas. Perhaps something else. There seemed to be some sort of electrical phenomenon. Coins fused in the pockets of victims though oddly their clothes and corpses were not burned. When a committee of businessmen and reporters tried to chart the course of the fire—following what they believed was the path of the "fire tornado"—"the more ground they covered on their walking tour, the more mysterious that hellish night seemed," noted *Firestorm at Peshtigo.* "Trees seemed to have been blown down, rather than burned down, yanked viciously from the ground by their roots. In one spot, the hot sand had been spun into a glass sheet around a tree trunk. It takes temperatures of more than 1,800 degrees to transform sand into glass."

Mysteries—deep ones—remained, and Father Pernin, in his own booklet, went on to discuss what he called "extraordinary phenomena and peculiar characteristics" of the "strange fire," including the scene at the river where "I had noticed on casting my eye upwards a sea of flame, as it were, the immense waves of which were in a state of violent commotion, rolling tumultuously one over the other, and all at a prodigious height in the sky, and, consequently, far from any combustible material. Strange to say there were many corpses found, bearing about them no traces of scars or burns, and yet in the pockets of their habiliments, equally uninjured, watches, cents, and other articles in metal . . . completely melted."

Yes, it was dry. Yes, there were winds. Yes, there were campfires. But this was a holocaust that moved in some places faster than a train and burned hotter than a crematorium. One family had witnessed "a bright light approaching, in size as large as a half-bushel measure." It cleared the house, said *Firestorm at Peshtigo*, and had "seemed to disappear into the darkness. Next they heard the 'great explosion' and the ground beneath their feet shook. Suddenly, the atmosphere changed, growing warmer and warmer by the second. Hot puffs of wind swirled around them and at once [a house] was on fire."

"[A number of people] asserted that they witnessed a phenomenon which may be classed with the marvelous," added Father Pernin. "They saw a large black object, resembling a balloon, which object revolved in the air with great rapidity, advancing above the summits of the trees towards a house which it seemed to single out for destruction. Barely had it touched the latter when the balloon burst with a loud report, like that of a bombshell, and, at the same moment, rivulets of fire streamed out in all directions."

During the Middle Ages and the chastisement of "Black Death," strange and sinister objects in the sky had likewise been reported.

But if Peshtigo-Chicago reminded us of anything, it was further back, at Pompeii, Italy, where in 79 A.D. Vesuvius had erupted and for three terrifying days caused that wayward city to suffer through soot, heat, quakes, and darkness. Sheets of fire had leapt from the volcano and terror had gripped a people who according to Pliny the Younger "debated whether to stay indoors or take their chance in the open, for the buildings were now shaking with violent shocks, and seemed to be swaying to and fro as if they were torn from their foundations. Outside, on the other hand, there was the danger of falling pumice stones. The flames and smell of sulfur which heralded the approaching fire drove the others to take flight." The historian Pliny had recounted that there'd been "a horrible black cloud ripped by sudden bursts of fire, writhing snakelike and revealing sudden flashes larger than lightning." In Wisconsin—near the first apparition site approved by the Church—the flames split boulders and melted church bells (as well as the wheels on rail cars).

"What wind had hurled train cars loaded with logs into the air and ravaged trees so thoroughly they were now twisted, torn from the ground by their roots?" asked Gess and Lutz. "On October 10 no one could say precisely what had hit the states of Illinois, Wisconsin, and Michigan, nor could they explain the strange phenomena of that night except to recall its horrors.

"Even as they choked out their descriptions of fire from Heaven or the earth shaking beneath their feet like an explosion or earthquake, they were still at a loss to capture the astonishing night in words."

29

In some way, what we faced, one of the events, would bear fire.

Wildfire? Volcanic? Astronomic?

Just as smaller fires led up to Peshtigo, so did smaller events foretell of what would come in our own era.

It would not be fire only.

Like fire, however, it would purge.

As a mystic said during a flooding of the Mississippi, "God will shake everything that can be shaken, and only that which cannot be shaken will remain. The flooding you see is but a warning; even now it divides your land. Travel is hard in the waters, but not as hard as it can be when shaking follows in the days to come." Such events, he said, were warnings to *watch the areas that already had been affected*—boding ominously when it came to the largest American city, which had seen terrorism, financial upheaval, weather swerves, a tropical storm, and a hurricane in recent years.

Where there have been hurricanes, larger ones. Where there has been cold, greater frigidity. Where there have been heat waves, scorching days. Where there have been fluctuations, more drastic ones. Where there has been ice, a thicker and more widespread freeze. Where there have been rumblings—well, no one knew, what the rumblings actually were; they were lately in Texas and Illinois and Upstate New York; they were in New Jersey (across three counties). Roars. Blasts. In Hawaii a massive boom was felt physically by witnesses as an atmospheric pressure. Mining? Secret military testing? In 2011 an unusual quake under the Pacific seemed to indicate that a tectonic plate was dividing into twos, with unknown future repercussions. (Such plates held continents.)

As for the sky: comets, fireballs.

Some even claimed the great Wisconsin, Michigan, and Chicago fires had been caused by one.

This was Comet Biela, which was discovered in 1772 and made a visible appearance every 6.7 years.

Upon one of its passes, in 1846, it was noted that Biela had split in half: there were suddenly *two* comets. (One might note that 1846 was also the year of the apparition at LaSalette, where among the messages was one saying, *"The fire of Heaven will fall and consume three cities"*).

Both chunks of Biela had tails and more remarkably, there was an arc of luminosity, a "gaseous prolongation," between them—a bridge of some type of cosmic material that stretched, upon the comets' return in 1852, for what was estimated as more than a million miles. The question: might earth have passed through the "gaseous prolongation" of Biela?

In 1832, earth had intersected the comet's orbit just a month after it passed. In 1872—a year after the fires—there had been a startling, unexpected meteor shower from the comet's remnants. That was just months after a blaze that had odd characteristics skyward. As one observer in Wisconsin noted, the fire "did not come upon them gradually from burning trees and other objects to the windward, but the first notice they had of it was a whirlwind of flame in great clouds from above the tops of trees, which fell upon and entirely enveloped everything." The trajectory of the flames was such that it had been as if someone had sprayed a fiery blast from the shores of Michigan in a triangle that fanned westward (hitting Illinois to the south and Wisconsin to the north). In Chicago, where winds were below thirty miles an hour—far less than in Wisconsin, where they took all the blame—there were nonetheless identical accounts of "a freakish wind" that "whipped flames in great walls of fire more than a hundred feet high, a meteorological phenomenon known as 'convection whirls'— masses of overheated air rising from the flames" and "spinning violently upon contact with cooler surrounding air," said another historical account. "The wind, blowing like a hurricane, howling like a myriad of evil spirits," wrote one witness, "drove the flames before it with a force and fierceness which could never be described or imagined."

It was at Akita, Japan, we recall, that a mystic conveyed the prophecy warning that *"if men do not repent and better themselves, the Father will inflict a terrible punishment on all of humanity. It will be a punishment greater than the Deluge, such as one will never have seen before. Fire will fall from the sky and will wipe out a great part of humanity . . ."* At Fatima, the image in the third secret was of an angel ready to torch the earth.

That seemed like the warning of nuclear war, but it was interesting that the secrets of LaSalette had been given *the same year* that Biela was noticed to have split into two and foresaw a day when flames would consume *"all the works of man's pride"* and the moon and sun would only reflect a *"faint, reddish glow"* and *"water and fire"* would give the earth *"convulsions."* An obscure mystic who claimed communication from what was apparently a "flame" of light foresaw that "there will be two days of awful darkness, different from those announced. The whole sky will be violet and red, so low that the tops of big trees won't be visible. These two days will serve as a warning to you, and be like a proof of His goodness to you, as well as proof of the imminence of God's anger on earth. During these two days, the trees which still have some leaves will be burnt—it will be as if a great fire had been lit over the entire earth. In the year which follows, fruit trees will not produce any fruit. The rain, which will fall from this low sky, will have an awful smell and will be like hailstones of fire; wherever those hailstorms will fall, a mark of a visible burn will be left behind. The water from this rain will be black, a frightening black, and almost the entire earth will be marked by this stain, but it will not harm the food of Christians. The Flame says that in Brittany, during those two days of darkness, a light will appear in this low sky, but it will not be seen because we won't be allowed to put our faces to a door opening; otherwise, a burning flash of lightning will shoot down and darken the pupil of the eye."

It a was a tough situation to discern, but we could certainly say: major change loomed.

As the 2004 prophecy said, there was going to be *"a major disruption in a region of the world that will affect everyone."* Only through prayer—the Rosary—would we find the correct perspective. Only then would there be clarity, or at least enhanced indications of the future. Seers and locutionists were to be held with suspicion when their prophecies were too detailed (or frequent). Nor could we determine it through mere intellect. There was mercy. God's Plans were known to change.

Frequently, a prophecy was what would happen if matters continued as they were at the moment of the prophecy.

Some events were subject to alteration.

There would be protection. At Medjugorje, the Blessed Mother had made five promises to shield faithful who prayed for, "those who do not know the Love of God" (atheists). The promises: *"I will strengthen you. I will fill you with my graces. With my love, I will protect you from the evil spirit. I will be with you. With my presence, I will console you in difficult moments."* The prayer: *"In the Name of Jesus, Who said that anything we ask in His Name will be given to those who believe, I ask that those who have not come to know the love of the Heavenly Father will be blessed with the knowledge that they are loved by Him beyond all human reasoning and understanding. Please grant them the gift to feel His love as it enfolds them to such an extent that they will be unable to resist or deny it. May the knowledge of the Heavenly Father's infinite love stir within their hearts the desire to return that love to Him, and to reflect it to all others. May their lives be a pure reflection of His resplendent love. I ask this in the name of the Father, and the Son, and the Holy Spirit, through the Immaculate Heart of Mary. Amen."*

God—through Mary—could protect us from *anything*.

That had been clear at Peshtigo when the wood tabernacle had survived along with the site of apparition. "When the right time arrived, I forcibly opened the tiny door [of the tabernacle]," Father Pernin had recalled. "There—circumstance as wonderful as the preservation of the tabernacle in the midst of the conflagration—I found the consecrated Host intact in the monstrance while the violent concussions the ciborium must have undergone had not caused it even to open. Water had not penetrated within, and the flames had respected the interior as well as exterior, even to the silky tissue lining the sides. All was in a state of perfect preservation!"

As at Sodom, there were angels to guide us.

Now, we faced a similar and initially regional incident.

The 2004 prophecy called it a *"major disruption."* The 2010 one used the term *"initial event."* It seemed to be something that'd come in the flurry of what the original 1990 message called *"regional chastisements."* In 2004 the word "region" was even used in describing that "disruption." It would *"draw the curtain."* But it would be a gradual process. In the *"transgressions"* of man was found *"the enemy of Creation"* (2010). A *"huge light"* would be seen. If not for the intervention of Heaven, *"what God created on earth"* would *"soon be damaged beyond recovery"* (2004). A *"very dramatic effect"* was in progress as regarded *"the support structure of what man calls nature"* (2004). Before the event occurred, there would be *"premature expectation"* (2010). The event to come would *"surprise everyone who has offered a prognostication"* (2004)—but would be in line with their expectations of something major, something without precedent, at least not in current life spans, something that was a game-changer. The fact that it would be something unprecedented had been stated directly in 2004 when it said that after the *"huge light,"* the Lord would *"act in a way I have not acted before."* Dark spirits were materializing (the *"darkness . . . expected"*) due to the *"pretense and aspirations of man"* (2010), or what the previous missive had called the *"arrogant and wayward course"* of scientists (2004). The *"disruption"* (2004) was going to be related—it seemed, taking the two latest locutions together—to the *"crescendo"* (2010).

"Blessed are those who fear God's judgment," said Mary in Argentina. *"It is your duty to teach the Almighty's justice, and blessed is he who learns it. The devil wants to have full*

domination over the earth, He wants to destroy. Everyone is aware that the earth is in great danger. This is what mankind's ambition leads to! Stay with the Lord and fear nothing, fear no attack, because nothing can prevail against God, my dears. He gives safety to His beloved fold. Daughter, the prince of evil pours out his venom today with all his might, because he knows that his sorry reign is ending, little is left to him. His end is near. My daughter, there is darkness and loss everywhere! Evil continues to spread; it is the evil one in his apparent victory! The work of God will finish with him. God's justice will save the just. With the Holy Rosary any danger can be faced, as Christ and Christ's mother are present in it. My daughter, the evil one is triumphant now, it is true, but it is a victory that will last briefly. God's warning is over the world. I tell my children: break the bonds that tie you to the materialistic world you live in. The coming of the Lord is imminent and certainly for that hour the soul of the Christian should be prepared. This is not a time of anguish, but a time for hope. They are not days of weakness but of fortitude. They are not days of anxiety but of peace. Where there is forgiveness, there is love; where there is love, there is no hatred; and where there is no hatred, peace reigns."

We were—said Mary—in *"dramatic moments."* There would be a happening so unusual it would jar the world, followed in quick succession by regional chastisements over a period of several years that would join as the smaller fires in Wisconsin had joined and turn into two major stages of purification. Each stage would consist of an event or series of events, with one of them prolonged—in my discernment. The landscape would be reduced to the simplicity of agrarian cultures. We would be more pastoral than agricultural, as Abel had been pastoral before he was slain by Cain the agronomist (and mass producer). There would be roaming bands of homeless as Moses roamed with the

Israelites. This would come after natural events, military conflicts, and the breakdown of infrastructure. Eventually, we would settle into peaceful communities, some small, some large, none megalithic, with no superpower. The traditions that started with scientists such as Sir Francis Bacon and had roots in the sixteenth century (with mass production first of clocks and watches, of weaponry, and then iron-ore processing, and gunboat engines, and then cars, soon food—from farms to fast-food chains, in a way that soon dominated all manufacturing and dehumanized mankind and created the fascination and reverence for technology propelled as it was by the magic of electricity) would come to an end, perhaps in a grinding fashion but also perhaps a scorching one.

The 1990 prophecy did not mention a global inferno. No. It had said that after initial regional chastisements would arrive *"a warning that involves not fire from the sky but fear of fire from the sky, and strange loud rumblings. This, according to mankind's response, will then be followed by another chastisement, or the inevitable onset of the change of era,"* indicating a sequence of events: a warning before a much larger event or series of them, to do with nature.

It would be something in the natural.

Nature, said LaSalette, was *"asking vengeance because of man"* and because it had been subject to the *"spirit"* of *"angels of hell."*

On January 25, 1991, a month after the 1990 prophecy, the Blessed Mother at Medjugorje had said, *"Dear children, today, like never before, I invite you to prayer. Let your prayer be a prayer for peace. Satan is strong and desires to destroy not only human life, but also nature and the planet on which you live."* Purification would come to halt this. "Nature expresses a design of love and truth," Benedict XVI had said. "It is prior to us, and it has been given to us by God as the setting for our life. Nature speaks to us of the Creator (*Romans* 1:20) and His love for humanity. It is destined to be recapitulated in Christ at the end of time (*Ephesians* 1:9-10, *Colossians* 1:19-20)." It was the "three a.m. hour." It was the "fourth watch" of the night. In fact, many continued to wake up precisely at the time, when the "veil" seemed thin. Some felt the call to intercede. Some felt engaged with the enemy. Some heard prophecy. Or they looked to the clock and it said "11:11" (as in eleventh hour). Forty thousand years ago the magnetic poles of the earth had reversed such that a compass would have shown north to the south, at the same time that there were radical changes in climate and the eruption of a massive Italian volcano at the Phlegraean Fields near Naples, to give us an idea of a sequence. There would be great societal distress. The spirit of *diaballein*, which meant "to throw through," was the spirit of division, which led to civil or regional or racial or religious wars. This would come. There would be roaming gangs; they would look for liquor, for cash and ammunition and guns, for canned goods in the cities and suburbs and they would seek the crops of the hinterlands. Only God would afford protection, and only He would instruct us on how to prepare.

Riots and something like civil war and certainly marauders would come if the shortages, if a disruption in the trucking system, if electrical or water shortages lasted beyond a few days. There would be an *air* of disturbance. It would be the Era of Disruption. It would be the period of profound reorientation. There would be one event after another—unrelated to the untrained eye and yet incredible in the way each would follow the other and dovetail, bringing huge problems to the electrical grid and manufacturing corridors and causing a tailspin (and then a dismantling) of the financial sector.

For weeks, there would be no commerce in one part or more parts of a major country.

This would be a first "sign" of major happenings: a regional disaster greater than *Katrina*.

One event would magnify the next—though at first in a way that seemed separate. That would change. It would become obvious. Somewhere and somehow would be an event that no one had prophesied, that no one had speculated upon, that no one in any walk of modern history had walked, and when all was said and done (without return to the Lord) America would be a collection of local enclaves, regional alliances, and republics (perhaps the "Northeast," the "Great South," "Espanola," "Dakota," and the "Great Midwest"). Would Christians—Catholics—one day feel the need to gather along the lower rim of the nation in a swath from say western Florida, Louisiana, and Texas to parts of New Mexico or California?

Here we arrived to the last unexamined part of the 2010 prophetic addition, whereby it said, *"Only those in union with God will be able to see in the darkness which so many expected and that already is upon the earth. New Mexico I have ordained as a beacon of light and also the place near the water where the cross stands."*

New Mexico? Was it because of the mountains? Did that lend it a mystical aspect?

It was a state with many devout Catholics—Mexicans had long migrated here and the history of its Catholicism was as old or nearly as old as anywhere in the United States. In and near Santa Fe was an explosion of amazing sites: a mysterious staircase that legend said was built by Saint Joseph, a church dedicated to the Archangel Michael (the oldest still-standing church in the country and one that possessed almost tangible power), the oldest shrine in the United States dedicated to the Virgin of the Guadalupe, and the oldest statue in the U.S. of Mary (*La Conquistadora*).

Not far away, to the northeast of Santa Fe, at Chimayó, was a Crucifix that had been unearthed after a resident saw a strange light radiating from the ground, and to the north, in Taos, was a portrait of Jesus that many said seemed to turn color. As one report said, "the life-size image of Jesus standing on the shore of the Sea of Galilee fades to a shadow as the wispy white clouds in pale blue sky and green water begin to glow around Him, as if all were bathed in moon-light. Soon the silhouette of Jesus grows three-dimensional and appears more like a dark statue than flat image. His robes seem to billow in a breeze. Over his left shoulder the shadow of a Cross is distinct to most. Some can see a halo over his head and the bow of a small fishing boat on the shore."

It was part of that range called the Sangre de Cristo which in northern New Mexico included a town called Angel Fire.

As for the Cross by the water: the strongest candidate seemed to be another old city—in fact, *the* oldest in America, a tad older than Santa Fe—of Saint Augustine. There in northeastern Florida, the first documented Mass on North American soil had taken place and a shrine dedicated to Our Lady of *La Leche* ("the milk") was the continent's oldest Marian shrine—with a 208-foot Cross that overlooked the Atlantic and stood as the tallest in America. I could vouch for the strong feeling under the Cross, visible miles out—a beacon at least to ships. I had no idea if this had anything to do with the prophecy. There were also towering crosses in Texas and Illinois. Some cited other states. But might the spot of the first American Mass (and the first thanksgiving, predating Plymouth) be pivotal in renewal or as a refuge?

Everyone was looking for the best place to live when the truth was that our peace and refuge were inside—that one could have the gift of prophecy and all knowledge of mysteries and faith to move a mountain, but that without love, it was "nothing." We could run but we could not hide. Events would come. There would be "upheaval in a region of the world," as a Medjugorje seer phrased it; there was the Muslim equation. *Religious wars.* There would be upheaval and the breakdown that would be manipulated by a false savior who would influence the new world order that rose to solve the calamities but that "savior" would be unmasked as false by seeing that he was a *temporal* savior, a savior who worked in the material, in pride, one who as Segatashya said would come *"and boast that he is the great leader of man, that he can end drought, stop flooding, and heal millions who are sickened with disease. He may perform miracles, he will brag of his great deeds, and the people of the world will flock to him to call him the Christ. But he is not Christ. He is Satan in disguise. He will claim to be doing what Christ did in the past—healing the sick and feeding the hungry— but he lies. Satan will come to famine-wracked nations with great quantities of food, but he will expect to be worshipped in exchange."*

30

The real Christ would come after the *"artifice"* and arrogance were *"broken"* in the wake of the evil personage who would not be able to rebuild the societies of men into new empires of falsity or at least not in a new era begun by a manifestation of Jesus that Gladys said was "imminent" and that Esperanza claimed (in a 2002 interview) would be "different than what people think; He's going to come in silence; people will realize He is among us little by little; He will disappear for some days and appear again; He will bilocate; He will multiply Himself; He will come and knock on every door; there is not much time for that; I will say from ten to twenty years"—while the 1990 prophecy spoke in terms of what seemed like outright apparitions; certainly, His Spirit would be all around; He allegedly had told Segatashya that *"wherever you are—if you are on a mountaintop, I will seek you out; if you are under a bridge, I will find you. Call to Me for strength and courage when the dark days come, and I will give you strength. Everywhere in the world people will start to have dreams about Me, and they will be filled by the Holy Spirit. But sinners will not be filled with the Holy Spirit, and they will seek out the demons who claim to represent God. The planet will tremble and the joy of the righteous will be overwhelming. A great rainbow of countless colors will traverse the sky, and a white cloud will form in the heavens. At that moment you will see Me emerge from the clouds carrying My Cross. I will dispatch all My angels across earth to assemble all the people of the world. My Cross shall make the good and wicked alike tremble. After all souls chosen by God have been led into Heaven, a great fire will erupt from deep within the earth and the world will be consumed in flames, and all those who rejected God and refused to believe will burn in the fire."* Would there be the fear of nuclear rain? Was fire a symbol?

The Lord would come as He had not before. It would be stealth and unexpected and sudden and startling and quiet before it was blazing, before, allegedly, there was resplendence, before we all heard about it from a distance.

Believed. Disbelieved. There were countless ways to envision a manifestation. Would it be in a pillar of light, towering in the sky, a column of luminosity, or a simple shroud of radiance as the Blessed Mother emanated radiance? The prophecy had said it would be *similar* to the apparitions but did not specify that it would be an apparition itself although we could assume so. It would be some form of manifestation and it would clearly be more potent than historical visions; perhaps those in the presence of the Light would be forced to their knees; perhaps everyone present— not just seers—would see Him; perhaps the light would be visible for miles. But most probably it would be local. He would come as she has come: to a vicinity, luminously.

Like appearances of Mary, He would come in *"light and power"* but with more force. It had been described in 1990 as a *"series"* of *"supernatural events."* By a series of such events, did it mean a number of places around the world or that specific locale? And if a specific locale, would it be one of the spots mentioned as a "beacon of light," or perhaps

South America, where His *"hand"* would be *"evident"*? There would be the blaze. There would be a mountain, somewhere. In *Deuteronomy* (5:4), the Lord spoke on a mountain "in the midst of fire" that had caused fear in those who beheld it. Jesus Himself said to His disciples: "I have come to set the earth on fire, and how I wish it were already blazing!" (*Luke* 12:49). Fire was good. Fire was a symbol of the Holy Spirit—when it was Godly fire. In nature, fire meant renewal—clearing away the dead brush, the decayed leaves, the moldy undergrowth. After a fire, life sprung from the ashes; it often renewed a forest—brought it back to its basics. And so the same would be with us spiritually.

When God destroyed idols—when He directed their destruction—it was with fire.

There was the question of whether the manifestation would occur at the same time as chastisements and this too was unclear though one could surmise that at least some warnings, some chastisements, will have happened, for the prophecy had said that the pretenses of the world *"will have been broken,"* which brought to mind the prophecy's allusion to September 11 and how that would break the *"pride"* of New York.

It was a disaster—a collapse—that had rattled (and temporarily broken) that stronghold.

Something of similar but larger nature loomed—a number of things.

Would the Lord manifest before, during, or after them?

The 1990 prophecy mentioned His manifestation after it mentioned an antichrist, but order of mention did not always imply order in chronology. For example, the allusion to September 11 had come after the discussion of chastisements, fear of fire, and the antichrist, as well as the manifestation—when of course it already had occurred, while the aforementioned events had not.

This much was clear: there would at least be a substantial breakdown before His manifestation. That was evident by His alleged comment in 1990 that He would not appear on television, be chauffeured in a car, or be whisked by jet—that He would not come into a world of unnatural convenience and technology.

There were many mysteries but also a formula, for those who discerned it as authentic.

We only knew that *no one knew*. In *Revelation* (7:9), John had a vision "of a great multitude, which no one could count, from every nation, race, people, and tongue. They stood before the throne and before the Lamb, wearing white robes and holding palm branches in their hands. Then one of the elders said to me, 'These are the ones who have survived the time of great distress; they have washed their robes and made them white in the blood of the Lamb. For this reason they stand before God's throne and worship him day and night in his temple. The one who sits on the throne will shelter them. They will not hunger or thirst anymore, nor will the sun or any heat strike them. For the Lamb who is in the center of the throne will shepherd them and lead them to springs of life-giving water, and God will wipe away every tear from their eyes.'"

Many were those with what they believed to be inklings.

"I had a dream that changed my entire life," a woman named Linette Robertson from Winnipeg, in Manitoba, Canada, wrote me. "I remember everything about this dream, because our Father 'appeared' to me and He made me understand many things about the Eucharist and my life. I had the dream in July of 1994. During a part of my dream I was walking up a hill on a rocky road and it was dusk. There were cars lined up on each side of me. Everyone—including myself—was in expectation of something huge, something magnanimous, about to happen. I was waving to some people I knew. Then, suddenly, someone yelled to 'Look, up in the sky!' and I saw a very large, shining-white, thick bolt of lightning (straight down with no zig-zags) and it split the sky in two. The entire sky opened and I had the Beatific Vision: colors I had never seen before and perfect clouds and purple sky."

Lightning. *A great distress.* An illumination. The real fire we need to fear was that in eternity—for hell did exist. So did heaven. We needed to prepare for future events but none more so than our eternal destinations and those of others—especially those who, through worldliness, through materialism, through hate, were at greatest risk. "We all know that there are persons on this earth who simply don't admit that God exists, even though He helps them," said the seer Vicka Ivanković. "He always tries to nudge them onto the path of holiness. They just say they don't believe, and they deny Him. They deny Him, even when it comes time to die. And they continue to deny Him after they are dead. It's their choice. It is their will that they go to tell. They choose hell." The more they are against the Will of God, she added, "the deeper they enter into the fire, and the deeper they go, the more they rage against Him. When they come out of the fire, they don't have human shape anymore; they are more like grotesque animals; but unlike anything on earth, as if they were never human beings before. They were horrible. Ugly. Angry. And each was different; no two looked alike. When they came out, they were raging and smashing everything around and hissing and gnashing and screeching." It was so awful that another seer who had been with Vicka during this "journey" refused to speak of it. The seer Marija Pavlović, meanwhile, saw a beautiful young woman enter the fire, only to come out as half-human, half-animal. "In the moment of death, God gives us the light to see ourselves as we really are," she commented. "God gives freedom of choice to everybody during his life on earth. The one who lives in sin on earth can see what he has done and recognize himself as he really is. When he sees himself and his life, the only possible place for him is hell. He chooses hell, because that is what he is. That is where he fits. It is his own wish. God does not make the choice. God condemns no one. We condemn ourselves. Every individual has free choice. God gave us freedom."

At Kibeho three seers reported mystical "journeys" to the hereafter, the first Alphonsine Mumureke, whose episode occurred on March 20, 1982, when the Blessed Mother invited her on a trip to a "special place" and warned her to tell the director of the school that while it would appear as if she were dead during this "journey," he shouldn't declare her as such and have her buried. "My body will be here," the girl told him. "But I'll be away until Sunday." A note was also penned to the bishop, as detailed in the book *Kibeho*, by Father Gabriel Maindron, and *Our Lady of Kibeho*, by Immaculée Ilibagiza (with Steve Erwin). That Saturday Alphonsine was found lying in bed at the school dormitory in what appeared to be a deep slumber, still fully dressed, her skin waxen, her hands neatly folded over her chest. Those who came into the room were unable to budge her, despite shouting into her ears. Witnesses included a nun, two priests, and an abbot named Augustin Misago who would later become bishop and approve construction of a shrine there. An official from Red Cross was summoned as was a nurse, and a stethoscope found Alphonsine's pulse to be impossibly slow. Her blood pressure, pulse, and lungs gave scant evidence of life (her breathing only once or twice a minute, and barely perceptible). The girl was in this deathlike sleep for eighteen hours, as also was to occur, but for longer periods, to Anathalie and another visionary named Vestine Salina—who went out on Good Friday and "returned" on Easter morning. In their descriptions was a high place in Heaven which Anathalie called "Isangano" ("the place of communion") with seven incomparably handsome men in pure white cloaks in a circle creating music but with no instruments, "each note filled with a different sensation of contentment and joy," in Ilibagiza's words.

There was also a place where the Blessed Mother showed her "millions of people dressed in white"—not quite as blissful as the seven but still "overwhelmingly happy."

This was "Isenderezwa z'ibyishimo" or the "place of the cherished of God."

But there were also nether regions seen by all the seers, who had their experiences at different times during the early 1980s. One such place was dim as dusk. "Below us were people dressed in clothes of dreary and duller colors in comparison to the other worlds we'd seen," said Anathalie. The people here were content, but still suffering. It was called "Isesengurwa," or a "place of purification" for those who "persevered."

"The last place we visited was a land of twilight where the only illumination was an unpleasant shade of red that reminded me of congealed blood," said this seer. "The heat that rose from that world was stifling and dry—it brushed my face like a flame, and I feared that my skin would blister and crack. I couldn't look at the countless people who populated that unhappy place because their misery and anguish pained me so greatly. Mary didn't have to say the name of this place . . . I knew I was in hell." Alphonsine described a "place of despair" where the road leading away from God's Light ends. "Our Lady showed me an abyss filled with fire to explain that this is the eternal fire," Vestine testified. "But she told me that hell is not fire. It is the eternal suffering of not seeing God, of being deprived of God."

And so it was that there was spiritual fire (the fire of hell, the fire of the Holy Spirit: our choice) and the fire here on earth.

"The Blessed Mother has said that those who are still alive when the permanent sign comes will witness many conversions among the people because of the sign," said the seer Marija Pavlović.

It would not be a barren, *"depopulated"* world, but major, tragic events—perhaps fiery ones—loomed.

"Many people ask whether the Blessed Mother's appearances here at Medjugorje mean that we have entered the end of times," said an interviewer to seer Mirjana Soldo. "Has the Blessed Mother said anything about the apocalypse or the Second Coming of Christ?"

"That is part of the secrets," Mirjana replied. "I would not like to talk about it."

"Will many people die between the time of the first chastisement or event or admonition and the Permanent Sign promised at Medjugorje?"

Replied the visionary: "After the visible sign those still alive will have little time for conversion."

Said a "word of knowledge" to the 1990 recipient: *"When you see the great smoke rise, Satan will have touched the earth. His manifestation will be near. He will seek to destroy what Christ has built, as Jesus came to destroy the work of the devil. In the end, the Cross will predominate, but not before the end of an era that has strayed."*

Back in Africa—at Kibeho—the visionaries who had not met with Church approbation (as had those three), especially the pagan boy Segatashya, were adamant, to repeat, that "the end" was near. "On the very last day, the planet will tremble and the joy of the righteous will be overwhelming," he quoted Jesus as telling him. "After all souls chosen by God have been led into Heaven, a great fire will erupt from deep within the earth and the world will be consumed in flames, and all those who rejected God and refused to believe will burn in the fire."

"We ask you, brothers and sisters, with regard to the coming of our Lord Jesus Christ and our assembling with Him, not to be shaken out of your minds suddenly, or to be alarmed either by a 'spirit,' or by an oral statement, or by a letter allegedly from us to the effect that the day of the Lord is at hand," said Paul in *2 Thessalonians*. "Let no one deceive you in any way. To this end he has also called you through our Gospel to possess the glory of our Lord Jesus Christ. Therefore, brothers and sisters, stand firm and hold fast to the traditions that you were taught, either by an oral statement or by a letter of ours."

Stand fast. Have no fear. A volcano? A bomb? Before a manifestation of Jesus, it seemed clear, there would be a great manifestation of evil—the devil laying his actual and dastardly and foul finger directly upon the earth: no longer just an influence, but a malevolent effect, a large one. To manifest was to make clear to the eye or understanding. It proved. It put beyond doubt. There was going to be a major demonic effect. In seeking to destroy what Christ had built, this raised the possibility of direct involvement with the Church. An attack? An infiltration?

We knew there was going to be a major disruption; there would be plural chastisements; we were headed for the crescendo; the angels had their instructions; not until the initial event would the curtain be drawn; it would reveal the entirety of the plan; but it would be parted only slowly; the plan would become clear *"in the woes of purification."* Might the *"initial event"* be something to do with the smoke? It seemed like it had something to do with the *"huge light."* The light would foretell of God's action—the smoke would foretell of Satan's.

How close together would they be? Would they inter-weave?

These were all questions that flowed like a parlor game and to which there were and could be no answers.

It was one mystery heaped upon another.

What we knew was that something was *coming*, approaching the doorstep, about to take a final step toward the threshold.

The *"strange loud rumblings,"* the regional chastisements, already had seen their precursors; the same was true for solar disruptions, for agricultural problems, for economic woes, for persecution.

What would a real persecution be like? Might there be a time again as in the days of the Apostles and ancient Rome, seeing that we were imitating Rome in so many ways? Might believers be corralled, separated some day, perhaps even sent to encampments? Would it truly involve the attempt—outright—to quash all that was Christian?

For that to occur there would have to be a total societal breakdown, a period of upheaval and chaos under the direction of false leaders until a manifestation signaled the return of earth to what God had intended. There would be a peasant lifestyle and when we thought of peasants we thought of those who lived close to the land and transportation that was simple and biological (perhaps by way of foot, bicycle, or a new energy that depleted nothing—with an accent on local production and plots of land that sustained a family or an extended family in a way that was natural. Would it be the end of the urban culture? Would it occur before or during a reorganization of nations—if there were to be nations as we know them? What would compose the structure of authority in a world that would be vastly and perhaps traumatically simplified?

It was not implausible when one looked at cultural, economic, and religious dissension to foresee regions that would coalesce into much larger confederacies, perhaps, in the Western Hemisphere, one including Canada, the U.S., and Mexico (also South America?).

The Lord was going to appear in a series of events—after the breakdown, after the plague, after the attempt by the nefarious one to control a new order. Storms headed—strange storms—for population centers. So did some kind of event so out of the norm that no one would expect it. Yet, we were called to be vigilant. "When you see a cloud rising in the west you say immediately that it is going to rain—and so it does; and when you notice that the wind is blowing from the south, you say that it is going to be hot—and so it is," Jesus said to the crowds. "You hypocrites! You know how to interpret the appearance of the earth and the sky, why do you not know how to interpret the present time?" (*Luke* 12:54).

At LaSalette the Blessed Mother reputedly had warned that there would be *"convulsions"* of fire and water, and perhaps here too had been precursors. Excessively parched land caused fires to erupt in 2012 on the hill of apparitions at Medjugorje—fires that at one point closed the sacred spot down to pilgrims. It brought to mind Saint Peter's quote ("But the day of the Lord will come like a thief, in which the heavens will pass away with a roar and the elements will be destroyed with intense heat, and the earth and its works will be burned up"), yet as N. T. Wright, a major New Testament scholar, wrote: "As with the rest of the New Testament, Peter is not saying that the present world of space, time and matter is going to be burnt up and destroyed. That is more like the view of ancient Stoicism—and of some modern ideas, too. What will happen, as many early Christian teachers said, is that some sort of 'fire,' literal or metaphorical, will come upon the whole earth, not to destroy, but to test everything out, and to purify it by burning up everything that doesn't meet the test."

There was also water: A flash flood on October 20, 2012, at Lourdes caused damage to bridges, the closing of the healing baths, and put the altar in the grotto itself—the very spot where Bernadette had seen the Virgin—under water, as if in keeping with *Revelation* 12:15: "And the serpent poured water like a river out of his mouth after the woman, so that he might cause her to be swept away with the flood."

Meanwhile, scientists were coming to believe that the earth's core was much hotter than they thought, perhaps as hot as the sun! What might come from beneath?

It was anyone's guess what might occur. A seer from Medjugorje likened the current stage as the beginning of a housecleaning in which everything is pushed out of place and even placed upside-down, before the scrubbing. Everywhere there were hints of a rearrangement. Would the trepidation over fire be due to some previously unseen and long-lasting discharge of electricity—a massive display of lightning—or some kind of light in the sky: a new phenomenon? And the sign: might it be similar in some way to an unexplained ray of light that had been witnessed on Cross Mountain in Hercegovina at the same time that a ray of light had been seen across the church of Saint James far below? One secret had been reduced. The others remained in place. More prayer was necessary. Much more. And fasting. Pertaining to Medjugorje, one could not help but recall that the original church had been badly damaged by a quake, and that an old man reputed to be a prophet back before the apparitions—one who foresaw Mary coming there—had also foreseen the appearance of a body of water. At the Vatican Museum, in a courtyard, near the gardens, was a work of modern art portraying a globe with huge cracks, splitting apart and revealing an inner globe. It had been fashioned in 1990. Off Portugal—off the land of Fatima—was a major underwater fault system.

"The trials of your time now head to the crescendo of meaning," said the prophecy.

"It is a final battle in which the trials of the future will serve as engagements complete unto themselves."

"The angels stand ready to assist those who unleash power with humility and belief."

"Only those in union with God will be able to see in the darkness which so many expected and that already is upon the earth."

"The world will not end but change."

It would be transformed—the world, the earth—to a simpler but eventually splendid state that was closer to but still a dull reflection of eternity.

Here was where our eyes need to be trained: on that place beyond this earth that lasts forever and is so full of love that there is no use trying to express it, a place of energy and luminosity and intelligence.

The living water.

The sea of fountains.

The luminous landscape with trees both familiar and unfamiliar.

The joy! In eternity, they say, is water that can be "breathed" and air that one can drink—this place where the entry is like jumping into a vast pool of milk (but instead of milk it is *Light*); not a dead branch on the trees; not a wilted leaf; the grass swaying in rhythm, emanating light, every single thing *alive* and radiating bliss and filled with the joy of praise for God, the streets, the paths, fashioned with crystallized gold and silver and jasper, buildings like ruby, transparent and yet solid, there but *not* there, crystallized, the building that are vastly larger than all the buildings in Washington combined, with columns taller than the Freedom Tower, more like art than construction—monuments to God, not Man; and golden channels through which the crystal water flows past meadows of huge white-petaled flowers that have gold at their center on vines that also at the same moment have beautiful large ripe grapes and other fruit and other kinds of flowers in this place more resplendent than what even Kincaid could paint, than Leonardo could capture, the music far, far beyond Mozart, the walls brilliantly hued, the birds with indescribable plumage, the people filled with a total sense of well-being: where colors are "heard" and music is "seen" on vistas where there are no more quakes, no more plague, no fire, no more storms, no darkness, no shadows, and no death among the souls who wear robes that are like pure spun cotton and glass in this place—this endless *series* of vistas—that go forth forever, the air filled with the aroma of lilacs and roses in combination and multiplied in ways we can't imagine.

Sparkling beauty. Sparkling happiness. Each drop of those living waters will have its own melody and tone, intermingled with the sounds all around, the music that has no beat because there is no time and seems to come from above but also below as if angels are orchestrating it to minister to the souls who have arrived in Heaven after the arduous earthen journey. Questions are answered as soon as they are formed; there is the need for no secrets; there is movement without the slightest effort.

It touches earth when we pray and our eyes fix on this existence where there are clouds of glory and flowers four feet across and trees that span miles with crystal "leaves" like diamonds and an aroma and humming set forth from gardens that seem endless and to our minds *are* endless and the sound of chimes and the sight of fruit that is picked with other fruit instantly taking its place and melting into the most delicious taste but without any form of sugar or residue, just an insuperable aftertaste, in this place where nothing can be defiled and where demons can not reach, towers and cities of light at great distances and angels of all kinds and sizes; where our tomorrows are God's yesterdays and where our tomorrows never end, so great is God that it will take eternity to explore.

This is what awaits us, our true home. Earth, we will see, was our place of exile. This is our true home. Earth was a place of tests, a place to learn—the greatest lesson of which is the test of love. *"Now I understand,"* one day we will say. *"Now it makes sense. I'm home. This is my home. I'm really home"*—thoughts that will come past the river or hedgerow or fence or gate at a point of no coming back, where we will be reunited with ancestors, all relatives, back to Adam, with whom we had a mission together. Big missions! Big tests from the One Who alone knows what is best for our sanctity and views us knowing what awaits us, what He has for us, if we but follow the prescription of His Son and our forefathers like Paul, who gave us all we needed when he told us, "Love is patient, love is kind. It does not envy, it does not boast, it is not proud. It does not dishonor others, it is not self-seeking, it is not easily angered, it keeps no record of wrongs. Love does not delight in evil but rejoices with the truth. It always protects, always trusts, always hopes, always perseveres" (*1 Corinthians* 13:4-7).

How can we fret, when this awaits us, if we have faith and purity, this reality where past and present and future are all as one and angels are clothed with the power to move the earth and bring judgment but also the power to defend and to keep God's children safe from all harm, all storms, all holocaust.

Let Heaven say: you are watched; you are defended. You are forever.

In the light of eternity, every earthly thing is a small matter, but for the salvation of the soul, which hinges on a simple vow:

"I will never hate," you must say. "I will not judge. I will live by love."

About the author:

A former investigative reporter, Michael H. Brown, 60, is the author of more than twenty-five books, most of them Catholic. He has appeared on numerous TV and radio shows, and contributed to publications from *Reader's Digest* to *The Atlantic Monthly*. He is the author of the Catholic bestsellers *The Final Hour*, *The God of Miracles*, and *The Other Side*, and lives in Palm Coast, Florida, with wife Lisa and three children. He is also director of the Catholic news website, Spirit Daily (www.spiritdaily.com).

Other Books by Michael H. Brown

THE OTHER SIDE

AFTER LIFE (Heaven, Hell, and Purgatory)

TOWER OF LIGHT (current prophecy)

THE GOD OF MIRACLES (real cases of answered prayers)

SENT TO EARTH: God and the Return of Ancient Disasters

SEVEN DAYS WITH MARY (devotional prayers)

SECRETS OF THE EUCHARIST

THE FINAL HOUR (the Blessed Mother's apparitions)

THE SEVEN

A LIFE OF BLESSINGs

Available at www.spiritdaily.com